WITHDRAWN

WJEC

Comr

Te

y

AS

Julian Mott
Anne Leeming
Edited by Dai Rudge

HODDER
EDUCATION

The publishers would like to thank the following for their kind permission to reproduce copyright material:

Photos
pp.1&2: Julian Mott; **p.12**: Andy Jones/Topics; **p.14**: courtesy of Tesco plc © Tesco plc; **p.34**: dbimages/ Alamy; **p.35t**: educationphotos.co.uk/walmsley; **p.35b**: Photofusion Picture Library/Alamy; **p.36**: courtesy of NPower Ltd © NPower 2006; **p.37**: Peter Titmuss/ Alamy; **p.43**: Philippe Psaila/Science Photo Library; **pp.47, 48 &49**: Andy Jones/Topics, with thanks to Tesco plc; **p.51**: courtesy of HSBC Bank plc © HSBC Bank plc; **p.55**: Steve Chenn/Corbis; **p.57b**: Anne Leeming; **pp.60&61**: courtesy of DRS Data Services Ltd © DRS Data Services Ltd; **p.67t**: Malcolm Fielding, The BOC Group plc/Science Photo Library; **p.67b**: Mauro Farmariello/ Science Photo Library; **p.68t**: Gustoimages/Science Photo Library; **p.68b**: Pasieko/Science Photo Library; **p.70t**: Pascal Goetgheluck/Science Photo Library; **p.70b** John Bavosi/ Science Photo Library; **p.71t**: D. Ouellette, Publiphoto Diffusion/Science Photo Library; **p.71b**: John Cole/Science Photo Library; **p.73**: Stuart Robertson/Topics, with thanks to the National Blood Service, Cambridge; **p.74**: Victor de Schwanberg/Science Photo Library, **p.78** *joystick, steering wheel, voice recognition kit*: courtesy of Saitek UK © Saitek UK; **p.73** *wireless 3D glasses*: courtesy of eDimensional, Inc © eDimensional, Inc; **p.78b**: Helen Duvall/Topics; **pp.79&80**: Andy Jones/Topics; **p.95**: courtesy of Luidia, Inc © Luidia, Inc 2008; **p.110**: Andy Jones/Topics; **p.119** Robert Harding Picture Library/Alamy; **p.129**: Julian Mott; **p.134t**: Steve Connolly; **p.134b**: courtesy of Saitek UK © Saitek UK; **p.135**: Martyn F. Chillmaid/Science Photo Library; **p.182**: Michael Donne/Science Photo Library

Other content
p.57t: BBC GCSE Bitesize webpage © BBC 2008, reproduced by permission; **p.72**: NHS Choices webpage © Crown copyright 2008, reproduced by permission; **p.82**: Tesco home shopping webpage © Tesco plc 2008, reproduced by permission; **p.83**: Everyman webpage © Everyman Media 2008, reproduced by permission; **p.104**: Totaltravel.com webpage © Totaltravel.com Pty Ltd, reproduced by permission; **p.148**: National Theatre registration webpage © National Theatre 2008, reproduced by permission

All WJEC material is reproduced by permission of the Welsh Joint Education Committee.

Every effort has been made to trace copyright holders of material reproduced in this book. Any omissions will be rectified in subsequent printings if notice is given to the publisher.

Hachette UK's policy is to use papers that are natural, renewable and recyclable products and made from wood grown in sustainable forests. The logging and manufacturing processes are expected to conform to the environmental regulations of the country of origin.

Orders: please contact Bookpoint Ltd, 130 Milton Park, Abingdon, Oxon OX14 4SB.
Telephone: (44) 01235 827720.
Fax: (44) 01235 400454.
Lines are open 9.00–5.00, Monday to Saturday, with a 24-hour message answering service. Visit our website at www.hoddereducation.co.uk

© Anne Leeming and Julian Mott 2009

First published in 2009 by
Hodder Education,
Part of Hachette UK
338 Euston Road
London NW1 3BH

Impression number   5   4   3
Year   2014   2013   2012

Although every effort has been made to ensure that website addresses are correct at the time of going to press, this type of data is subject to change. It is sometimes possible to find a relocated web page by typing into the URL window of your browser the address of the home page of its website.

Hodder Education cannot be held responsible for the content of any website mentioned in this book.

Cover photo: Chepko Danil/istockphoto
Typeset in Stone Sans and Gill Sans
Editorial and production by Topics – The Creative Partnership Ltd, Exeter
Printed in Dubai

A catalogue record for this title is available from the British Library

ISBN: 978 0340 976 050

Contents

Chapter 1

Data, Information and Knowledge
4.1.1

What is data?

Data consists of raw facts and figures. It is usually a series of values produced as a result of an event or transaction. Readings from sensors or facts collected in a survey are both examples of data.

If I buy an item in a supermarket a lot of data in the form of facts is collected, such as:

▶ 0753461 (my loyalty-card number)
▶ 060042350032 (the product identity number for an item bought – often called the barcode number)
▶ 563 (the weight in grams of a product, such as apples, purchased)
▶ 011420054132 (the number of my credit card used to pay for the goods).

All this data has been generated by an event – my buying some items in a supermarket.

If I pay a cheque into my bank account, this is an event that collects a record of the transaction. The record might contain details such as:

▶ my bank account number and sort code
▶ the bank account number and sort code for the cheque paid in
▶ the amount of the cheque.

Each of these details is represented as data in the form of numbers or other characters.

Data can be captured in many different ways. For example:

▶ barcodes on products can be scanned at a supermarket POS (point-of-sale) terminal using a barcode scanner
▶ humidity sensors can record the level of moisture in a greenhouse
▶ details of an account can be read by scanning the magnetic strip on a debit card
▶ the letters on a number plate can be recorded by a scanner reading an image produced by a traffic camera.

A data set such as **24, 67, 35, 55, 61, 82, 74** has little meaning unless the context is known. The numbers could represent the age of patients due to attend a doctor's surgery or the marks obtained by different members of a class in their ICT module exam.

Examples of data

The meaning of the data is not obvious without **context**. However, data is very useful when it is **processed** into a useable form to create **information**.

What is information?

£178.45
£279.67
£1877.45

78345.78 kWh

£1877.45
£6510.07
£8387.52

ed this quarter
orward
e

Examples of information

Information is data that has been processed by the computer. The data has a context and has been turned into a useable form which makes it understandable to the user.

For example, when the barcode of a product is scanned at a till, data is entered into a computer. The computer program looks up the name of the item and its price and calculates the total amount payable, which is then displayed on the till. This price is information because the data has been processed and a context added so that it is meaningful.

How information is displayed will affect its usefulness. Both the examples shown here are meaningful to the user.

What is knowledge?

Knowledge is derived from information by applying rules to it. Knowledge is the ability to make sense of information so that it can be used effectively. Knowledge is the interpretation of information.

When the manager of a camping shop is provided with a chart showing the monthly sales figures for different products, the decision to discontinue a particular product can be made as the information he or she has been given, together with his or her expertise and experience, has become knowledge.

Activity 1

Study Table 1 on the next page. Then copy and complete the following grid. You will need to be creative!

Data	Context	Information	Knowledge
19, 18, 23, 20, 22, 25	Responses to a question in a survey asking students whether they were happy with the access to computers in college, on a scale from 0 to 5		
	Time when each runner in a marathon crosses the finish line		
	Number of children aged 10 in each school in a county		

Data	Context	Information	Knowledge
Yes, No, No, Yes, No, No, No, Yes	Responses from a number of regular customers to a question in a survey carried out by a holiday company asking whether the customer would be interested in having a city break in Lima	The yes/no answers could each be added up and the percentage of customers who would be interested in the city break could be calculated.	A manager could use this information to decide whether or not to continue with plans to set up the city break. He would know what level of interest is needed to make it worthwhile.
3, 4, 5, 0, 1, 4, 6, 2, 8	Meic's marks for the questions in an ICT exam sat as a mock in school	Adding Meic's marks would provide a total mark for the exam. This could be converted into a percentage.	If Meic's teacher knew how the raw marks converted into UMS for that paper as well as the grade boundaries for UMS scores, she could establish the grade for the module.
120 70 135 60 122 60	Angharad's blood-pressure readings taken at different visits to her doctor	These readings could be displayed in a table in the form 120/70, 135/60, 122/60	Angharad's doctor could interpret these readings to make a judgement about her health and take appropriate action.
187213, 187794	The previous and current readings of a customer's electricity meter	Subtracting the first value from the second would give the number of units of electricity that the customer has used. This number can then be multiplied by the unit cost to determine the amount that the customer owes.	Looking at the pattern of the customer's previous electricity bills may indicate that the number of units used is abnormally high or low.

Table 1 Four examples of the relationship between data, information and knowledge

How data can arise: direct and indirect data capture

Data capture means the collection of data to enter into a computer. Data can be input into a computer in a variety of ways, depending on the source. For example:

▶ use of keyboard
▶ speech recognition by using a microphone
▶ use of webcam
▶ use of touch screen
▶ selection from list using a mouse
▶ use of sensors
▶ use of barcode reader
▶ transfer of pre-captured data from an external device, such as a digital camera.

Data can be captured directly or indirectly. **Direct data capture** is the collection of data for a particular purpose. Examples of direct data capture are:

▶ barcodes being read at a supermarket till so that the product can be identified
▶ account details being read directly from the chip embedded in a credit card
▶ an MICR device automatically reading the numbers on the bottom of a cheque
▶ data from an automatic weather station being downloaded into a computer.

Indirect data capture is the collection of data as a by-product from data collected for another purpose. Examples of indirect data capture are:

▶ using data collected from reading barcodes at a supermarket till to work out stock levels
▶ using the records of transactions generated at a store when a customer uses a loyalty card to build up a profile of the buying habits of the customer. The store could sell this customer profile to another company, enabling them to target mail at the customer for products that the customer is most likely to use.

Encoding data

Data has to be processed to produce information. In some circumstances, a code is used to represent the data to allow processing to be more effective and to produce more useful information for the user.

Common examples of the use of coding include:

▶ Gender is usually stored as **M** or **F** instead of 'Male' or 'Female'.
▶ Banks use branch sort codes such as **60-18-46** instead of the name of the branch.
▶ Dates of birth are coded as, for example, **06 02 1986** instead of '6th February 1986'.
▶ Airline baggage handlers use codes for destinations: for example, **LHR** means London Heathrow, **FRA** means Frankfurt.
▶ Postcodes: **SO9** identifies an area of Southampton; **SO9 5NH** is the university. A postcode written on an envelope can be converted into a series of dots at the sorting office for automatic sorting.

Codes are often easy to remember, such as LHR for London Heathrow.

Codes are used because:

▶ the code is usually short and quicker to enter; fewer errors are likely to be made
▶ the code takes up less storage space on disk and less main memory
▶ using a code ensures that the data stored is consistent. For example, it would be difficult to search a file for people with a given date of birth if some dates were stored in the form 25th May 1988 and others as May 25 1988.

It is possible to access a computer program on the Internet that outputs the full address when you enter a postcode and house number. Entering the postcode:

▶ is quicker as it is much shorter to type in than the full address
▶ allows an immediate check to be made to see if the postcode really exists
▶ avoids spelling the name of the street incorrectly.

Data entered into a computer is stored in code. However, if the data item is to become information it must be decoded before it is output. So at a supermarket till, the barcodes of the items are entered into the computer as data but information – the total cost for all the purchases – is displayed on the till.

▶ Loss of precision due to coding

Market research questionnaires often ask the subject to tick an age range like this:

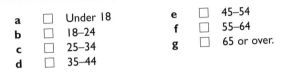

The answer is stored as code: for example, **c** for anyone aged 25–34. This coding is easy to use but leads to a loss of precision:

▶ People who are 25 are bracketed with people who are 34.
▶ If you wanted to know the average age, you could work out a figure that might be close but would not be exact.

The fewer the categories, the greater the loss of precision.

▶ Value judgements

A value judgement is a judgement that is based on a personal view. It is subjective rather than objective. It is entirely your own opinion and may differ completely from someone else's opinion. Examples of value judgements are if you say something is nice, attractive or ugly.

If someone says, 'I get up at 7 o'clock each morning,' this is not a value judgement but a statement of fact. If they say, 'I get up early each morning,' this is a value judgement. A milkman used to getting up at 3.30 wouldn't describe 7 o'clock as early. A student used to getting up at 11 o'clock might describe 7 o'clock as very early.

▶ Coding value judgements

Businesses are interested in our opinions. Do we like the taste of a product? Is the packaging attractive? Is it too expensive? These are some of the questions a market researcher might ask members of the public before a new product is launched. Information from this research will later be used to determine the price, the image and even whether the product is produced at all. It is likely that there will be a limited choice of responses. For example, if a new product costs £1.65, is it:

1 much too cheap
2 too cheap
3 about right
4 too expensive
5 much too expensive?

What happens if the customer thinks it is a little bit too expensive? Do they choose 'about right' or 'too expensive'?

Coding value judgements like this leads to a limited number of answers, none of which may be appropriate. The results may not be meaningful because different people will have different opinions about what 'too expensive' and 'much too expensive' mean.

Summary

▶ **Data** means raw facts and figures, records of transactions.

▶ **Data capture** is the collecting of data and can be carried out in many different ways.

▶ **Information** is data which has been processed to give it a context which gives it a meaning.

▶ **Knowledge** is derived from information by applying rules to it.

▶ Data frequently needs to be **encoded** when collected to enable effective processing.

▶ Advantages of encoding data:
   a fewer transcription errors
   b less time spent on data entry
   c greater data consistency
   d less memory required.

▶ Problems associated with encoding data:
   a coarsening of data
   b value judgements – judgements based on a personal view.

Chapter 1 Questions

1 Give **two** examples not mentioned in the chapter to illustrate what is meant by the term *data*. (2)

2 Give **two** examples not mentioned in the chapter to illustrate what is meant by the term *information*. (2)

3 Give **two** examples not mentioned in the chapter to illustrate what is meant by the term *knowledge*. (2)

4 Describe, using examples, **three** different methods of capturing data. (6)

5 Encoding value judgements can lead to reduced accuracy. As a result information from a questionnaire may be inaccurate. Explain, with the use of **two** appropriate examples, why this may happen. (4)

6 A checkout operator in a supermarket scans the barcodes of items being purchased by customers. The scanner is linked to an

electronic point-of-sale (EPOS) system. The software that is used contains functions to look up the prices and descriptions of the products that are scanned in order to produce an itemised receipt for the customer. The software also produces a daily sales summary report for the store manager.

State **one** item of data that is entered into the EPOS system and describe **two** items of information that are produced. (5)

7 Define the terms *information* and *knowledge* and discuss, using a suitable example, the relationship between them. (4) WJEC specimen

8 a Information is data which has been processed by the computer. Define the term *knowledge* and use a specific example to show how knowledge is derived from information. (3)

b Give **two** reasons why data is encoded and give an example of a possible problem with encoding data. (3) WJEC June 07

2

The Value, Importance and Quality of Information 4.1.2 & 4.1.3

Managers need information to help them to **make decisions** and plan future actions. Information is also needed to **monitor progress**. A salesperson might use their monthly sales statistics to check how well they are progressing towards meeting their annual target. The managing director of a company might use information showing the annual sales and profits of a newly opened store to monitor its progress.

When a new shampoo is launched, information obtained by market research and sales figures can help to monitor the progress of the shampoo's popularity. Market researchers might stop shoppers in a street or send questionnaires to a sample of homes. The questionnaire responses could provide information on whether people have heard about the product, whether they have used it and if they have, what they think of it! Sales figures will show how far sales are reaching targets.

Information can be used to help **target resources** such as money or personnel to a section of a business that could provide it with a competitive advantage.

Having information can allow a company to **gain advantage** over competitors. Information can identify gaps in a particular market, which can then be filled. For example, market research may show that many people would like to buy shampoo in a large bottle with a dispenser that can be used to transfer the shampoo into very small bottles that can be carried around easily. The company could be the first to produce and sell shampoo dispenser kits thus gaining increased sales.

Information allows a manager to **spot trends**. By analysing their sales figures over several years, a chain of garden centres noticed that their sales of garden gnomes were steadily declining whilst sales of water-fountain kits were increasing. On the basis of this information the company made the **strategic decision** to alter the range of products it sold. They decided to reduce the range of gnomes stocked whilst increasing their range of fountain kits.

Information is said to be of good quality if it is **accurate**, **up to date** and **complete**.

Accurate

How accurate information needs to be depends upon how it will be used. For example, the information in a bank statement must be exactly right to the nearest penny, otherwise the account holder could make inappropriate decisions over spending and would be fully justified in complaining to the bank. When reporting overall A-level pass rates at a school a figure to the nearest 1% would usually be sufficiently accurate.

The accuracy of information is very important. For example, inaccurate stock figures may cause a store manager to reorder the wrong amounts. This could result in items not being available for customers or too much stock being held, which would take up extra space and tie up capital. When a customer receives a domestic gas or electricity bill for thousands of pounds it could be because a meter has been misread. If a wrong phone number is written down in a conversation it could become impossible to contact a person or company.

Sometimes inaccurate data can even have life-threatening results. If an automatic system using sensors to collect data were to develop a fault, inaccurate data could be gathered. This could lead to a catastrophe: for example, if the system was in a chemical plant it could cause an explosion.

Up to date

If information is out of date, then wrong decisions can be made. It is very important that all reports produced include a date so that the person receiving them knows how old they are. In certain circumstances, a time is also required. This enables the reader of the report to know exactly when it was produced. Information changes over time and without a date the reader might make a wrong decision, unaware that the information is out of date.

If a list of names and addresses used for mail shots is five years out of date, many letters may be sent to the wrong address as some people listed may have moved or even died during that time. Letters sent to deceased people can cause great heartache for their surviving relatives. It would be a waste of time and money for a company to send out letters to out-of-date addresses. The older the mailing list, the fewer the 'hits', and consequently the fewer the responses.

In order to determine the number of AS ICT classes to run in a college, the administrator would need to know the number of students wishing to follow the course this year. Last year's figures might be quite different; if they were used instead of this year's numbers then too few classes might be set up.

A sales manager for a large company selling office furniture throughout the UK will need to decide which salespeople have been doing badly and need extra support and which products to choose for extra production or promotion. Using information based on an earlier month's figures rather than the most recent could result in incorrect decisions leading to reduced sales and profit.

When employees of a cinema are taking a booking for the evening performance of a film, they need to know which seats are still available at the time of booking, not the ones that were available at the start of the day.

▶ Keeping information up to date

Information has to be up to date to be useful. Keeping information up to date will affect the costs of producing it. The costs arise from the need to:

▶ collect up-to-date data
▶ enter the data into the system
▶ delete out-of-date data.

Traditionally many computer systems operated in batch mode, in which data was collected over a period of time – a day, a week or even a month – before processing took place. The information then produced was only as up to date as the most recent processing run. Transaction processing updates with new data as it arises, processing each change as it occurs. Information produced from a transaction processing system is always as up to date as possible, but such a system is more costly to run as faster processing, more sophisticated hardware and faster communications might be required.

Organisations need to have systems in place to ensure that changes in data can be collected. This can be very complicated and time consuming as changes can include altered marital status and perhaps a change in surname, a change in telephone number as well as address. Data will need to be updated frequently with details of changes typed in. Very often when a patient attends a doctor's or dentist's clinic the receptionist will quickly check basic data with them to ensure that it is up to date.

It is very important that a school or college has up-to-date information about its students. Current contact addresses and telephone numbers are essential. A system could be in place whereby students fill in a form whenever any changes occur. However, such a method would not be foolproof. To catch missed changes, every student might be given a printout of their personal details and qualifications every year or even every term for checking. Any changes would be added and the student would be expected to sign the form. The data held electronically would then be updated. Such a process would cost money. Each student's details would need to be printed out and distributed; missing students would need to be chased up; every sheet would need to be checked for changes and the changes entered. The data could be kept even more up to date if printouts were issued and checked every week, but the cost in both time and money would make this unproductive for the few changes occurring each week.

Many organisations try to gather address changes and other details from customers by including a form with every invoice that allows the customer to enter changes easily. It is then a simple matter for this changed data to be entered onto the database.

Name and address lists used for targeted mailing will soon get out of date. It is no use having a mailing list when the addresses are no longer correct. When people move house, mail continues to be sent to the old address until the relevant mailing list is updated. Systems need to be put in place that will enable entries to be deleted when no longer current and new names to be added. It is crucial that out-of-date data is deleted as soon as possible.

Organisations which keep a database of customers will probably record the date when the customer last made contact in some way – by making a purchase or an enquiry. People who have made no contact for a set period of time can then be deleted from the database. Some organisations may periodically buy up-to-date lists.

Complete

If a marketing manager is deciding whether the sale of a particular product should be discontinued, their decision could be impaired if they do not have figures for overseas sales.

Many examples can be found when incomplete information has an effect. If the address on a letter is incomplete, without a postcode, there is likely to be a delay in delivery. A badly filled in, incomplete order can result in the non-delivery of some items.

Ideally all the information needed for a particular decision should be available. However, this rarely happens. In reality, good information is often incomplete, but complete enough to meet the needs of the situation.

Activity 1

For each of the following situations, state why the information might lead to an inappropriate decision being made. Describe the possible consequences of the decision.

1 The purchasing manager of a mail-order company is looking at a list of stock levels for their products before placing orders prior to the Christmas rush. The list was produced in June.
2 Two trained teachers are considering setting up a new after-school club in the local area to start in September 2009. They have information from the local council on the number of children under the age of 11 attending a local state primary school which was produced in June 2005.
3 A bakery wishes to determine ways of increasing profits. They want to know whether they could sell more loaves and which are the most popular. The manager is given the number of loaves of each type baked each day for the last 12 months.
4 The manager of a holiday company has to prebook places in hotels for the 2009 season. They have the results of a market research survey of holiday preferences from members of the public that was carried out in 2003.

Case Study 1 – Lorry using satnav gets stuck

A road in Carmarthenshire was blocked for more than three hours by an articulated lorry. The huge vehicle was stuck fast between a wall and a hedge on a sharp bend. 'The lorry driver told us he had been using his satnav,' said local residents. 'This is the third time that the road has been blocked in recent months. It's high time the council put up a warning sign!'

1 What caused the problem?
2 Explain, with the help of an example in **each** case, why a driver needs satnav information to be:
   a accurate
   b up to date
   c complete.

Satnav in use

The cost of getting good-quality information

Reminder

Up-to-date, accurate and complete information adds value to an organisation by aiding decision making, monitoring progress (both that of the company and that of the individual) and allowing the targeting of resources. Thus the organisation can gain competitive advantage.

Obtaining good-quality information incurs costs in terms of money, time and human resources.

Financial costs will be incurred in a variety of ways when setting up systems, including hardware and software costs, running costs such as paper, ink and electricity, and communication costs. Getting good-quality information is **time consuming** as data has to be collected, input and processed before information is available. There are likely to be **human-resource costs** as specialist staff may be required to run the new systems. This could cause job losses among existing staff, or retraining to enable them to acquire new skills.

There are a range of costs involved in **data collection** (both **direct** and **indirect**). An expert will be needed to design any form that is to be used. If information is obtained through a survey, costs will arise in setting up questionnaires, as well as the costs of carrying out any interviews. Employees may need to spend time going through documents to extract the required information. Sometimes information is bought from another company.

Once data has been collected it needs to be entered into the ICT system. This **data entry** will incur costs as people will need to be employed to type in the data, which will take time. Specialist input devices such as barcode scanners or optical mark readers may be needed.

The data entered will need to be **processed**, incurring more costs. A technician may be needed to run the computer, carrying out such tasks as refilling printers with paper, ensuring that the correct backing storage media are loaded and distributing the information output to the appropriate people.

There will be further costs from **maintenance** of the system. From time to time equipment will need to be repaired, changes will need to be made to software, regular backups will need to be taken and stored. The data itself will require maintenance as records that are no longer needed are deleted and other changes made.

How information can improve the quality of decision making

If users believe that the information that they are given is accurate, correctly targeted to their needs, complete, relevant, up to date and presented in a form that they can easily understand, then they have confidence that they can use it when making decisions. Good information allows managers to make decisions that they would be unable to make without it. For example, information gained from analysis of previous sales and market research could allow a sales manager to set the price of a product so that the company gains an advantage over competitors whilst still maintaining high profits. With sound information, the company could also gain competitive advantage by identifying gaps in a particular market which can then be filled.

Trends can be spotted from good information which can lead to money-saving decisions. For example, an analysis of sales could indicate that a particular product is out of fashion so the decision is made to discontinue the line.

Good information can ensure that resources target where they will be most effective. Advertising and marketing is a waste of time and money unless it is aimed at people likely to buy a product. Good information will provide details of these people. Information about customers' buying habits can lead to a company becoming more profitable and is such a valuable commodity that a company will often buy the information if it cannot produce it itself.

Case Study 2 – Supermarket loyalty cards

The use of loyalty cards is common in supermarkets and other large stores. Customers have to fill in an application form to obtain a card; this requires them to give their name, address and other information. The loyalty card is used whenever a customer purchases goods and points are allocated according to the amount spent. The points can then be used to make further purchases.

The use of loyalty cards means that special-offer information and vouchers can be sent to customers. The loyalty card identifies both the customer and the types of goods they buy. Its identity number is input into the computerised till when details of purchases have been gathered from the barcodes on the products. Thus special offers sent to a customer can be for products that are likely to be of interest.

This information relating to the purchasing patterns of a customer is of use to other organisations besides the supermarket or store itself. For example, a list of names and addresses of people who regularly purchase cat food would be valuable to a company selling pet insurance products.

1 List **three** other types of company that would be interested in purchasing the list of names and addresses of pet owners.
2 List **five** types of company that would be interested in purchasing a list of names and addresses of people who regularly buy baby food. Explain why it would be important that the list should not be more than three months old.
3 Explain why it is worthwhile for the organisations listed above to buy the list of names and addresses from the supermarket.

Supermarket loyalty card

How to find information

There is a wealth of sources of information available to a user. Many of these are accessed using a computer system.

▶ Electronic methods

Information can be acquired over the Internet or from CD-ROMs. Many users have access to intranets, either at work or through an organisation of which they are a member.

Using the Internet, a user can search the World Wide Web using a search engine. By carrying out a **keyword search**, typing in a word or words relating to the topic of interest, pages holding relevant information can be found. Very often, the information available over the Internet is more up to date than that available elsewhere. For example, there are many news sites that are continually being updated. The Web provides a huge and varied choice of information which can be accessed very quickly but care needs to be taken to ensure that information found is appropriate to the needs of the user. Increasingly, information is provided in a variety of formats not just as text. Video and sound clips are becoming more common; these are often combined to form **virtual tours**.

E-mail can be used to exchange information between people. It is often possible for an individual to receive information by e-mail from an expert who is perhaps associated with a help desk.

Bulletin boards can be a useful source of information within a limited field. A user can post questions there and reach a wide audience of people interested in the same area.

Software encyclopedias are available **on line** or on **CD-ROM**. These allow keyword searches to be made quickly and easily. If copyright restrictions permit, pictures and diagrams can be copied and pasted into reports. CD-ROMs are easy to carry around. Online encyclopedias can provide up-to-date information and often include interactive resources which help understanding.

Chat software allows a user to ask another person, such as a colleague or fellow student, a question. This can be done quickly in real time; any query can be followed up with further questions. This method of obtaining information is useful if someone has a query over the use of software or about the nature of an assignment.

Teletext and **interactive television** are both sources of up-to-date information.

▶ Non-electronic sources

You do not need to have access to a computer to get information. Books, newspapers and magazines are all useful sources. These can be used in the home, the workplace or in a library and are easy to carry around. Manuals also provide easily accessible information.

Information can also be acquired from another person in conversation. This often happens in the workplace either formally, for example in a meeting, or informally, perhaps when two people meet in a corridor.

Activity 2

Copy and fill in the grid below. For each example, choose a **different** source of information.

Information	Source	Justification
The weather forecast for the day		
How to install a new piece of software		
Details of the historical background to the Welsh Assembly		
The question that you have to answer for your ICT homework this week		
Some background details about your favourite band		
The time of day that a film is showing on TV		
The telephone number of a person that you haven't phoned before		
The current exchange rate for the euro		

Summary

▶ Good information should be **accurate**, **up to date** and **complete**.

▶ Good information adds value to organisations by:
  a aiding decision making
  b monitoring progress
  c allowing the targeting of resources
  d giving a competitive advantage.

▶ Ensuring that information is of a high quality is costly. These costs can be in terms of:
  a money
  b time
  c human resources.

▶ Good information can improve the quality of decision making as it has user confidence.

▶ Information can come from a variety of sources, both ICT and non-ICT based.

Chapter 2 Questions

1 A report has been produced by an ICT system for the sales manager of a company. She complains that she does not know when the report was produced, or how up to date the contents of the report are.

a Explain why up-to-date information will be important to the sales manager and what could be done to ensure that she knows when the information was produced. **(4)**

b Discuss other factors that may affect the quality of the information produced for the report. **(8)**

2 The owners of a holiday company are considering organising some special deals for 2009. They use data obtained from customers who took one of their holidays during the year 2005 to decide what to offer. One of the owners, James, says that the information produced is not suitable for making the decisions.

Explain what makes James unsure of the usefulness of the information and discuss the implications for the holiday company of making decisions based on it. **(5)**

3 State **three** factors that affect the value and importance of information. Give an example that shows clearly how **each** factor affects the information's value. **(6)**

4 The owner of a video store is considering updating the manual record-keeping system to an ICT-based system to get better-quality information.

   a Describe **two** factors **other** than the financial costs of purchasing new hardware and software that must be considered in setting up and maintaining the system. **(2 x 2)**
   b State **two** advantages that up-to-date, accurate and complete information will give the store owner. **(2) WJEC Jan 05**

5 a There are financial costs involved in getting good-quality information. State **two other** costs and, giving a different example for **each** one, show how these costs arise. **(4)**
   b Give **one** example of a problem that could arise if information is not:
   i   up to date **(1)**
   ii complete **(1)**
   iii accurate. **(1)**

   Use distinctly different examples in **each** case. **WJEC Jan 06**

6 Good-quality information must use *accurate* and *valid* data.

   a In addition to being *accurate* and *valid* outline **two other** factors which would give good-quality information. **(2)**
   b Discuss, using an example, **one** way in which good-quality information can add value to an organisation by aiding the decision-making process. **(2) WJEC June 06**

7 A student wishes to find out about the Solar System.

   a Describe how the student could make use of **two** different, appropriate **electronic** sources of information to find out about the Solar System. **(2 x 2)**
   b Give **one non-electronic** source of information the student could use for this purpose. **(1) WJEC Jan 07**

8 a Discuss how up-to-date, accurate and complete information can add value to an organisation. **(3)**
   b Getting good-quality information costs money, time and human resources. Describe with suitable **distinct** examples how such costs could arise. **(3) WJEC June 07**

9 a A company improved its performance by having *up-to-date, accurate* and *complete* information. Describe **two** ways in which such information has added value to the company. Illustrate your answers with suitable differing examples. **(2 x 2)**
   b Other than data collection, describe **two** of the costs in terms of money, time and human resources in obtaining good-quality information. Use a suitable **different** example to illustrate your answer in **each** case. **(4) WJEC Jan 08**

Validation and Verification
4.1.4

Errors

▶ Why are errors a problem?

Some errors in data can lead to catastrophic results, whilst others can affect the acceptability of a computer system. As businesses and other organisations are dependent on information from computers, it is essential to try to reduce the occurrence of data errors and so ensure that the information is as accurate as possible.

▶ Results of errors

There are many examples in newspapers of the results of errors occurring in computer systems. These include pensioners receiving gas bills for millions of pounds and others getting letters threatening legal action unless an outstanding payment of £000.00 is received within ten days. An error in a program caused a newly developed fighter plane to turn upside down when it crossed the Equator. (Luckily this was detected during simulation testing.)

▶ When errors can occur

Errors can occur at several stages in a system:
- ▶ when the data is captured
- ▶ when data initially collected on paper is **transcribed** (copied), usually via a keyboard, and entered into a computer
- ▶ when data is transmitted within a computer system, particularly over a network link
- ▶ when data is being processed by software.

▶ Errors in data capture and entry

The majority of errors are introduced at data entry. Consequently automated methods are used whenever possible. For example, using barcode readers at a supermarket checkout means that no data needs to be keyed in, thus saving time and removing the chance of transcription errors. However no method of data entry can guarantee to be error free.

It is not always possible to use automated data entry methods. For example, in many supermarkets fresh products such as vegetables are weighed at the checkout and the appropriate code is keyed in. If the operator wrongly identifies the vegetable or mistypes the code, then incorrect data is input. In some systems the operator can enter a number for multiple items rather than scanning each item separately. Mis-keying could result in a customer being charged for 50 tins of baked beans instead of 5!

Many errors occur when data is originally captured. Application forms, mail-order requests, census forms and details of car repairs undertaken are all examples where data is often first captured on paper. Errors can be recorded at this stage. A common mistake is to enter a date of birth with the current year. Forms that do not clearly indicate what is required also lead to errors.

▶ Transcription errors

Whenever data is manually copied there is a chance that errors will be made. These copying errors are known as transcription errors. They can occur when the person involved misreads what is written or mishears what is said. Poor handwriting and unclear speech over the telephone are both likely to lead to transcription errors. Long codes made up of numbers or letters that have no particular meaning to the person keying in the data are particularly vulnerable to error. The skill and accuracy of the typing of the data inputter will have a major effect on the number of transcription errors made.

If computer operators are interrupted when entering data from a pile of paper documents they may miss out a page or enter data from the same page twice.

A common form of transcription error is a **transpositional** error, where the order of two characters is mistakenly swapped. A code number 134638 could easily be mistyped as 136438. It is likely that this code number is being used to identify something such as a bank account, a hospital patient or a product. Entering the wrong code could have serious consequences, resulting in the wrong person's bank account being debited, the wrong patient's notes being updated with a drug prescription or the wrong product being ordered for a customer.

Activity 1

For each of the transcription errors below explain what is wrong and why the error is likely to have been made:

1 SO23 5RT entered as S023 SRT
2 Leeming entered as Lemming
3 419863 entered as 419683
4 2000000 entered as 200000
5 Hatherley Road entered as Haverly Road
6 238.591 entered as 2385.91
7 23/5/89 entered as 23/5/09
8 199503 entered as 195503.

▶ Reducing data capture and transcription error

The use of automatic data entry, where there is no need for the keying in of data, removes the possibility of transcription errors. In a computerised system for a lending library, a hand-held scanner is used to record the reader's identification number from a barcode on their membership card as well as the accession number held as a barcode in the book.

Methods of recording the current reading of a householder's electricity meter have developed through the following systems:

▶ a form filled in by the reader that was later transcribed using key to disk
▶ a pre-printed OMR (optical mark recognition) card where appropriate boxes were shaded to represent the digits
▶ a hand-held computer with data relating to the customer's account so that data can be entered and checked at the house.

> OMR technology scans a form for the presence of marks in preset positions.

A turnaround document is a document produced as output from one computerised system and later used as an input to another system. Using a turnaround document that can be read in by an OCR reader minimises the amount of data that has to be keyed in.

As transpositional errors are a very common form of typing error, it is crucial to avoid these as far as possible. Paper forms need to be designed with great care so that the chances of errors being made are kept to a minimum.

A data entry screen should be designed to follow the layout of data on the paper form. Mistakes are more likely to be made if the eye has to jump around the page to find an appropriate data field.

The greater the number of characters that need to be keyed in, the greater the chance of error. Wherever possible codes should be used.

To ensure that only valid choices can be entered, options can be given for the user to choose, in the form of either tick boxes or drop-down lists.

Human errors such as transcription errors can be detected using two techniques – validation and verification.

Activity 2

For each of the following systems, suggest how a method of data capture could remove the need for data transcription.

1 In a school library, the name and class of the student together with the book accession number and return date are keyed in whenever a student borrows a book.
2 Lists of marks awarded to students in their AS-level coursework are sent in to the examination board from centres. On receipt of these lists the marks are keyed in by administrative assistants.

3 Employees in an office write down the time of their arrival and departure in a book. These figures are keyed in using DDE (direct data entry) at the end of the week so that overtime pay can be calculated.

4 Members of a postal book club can order books by telephone. A clerk takes details of members' account numbers and the codes of the books required then keys in the data using a DDE system.

Verification

Verification is a method of checking that no changes have been made to the data during data entry. It often involves double entry of data.

Verification is used to check that no changes are made to data as it is copied from one medium to another.

One common method of verification involves the **double entry** of data into the computer. The computer automatically compares the two versions and tells the user if they're not the same. For example, when network users change their password, they have to type in the new password twice to verify it. When bank employees key in the amount written on a cheque, the amount will be entered again by a second person and the two entered values compared by software before the entry is accepted.

Proofreading, where a user **visually checks** an entry, is another form of verification. When a customer is purchasing goods on line they have to enter product and payment details. Most systems will ask them to read and confirm that their details are correct. After writing a chapter of this book the author proofread it by checking through the document to find errors that had not been picked up by the spell-check function of the word processor.

A third method of verification is to print out a copy of details that have been entered and **send the printout** to the originator of the data for checking. At a college, student details, such as address, date of birth and previous school, are entered into a database when the student enrolls. During the first week of term, each student is usually given a printout of their personal details. They are required to check the details, note any errors and sign to confirm that the check has been carried out.

Validation

Validation is computerised checking that detects any data that is not reasonable or is incomplete. There are many different validation techniques that can be included in a program. One or more might be included for a particular data item. The most common techniques are:

▶ **Presence check:** This checks that an entry has been made for the field. For example, the surname field in an order form cannot be left blank.

Validation is a method of checking by computer program that data entered into a computer system is reasonable and obeys preset rules.

▶ **Range check:** This checks that a value lies within in a certain range of values. For example, the month of a year must be between 1 and 12. Numbers less than 1 or greater than 12 would be rejected. In the same way, a mark gained in a test could be checked to be between 0 and 50.

▶ **Type check:** This checks whether data is text or numeric, etc.

▶ **Format check** (type or picture check): This checks that data is of the right format, that it is made up of the correct combination of alphabetic and numeric characters. A National Insurance number must be of the form XX 99 99 99 X. The first two and the last character must be letters. The other six characters are numbers. Any other format is rejected. A format check is commonly used with a date field.

▶ **Cross-field check:** This checks that data in two fields corresponds. For example, if someone's gender is stored as F (female), their title cannot be Mr. If the month in a date is 04, the day cannot be 31 as there are only 30 days in April.

▶ **Look-up list of fixed values:** This checks that the data is one of the entries in the list of acceptable values. For example, the day of the week must be from the list Monday, Tuesday and so on.

▶ **Check digits:** These are used to check the validity of code numbers used for identification, for example, product codes in a supermarket, bank account numbers, credit-card numbers or student identification numbers. These numbers are long and prone to data entry errors. It is crucial that such numbers are entered correctly so that the right record in the file or database is identified. The check digit is an extra digit added to the end of the original code. The value of the check digit is determined by the value and positioning of the other digits: for any given code there is only one possible check digit. When the code has been entered, the check digit is recalculated and compared to the entered value. If the two digits do not match, an error is reported.

Case Study 1 – Validation of meter readings

An electricity company reads the meters in individual houses. These readings will be validated by a range check to make sure that they are within a sensible range. The records are fed into the computer.

The computer can check that the details for every house have been entered by checking that a control total, the number of houses, is correct. Of course, one house may have been omitted and another entered twice. This can be checked by making sure that no customer number is repeated.

1 When the bill is calculated it should be validated by another range check to make sure that it is not ridiculously high or low. List **three** validation checks that could be made on the customer number. Explain the purpose of each test.

2 Another field that has data entered into it is the date that the reading is taken. Give **three** validation checks that could be made on the date. Explain the purpose of each test.

Activity 3

What could be a consequence of making an error when entering:

1 the examination number for a student's exam result

2 a patient number in a hospital

3 the product code when ordering an item of clothing on line

4 the account number when making a bank transfer.

Activity 4

Generic software packages such as spreadsheets and database management systems have the facility to add data validation checks. Figure 1 shows data validation being added to a Microsoft Excel spreadsheet.

Set up a spreadsheet that allows the user to enter the data shown in the table below. The validation checks shown should be added. Suitable error messages for invalid data entry should be displayed.

Data item	Validation checks
Name	Maximum 25 characters
Team	One of: Basingstoke Bashers, Andover Athletic, Salisbury Stars, Winchester Wanderers, Southampton Swifts.
Position played	Whole number between 1 and 12

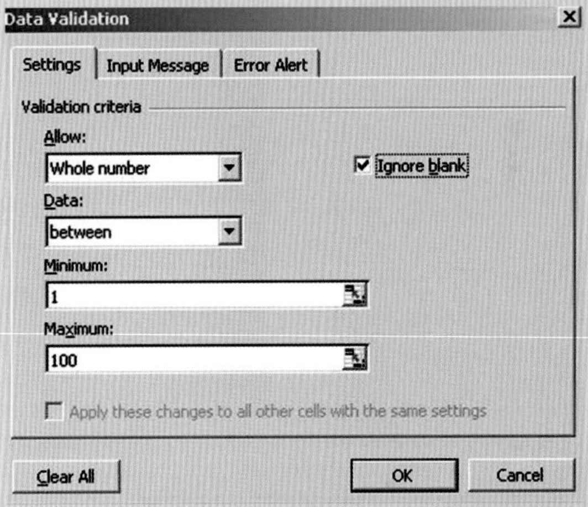

Figure 1 Data validation being added to a Microsoft Excel spreadsheet

► Accuracy versus validity

Validation checks can ensure that the data entered is reasonable and sensible, that it obeys set rules. Such checks however cannot ensure that the data entered accurately represents the source data.

It is possible that data entered could be **valid** but **inaccurate**. A temperature sensor recording the temperature in a furnace may give valid data, a number within a certain range, but the data may not accurately reflect the temperature if the sensor is not set up correctly. If '25 The Glebe', the address of a customer, is entered as '52 The Glebe' or even '61 Brockhampton Road', no validation error would be detected as both are reasonable addresses. However, neither is an accurate address for the customer. A person's date of birth entered as 25/03/1975 is a valid date but would be inaccurate if they had been born in April.

Activity 5

State which of the following errors could be detected using validation checks. For those that could be detected, suggest a suitable check.

1 Car registration of 234 B 65
2 Date of birth for a sixth-form-college student of 12/4/1999
3 Entry of a quantity of 20 tins of dog food instead of 2
4 Name of Lian instead of Liam
5 Entry of a quantity of 2000 tins of dog food instead of 2
6 Date of admission to hospital of 31/04/2005
7 Shoe size of 5½ instead of 6½
8 UMS score of 650 for A-level ICT.

Further errors

▶ Transmission errors

Data that has been entered correctly in a system can become corrupted when it is transmitted within a computer or when sent from one computer to another. This may be due to a poor connection or 'noise' on the line. All data is held within a computer and transmitted in binary coded form: everything is represented by a string of ones and zeros. Data corruption will result in one or more zeros being altered to ones, or ones being altered to zeros. It is likely that the resulting string of bits would be interpreted as another character, graphic, etc.

For example, if just three bits were corrupted when transmitting the characters ICT in ASCII the result could become HGV:

1001001 (I)	1000011 (C)	1010100 (T)
1001000 (H)	1000111 (G)	1010110 (V)

Transmission errors can be avoided by the receiving computer sending the same message back to the original sender. If the two messages are the same, the data will be correct.

The use of **parity** is a method that enables the detection of errors. A **parity bit** is an extra bit that is added to a group of bits when data is being transmitted or stored. The parity bit is solely used to check that the other bits have not been corrupted. There are two types of parity – even and odd. When even parity is used the parity bit is chosen to be 0 or 1 so that the total number of transmitted bits set to 1 (including the parity bit) is even.

▶ Processing errors

Errors may occur owing to incorrectly written software. Experience shows that programmers produce 30–100 faults in every 1000 lines of code. Calculations could be worked out incorrectly, the wrong record could be updated in a file or certain types of transaction could be ignored.

Errors can also occur owing to omissions in the specification (the document that lays out what a new system is to do), where certain situations are not considered when the system is designed. Design must always assume that an operator can make errors.

One computer system tried to raise the temperature in a chemical process to 800 degrees when the operator had meant to enter 80, with the result that a poisonous chemical was released into the atmosphere.

A fatal error occurred when a patient received a lethal dose of radiation treatment for a cancerous tumour. The computer-controlled equipment had previously been used hundreds of times without causing an error. On this particular occasion the operator had altered the data entered by using the cursor keys in a particular way that had not been anticipated.

Other types of error can occur when the computer system is not operated correctly. For example, an incorrect file name can be entered and an out-of-date set of records used. A batch of data could be lost or forgotten so that a number of transactions are not entered into the system. Hardware failure, such as a disk corruption, can cause some data to be lost; power surges and the presence of a virus are other possible causes of error.

Activity 6

1 Discuss possible causes of the following (there may be a number of possibilities) and suggest solutions.

a A tenant is sent a letter that states that rent is overdue when in fact it has been paid in full.

b An electricity bill demanding a payment of 2p is sent out.

c A customer receives a copy of *Madagascar* instead of

Brynbedw
6th Form College

Please complete the form in black ink using BLOCK CAPITALS

Surname	
Forename(s)	
Home address	

Telephone number	Postcode
Date of birth	Age on 1/9/2009 yrs mths
Previous school	

Ethnic origin (please tick)

White ☐	Black Caribbean ☐	Black African ☐	Black Other ☐	Indian ☐
Pakistani ☐	Bangladeshi ☐	Chinese ☐	Other ☐	Info refused ☐

Provisional Course for September 2009

Please indicate which courses you are interested in. Please list, in order of preference, the subject name and the level (AS, A2, GCSE, BTEC).

Subject	Level

Current Courses of Study

Please list the GCSE subjects that you are currently studying, or have already taken, indicating which level paper you are being entered for (higher, intermediate or foundation). Please ask your school to add your predicted (or actual) grades.

Subject	Level	Predicted Grade

APPLICATION FORM 2009

Figure 2 Application form for Brynbedw 6th Form College

Summary

▶ The information produced by a system is only as good as the quality of the data that is input.

▶ Errors in data can have far-reaching effects.

▶ Errors can occur when data is:
  a captured
  b transcribed
  c transmitted
  d processed.

▶ Errors can be reduced in a variety of ways, including:
  a using automatic data capture methods such as OCR or OMR that remove the need for transcription

  b verification checks
  c validation checks such as presence check, range check, type check, format check, cross-field check, look-up list, check digit
  d thorough analysis and specification that takes into account all possible circumstances
  e thorough testing.

▶ Data that is valid may not be accurate or correct.

Chapter 3 Questions

1 Items stored in a computerised stock-control sheet are uniquely identified by a product code. The format of the product code is XXX99, where X is a capital letter (L, M or N) and 9 is a digit. The product has a range from LLL00 to NNN99.

   Name and describe **three** validation checks that could be used on this product code. (6)

2 Banks use *verification* and *validation* methods to reduce data entry errors in their online banking systems.
   a Define the term *verification*. Name and describe **one** verification method used in online banking systems. (3)
   b Define the term *validation*. Name and describe **one** validation method used in online banking systems. (3) **WJEC specimen**

3 Validation and verification are very important in online shopping systems. Describe, using suitable relevant examples, how these methods are used to reduce data entry errors in online shopping systems. (2 x 2) **WJEC Jan 08**

4 a Errors in data can occur during *data collection*, *data entry* and *data processing*. Describe how **each** of these three types of error could occur. (3)
   b The purpose of verification and validation is to minimise errors in data. Distinguish between verification and validation and give an example of a validation method. (3) **WJEC June 07**

5 Good-quality information must use *accurate* and *valid* data.
   a Define the term *accurate data*. (1)
   b Data may pass a *validity* check but still be *inaccurate*. Using a suitable example, explain the difference between validity and accuracy. (2) **WJEC June 06**

The text of this chapter requires about 90 Kb of storage. A typical photograph could require about 5000 Kb.

Investigate the storage available on the computer that you use. (You can do this by using the **My Computer** utility in Windows.)

1 What is the capacity for the hard disk? How much is currently being used?
2 Draw up a table showing the storage required for **five** programs that you use frequently.
3 Copy and complete the following table. Use the Internet to find out the range of storage available for each device and explain what data is stored.

Devices	Range of storage	What storage is used for
Mobile phones		
Memory cards for digital cameras		
Memory sticks		
Digital video recorders		

▶ Speed of searching

ICT systems can search through large volumes of data very quickly. For example, files can be located via the name of the file, the date of creation or particular text stored within the file.

Consider a computer system used by the police that stores details of the fingerprints of hundreds of thousands of people in digitally coded form. When a fingerprint is detected at the scene of a crime, a search needs to be made to see if the print matches any that are held. Without a computer system this task could not be undertaken for all the thousands of stored prints within a realistic time.

▶ Greater accuracy and speed of data communication

Without ICT systems, individuals are limited to the use of human contact, the postal or telephone service for communication. ICT systems can link to other ICT systems and other electronic devices, almost anywhere in the world. Wireless connections are becoming more commonly used. They are more flexible but can only be used over short distances and performance does not match that of hard-wired systems.

The Internet allows people to communicate with other users worldwide via e-mail as well as to access and transfer huge amounts of data through the World Wide Web. A holiday company will store details of all available holidays together with bookings that have been made on a central computer system. This will be available to travel agents in many different locations who can link their computer system to the central data store. This enables a travel agent both to have access to up-to-date information on holiday availability, and to make immediate bookings while their client is with them. Alternatively, the booking could be made directly by the customer with no travel agent involved.

The home user has a wealth of information available over the Internet. The site http://www.ratedtrader.com provides householders with access to a range of local traders such as plumbers and electricians. It is also possible to find out the postcode for any address in the UK.

News bulletins and weather forecasts are readily available on a number of websites and can be accessed from some mobile phones and televisions as well as from computers.

Banks offer online services. With online access an account holder can view both the balance in their account and all transactions that have been made. Standing orders can be set up and payments and transfers made.

Activity 2

ICT allows all the following to be done:
- finding out a postcode by accessing the website www.royalmail.com
- using a tourist information booth with touch-screen display to find out about local attractions
- finding a suitable plumber by accessing the website www.ratedtrader.com
- getting the next day's weather forecast for a town abroad
- booking a ticket for a flight from Glasgow to Southampton
- setting up a transfer from your current account to your savings account.

For each of the above describe how the information could have been obtained before the development of ICT systems. For example, it was possible to find out postcodes by visiting a post office, where books listing postcodes were kept.

Case Study 1 – Ken is off to New York

Ken is an executive working for an international media company. He lives in South East London and commutes every day to Central London. Today he is flying to New York to attend a conference.

As he eats his breakfast, he checks that there is no delay to his flight by accessing the airline's website using his home computer. He also checks in to his flight using the airline's online facility. He is able to print out his boarding pass, the document that displays his seat number and is required to allow him onto the aeroplane. He had previously purchased his e-ticket on line.

He has booked a taxi to take him to the airport and uses the journey time to check his e-mails using his PDA. He responds to a few urgent messages.

Ken books in his luggage and then goes to the airline's executive lounge. This is a WiFi hotspot so he is able to use his laptop computer to access the Internet. He searches for some material relevant for the conference that he is attending.

His flight is called, so Ken logs off his computer and boards the plane.

1 As an alternative to confirming his booking from his home computer, Ken could have used an airport check-in kiosk. Find out more about these kiosks from an airline's website such as http://www.britishairways.com
List the features offered.

2 List the information that Ken has acquired and the services that he has accessed using ICT during the morning.

3 Describe the advantages to Ken of the accessibility of information and services that ICT provides.

▶ Different output formats

Storing data digitally allows it to be processed into information that can be presented in a variety of ways. Better presentation of items such as invoices, letters and other documents, as well as a well presented and accessible website, can improve the image of a company and may bring more customers and higher profits.

Information should be presented in a format that is appropriate for the intended audience. It is relatively straightforward to produce numerical information in a tabular form or using charts and graphs. A desktop publishing (DTP) or advanced word-processing package can be used to combine graphics and text to create posters, news-sheets and flyers.

Not all information is printed on paper. A report to a group of directors could be presented on a screen. Such a presentation could include graphs, tables and text.

Traditionally, acetate slides with information printed (or written) on them were used with an overhead projector (OHP). These slides are cheap to produce and only require a standard overhead projector and screen for display.

Nowadays many presentations are prepared using software such as Microsoft PowerPoint. Although individual slides can be printed onto acetate and displayed using an OHP, the package enables the information to be displayed as a slide show using an LCD projector and a screen. PowerPoint also gives the option of printing out the presentation so that the audience have a hard copy of the report to take away with them for later reference.

An LCD projector is connected to a computer and the image appearing on the computer screen is projected. Many rooms such as lecture rooms or classrooms have a ceiling-mounted LCD projector. This projector is permanently fixed and can easily be connected to a computer – for example, a laptop.

Electronic whiteboard in use in a classroom

LCD projectors can also be connected to video or DVD players where appropriate.

The use of electronic whiteboards together with LCD projectors has opened up further possibilities for presenters. For example, the user can add notes to the image on the screen, and store and print these annotations.

Electronic whiteboards may have a touch-screen feature, so that the presenter can navigate the screen using a finger to move the cursor and double clicking with taps on the screen. An alternative is to use a special 'pen'.

Case Study 2 – Public lending library

A lending library in Wintown has a very large stock of books, DVDs, CDs, audio tapes and videos that are loaned to members for a fixed time period. The computer system used to manage the flow of data in the library is linked via a wide area network to the central county computer.

The computer system records details of all loaned and returned items. Whenever a loan is made the system checks that it will not exceed the member's loan limit; also the member will be reminded if they have any overdue items.

An electronic catalogue of all items held by the library is maintained for the use of both staff and members. A member is able to check on line from home what books are available for loan and to reserve a book for collection later. The central county computer can be accessed to extend the search for a book countywide.

Once a week a mail-merge program is run that produces letters to be sent to all members who have items that are over a month overdue.

Every six months a summary is produced for the senior librarian that provides statistics on borrowing patterns. A list is also produced that contains the details of all items that have not been borrowed during the last period.

1 What is a mail-merge program?
2 Describe the data that you think will need to be brought together to produce the letters concerning overdue items.
3 Describe how each of the following capabilities relates to the Wintown library lending system:
   a fast processing
   b vast storage capacity
   c speed of searching for data
   d repetitive processing.

Case Study 3 – Gas billing system

A gas company delivers gas to over half a million customers. Details of all customers are held on the computer system and every three months bills are printed out and sent to the appropriate householders. Each bill is worked out from a meter reading taken from an individual property. Customers are often offered a discount if their bills are sent by e-mail and/or they make payments by direct debit every month, with an adjustment at the end of the year according to how much gas they have used.

Details of any payment made are used to update a customer's record. If payment is not made within a defined period the customer is sent a further bill as a reminder.

Each meter reader uses a hand-held device to record the number read from the meter. The device already contains details of the customer and house. At the end of each day the meter reader attaches their device to a connecter installed at their home. This is then connected via a telephone line to the company's wide area network. Details of the readings recorded are transferred to the central computer system and details of the households that the meter reader is to visit the next day are downloaded to the device.

1 What information, apart from the recent meter reading, will be needed to produce a customer's bill?
2 How could bills be produced if there were no ICT system?
3 Describe how each of the following capabilities relates to the gas billing system:
   a repetitive processing
   b vast storage capacity
   c greater accuracy and speed of data communication.

Case Study 4 – Airline bookings

Every airline maintains a centralised booking system for its flights. Travel agents all around the world can access the system to find out about seat availability as well as to make a booking. Travellers can cut out the travel agent by searching for flights over the Internet and booking directly using the airline's website.

Bookings can be made several months in advance. For many large airlines there will be thousands of flights available for booking at any one time.

Whenever bookings are made, details relating to the passengers are recorded, including dietary requirements. Seat numbers can be allocated, the total cost, including airport fees and other charges, is calculated and payment made by credit/debit card.

Many systems allow the travel agent to print the ticket for the customer at the time of booking. Travellers who book over the Internet do not get a ticket but receive a reference to give when they check in. Some airlines allow passengers to print their own boarding cards and check-in documents using a touch-screen computer system.

When passengers arrive at the airport they check in, their luggage is booked in and has a label attached that holds details of airport destination along with an identification code. All the details are recorded on the computer system.

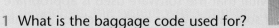

A number of lists need to be produced, including:
▶ a full passenger list for check-in clerks
▶ a list showing special dietary requirements for the caterers
▶ a list of passengers needing special service together with their seat numbers.

1 What is the baggage code used for?
2 Refer to the list of capabilities on page 30 and explain which apply to the airline booking system.
3 What problems could arise from having a booking system that is dependent upon ICT systems?

Limitations of ICT

The efficiency of a data processing system is affected by a number of factors, including:
▶ hardware
▶ software
▶ suitability of operating system
▶ communication
▶ input.

▶ Hardware

Although the technological advances have been made, financial and other constraints limit what an ICT system can be used for. For example, home users may not be able to produce the high-quality photographic prints that they wish to because they do not have an appropriate printer.

Speed is often a factor in determining the effectiveness of a data

Whenever new software is written, errors are created. The process of testing is designed to discover these errors. If **insufficient testing** is carried out, errors will go undetected. See Chapter 3, page 25 for examples.

Even when rigorous testing has taken place software may fail to operate successfully as part of an information system. This could be because the software was not designed for the situation in which it is being used. Perhaps the volume of the data and the size of the resulting files are much greater than those the software was designed for. A user might use the software in ways that had never been considered, causing it to behave in unexpected ways. It could be that the software is being used in a different environment.

New software cannot be tested for use with every combination of hardware and other software. Installing and using new software may cause an established system to fail.

The hardware resources provided to run the software may not be sufficient for it to run at its optimum. This could cause systems to run unacceptably slowly or even to crash frequently. New hardware could be released that the software will not work with; the software developers may not have been aware of these changes.

Another factor that can adversely affect the efficiency of a system is **poor communication with the user**. During the initial stages of a system's development – the analysis and design phases – it is very important that the users are listened to and their requirements fully understood. During the analysis phase, the systems analyst has to gain a full understanding of how the current system works as well as finding out what users require in a new system. If communications between users and analyst are not good, the analyst's understanding will be inaccurate or incomplete. The design phase covers all aspects of the system including specific designs for data entry screens, forms, reports and all procedures. These should be shared with users at all stages of development so that they can suggest appropriate changes.

If communications are poor at either stage of development, the final system will not reflect the real needs of the users and will be unlikely to run efficiently. The system may fail to take into account the data and processes that are required.

The **ability of the user** is a crucial factor. Without adequate training a user may not be able to use a data processing system effectively. Data entry errors could occur owing to lack of skill, and the full range of facilities of the system may not be used. It is crucial that users' skills levels are taken into account when a new system is developed and that adequate training is provided: with the wrong person in the job the most technically sophisticated system will not run efficiently.

Post-implementation procedures include the training of staff and the transfer from the old way of carrying out the tasks to the new systems. If these procedures are poorly planned and carried out the new system is unlikely to run efficiently. Users will lack confidence if they are not fully trained; they will take much longer to carry out tasks and make numerous mistakes.

Good **maintenance procedures** are crucial to the success of any data processing system. Files must be kept up to date. Consideration should be given at the design stage to ensure that adequate procedures are in place to deal with the backup and archiving of data. Backup is needed so that lost data can be restored. Archived data is data that is no longer current but may be needed for reference purposes. If no procedure is in place for archiving such data, files will become over full and the system will be slowed down – eventually failing to function at all.

Software such as virus protection programs needs to be kept up to date.

Maintenance also involves making changes to software after it has been implemented. There are a number of reasons for doing this. The changes might be made to put right errors in the original software that come to light after it is released. Changes could be made to improve performance of the software in some way – for example, the time taken to carry out a particular function. Also, modifications may be needed to meet changing needs, such as the introduction of the euro or to interface with a new operating system.

If maintenance is not carried out in an organised and structured way, the system will fail to perform as intended. Users are likely to become frustrated and will have to spend time finding ways of countering the weakness of the system. This will be a waste of time and energy.

Very often the **cost** of a proposed system will mean that a cheaper alternative is implemented owing to budget constraints; the costs of the better system might exceed possible benefits. This can result in a system that does not fully meet the needs of the user.

An organisation must ensure that adequate **hardware support** is provided otherwise the running of the system may be interrupted when hardware breaks down.

Summary

ICT systems have the following advantages over manual methods for processing data:

▶ repetitive processing
▶ speed of processing
▶ vast storage capability
▶ speed of searching for data
▶ greater accuracy and speed of data communication
▶ ability to produce different output formats.

There are a number of factors affecting the efficiency of data processing systems, including:

▶ hardware
▶ software
▶ suitability of operating system
▶ communications
▶ input.

Chapter 4 Questions

1 When Mrs Evans received her electricity bill she found that it was for £50000, which she knew was not correct. When she contacted the electricity company to complain, she was told 'the computer had got it wrong'. Describe a more likely explanation. (2)

2 Most employers now use computer systems to calculate their employees' wages and pay them straight into the employees' bank accounts. Describe **four** capabilities of ICT which make electronic payment advantageous to the employer. (8)

3 Over half the world's e-mails are believed to be spam. This is unrequested advertising sent to collections of e-mail addresses and offering to sell you anything from medication to a university degree. Describe **three** capabilities of ICT which have made spam so prevalent. (6)

4 A hospital is planning to provide all its doctors with hand-held computers. These computers will be useable anywhere in the hospital to access patient information and order medicines.
   a List **two** benefits to the hospital of introducing this system. (2)
   b Explain **one** disadvantage to the doctor of introducing this system. (2)

5 Information technology is widely used in business to process large amounts of data.
   a Discuss **two** advantages of ICT over manual methods of processing data, using suitable examples in each case. (4)
   b Describe **three** factors affecting the efficiency of data processing systems. (3) WJEC Jan 2008

5

Uses of ICT in Business and Education 4.1.6 (Part 1)

CAD/CAM

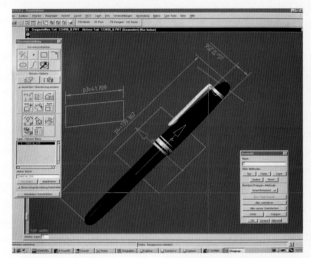

CAD package in use

Computer-aided design (CAD) is software that allows a user to draw accurate plans and designs.

For **CAD**, where high precision is required, **bitmapped graphics**, in which colour is assigned to individual pixels, are not appropriate. **Vector graphics** are used instead. With vector graphics the image is stored in terms of geometric data. For example, a circle is defined by its centre, its radius and its colour. Vector graphics enable the user to manipulate objects as entire units. For example, to change the length of a line or enlarge a circle the user simply has to select the chosen object on the screen then stretch or drag the image as required.

A bitmapped graphic would require repainting individual dots in the line or circle. With vector graphics, objects are described mathematically so they can be layered, rotated and magnified relatively easily.

CAD packages allow **three-dimensional (3D)** images to be designed and viewed from different angles. When a product such as an engine or a lamp is designed, there are considerable error risks if only two-dimensional (2D) plans are used. The ability to view a 3D image of the product design can help the designer visualise what it will eventually look like. Conversion from 2D to 3D allows the bare plan to be solidified so that non-experts can get a better feel for what the final product will look like.

Producing a 3D image requires considerable processing power and a large quantity of memory. CAD packages also allow the creation of wire drawings, which just show the outline structure of a design. These help with perspective and working out stresses and strain areas. They have the advantage of requiring less processing for display.

Many industries now use computer-aided design/computer-aided manufacturing (**CAD/CAM**) where the output from a CAD process is input to control a manufacturing process. CAM systems produce objects using **computer-controlled** machines.

Benetton, the fashion company, uses a CAD system to produce templates for items such as a pair of jeans in a range of sizes. The CAD system automatically calculates the best way to lay the templates on the fabric so as to minimise the wastage of materials and cuts the time taken to produce these templates from 24 to 2 hours.

Benetton links its CAD system to its CAM system. This enables designs created on the CAD system to be transferred directly to computer-controlled knitting machines, so increasing the flexibility of the systems still further.

Benetton finds that the quality of the computer-manufactured products is higher and more consistent, leading to increased productivity as fewer garments are wasted. The use of CAM should optimise the use of raw materials, so cutting down on wastage. The use of 3D designs allows the product to be viewed in its final form without the need to build a physical prototype. This reduces costs and development time.

CAD programs are also used in engineering and architecture. Users can draw accurate straight lines and arcs of different types and thickness. By zooming in, designs can be produced more accurately. Designs for complex items such a car or a school building can be produced in layers. Each layer will show different information. For example, in the design for a building one layer might show electrical wiring, another gas pipes, another plumbing, and so on. These layers can be displayed individually or all together.

▶ Features of CAD/CAM packages

CAD/CAM packages offer a range of features that make them appropriate for use in a wide range of design fields.

A user can **zoom** in on part of an image. This means that they can magnify and work in fine detail on a particular area. They can **rotate** the 3D image to see it from any angle, giving them a range of views from the outside of the object. This helps a designer to get a better idea of how the product will look.

CAD packages allow a database to be created within them which can be linked to the design. The amounts of different materials required to make the product can be built up. The system can produce **costings** for manufacture that can be used to see if production is feasible against a budget.

By using **hatching** or **rendering** the designer can display the effects of using different finishes or materials. This allows them to do 'what if' investigations to explore the best finishes for the product.

CAD packages can calculate the maximum **stresses** and **strains** on designed structures so that the suitability of design features can be checked against the requirements. By working out the weights that materials can take, the designer can avoid disasters later on when building takes place, as building should be well within the safety requirements.

For building designs a **walk-through** feature allows a user to visualise what the building will be like by 'visiting' the rooms displayed in 3D. The walk-through provides spatial awareness of what the design looks like in relation to other features.

The use of **clip-art** can speed up the design process. For example, when designing a hospital, a standard window can be selected from a number of existing designs. This window design can be replicated throughout the design for all similar windows, thus saving time and ensuring consistency.

▶ Hardware requirements for CAD/CAM packages

CAD/CAM packages require a computer with a high processor speed, large main memory (RAM) and a graphics card. Such resources are needed for the constant drawing and redrawing of the complex images.

Specialist input and output devices, including graphics tablets, are used. These allow the designer to draw on screen in a way that mimics drawing with pen and paper. Large, high-resolution screens are needed to display the images for the designer to work on. Very often large plotters are used to produce hard copies of the designs. CAM packages output to machines such as lathes, drills or routers.

▶ Advantages of using CAD/CAM software

- ▶ The designer can draw plans faster than by working manually.
- ▶ The zoom function allows the designer to magnify and work in fine detail on a particular area.
- ▶ Designs can be rotated and viewed from any angle, which helps the designer to get a better idea of how the product will look.
- ▶ Costings can be produced to help the customer see if manufacturing a product is feasible against its budget.
- ▶ The walk-through feature allows the designer and the customer to visualise what the final product will be like.
- ▶ Both the designer and the customer can see and modify designs before products are produced.
- ▶ Costs are reduced as there is less wastage in materials because designs can be tested by viewing in 3D and using features such as checking for stresses before products are manufactured.
- ▶ Simulations can be carried out to test would happen to the final product if certain elements of the design were to be altered.
- ▶ Since they are stored on computer, designs can easily be shared across departments.
- ▶ Testing can be carried out at the design stage.

▶ Disadvantages of using CAD/CAM software

- ▶ CAD/CAM software is very expensive.
- ▶ A high-specification computer with high memory capacity, a very fast processor and high-quality display screen is required.

▶ The computer could crash owing to a power failure or virus, making design or manufacture impossible until the system is restored.

▶ CAD packages have extensive features; to make good use of them a designer will need to have considerable training.

Special-purpose CAD packages are available for many areas such as kitchen or garden design. A garden design package will give the opportunity to view how the garden will look after one, two or even ten years with the chosen plants. Clip-art can be used to copy chosen plants into the design. Displaying the design in 3D and using the walk-through feature can provide a good idea of what the garden will look like once it is established.

Case Study 1 – The Trinity House Lighthouse Service

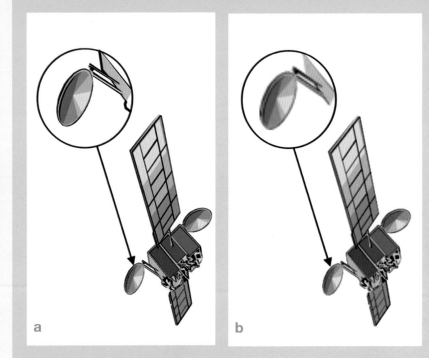

a
b

Figure 1 Part of the design for a lighthouse:

a **Vector graphic**
b **Bitmapped graphic**

Trinity House provides nearly 600 aids to navigation sites such as storm-lashed lighthouses and buoys. Project teams consisting of specialist engineers are responsible for projects from initial design through to completion.

A CAD program is used to generate drawings that are used in the manufacture, construction and installation of navigational equipment. Vector graphics enable the engineer to represent the various components and services as objects that can be copied or adapted for different applications. Layering can be used to differentiate services such as water supplies, electrical cabling and control systems.

Input is normally via a digitiser and tablet with the primary output device usually being a pen plotter or A3 laser printer.

1 Explain why a bitmapped graphics package is not appropriate for use by the Trinity House Lighthouse Service. Give at least **three** reasons.

2 Describe **three** features of a CAD package that make it suitable for use by the Lighthouse Service.

3 Explain why a digitiser and tablet are used for input rather than a mouse.

Computer-based shopping systems

Business today is unrecognisable compared with business in the days before computers. The electronic office is an obvious example of the effect of ICT on business. A modern office is likely to have a computer on every desk.

The work carried out in offices is generally the receipt, processing, storage and dispatch of information. A computer can do all these things more efficiently than traditional methods. The use of word processing and desktop publishing packages has meant that even very small businesses can produce material in a very professional manner and so enhance their image with both existing and potential customers. A document can be stored for later use and does not need to be retyped if it is needed again, perhaps with minor changes.

▶ EPOS systems

In most large shops an **electronic point-of-sale (EPOS)** till is used. It is set up to identify goods, look up prices and produce an itemised bill for the customer. EPOS tills are linked to a **local area network (LAN)** within the shop. The shop is linked by **wide area network (WAN)** to the company's warehouses and suppliers, enabling the ordering and distribution of goods from the warehouses. Queries can be sent from the shop to see if items of stock are available elsewhere.

Central office can receive sales and stock reports from each shop. The software also maintains sales and stock-level information for use by the store manager.

▶ Data entry

Hand-held barcode reader

For goods to be identified in a computerised system, every product must have a unique identifying code. For many products this is printed on the packaging as a barcode. A barcode consists of parallel black lines with white spaces in between. There are a number of input devices that can read a barcode.

The codes are read from the bars by a scanning device that detects patterns of reflected light and encodes them into computer-readable form. The device can be a **hand-held (wand) barcode reader**, which is moved over the barcode, or a fixed **flatbed** scanner, where the object is moved across the reader. The barcode has distinct right and left sides but can be read in either direction.

Laser flatbed scanners are frequently used in supermarkets to read the barcode which identifies the product. Products are passed over the scanner, which interprets the product identification code that is encoded in the barcode. The computer system can then find the price from a database.

A specialised **keypad** allows numbers to be entered if several of the same

Itemised till receipt from a supermarket

Shelf-edge computer (SEC)

Automatic till

items are purchased; this saves the operator from scanning every one. If, for some reason, the barcode cannot be read, a beep sound is made (through a loudspeaker) to alert the operator. The operator can then enter the **product identity code** or **article code**, which is printed underneath the barcode, using the keypad. As products are scanned, a **screen** displays details of the latest purchase together with the current total cost for the customer to view. There is a small **printer** attached to the EPOS till that outputs an itemised receipt with the name of the supermarket, the date and the amount owing together with a list of all items purchased.

Loose products such as fruit and vegetables will not be barcoded. These items must be weighed on special **scales** linked to the EPOS till. The scales use sensors to produce an electronic value equivalent to the weight. The operator must then type in at the keypad the appropriate product code for the fruit or vegetable. Alternatively, they may be able to select the product type from a series of images displayed on a special **touch-screen display** – if they are weighing red onions they touch the image of a red onion.

Shop staff working around the supermarket aisles may use specialist hand-held computers called SECs (**shelf-edge computers**). These can be used for implementing changes in price for specified products as well as recording information on stock levels on the shelves.

Many supermarkets allow customers to scan their own purchases. This may be achieved through the use of hand-held **self-scan** devices. Customers register to use these devices. As they select goods, they scan them before putting them in the basket. The device provides them with a running total for the cost of the items that they have selected. When they complete their shopping they go to a till. They will normally hand their scanner to the till operator, who will download the records of scanned goods and produce a bill. From time to time the operator will scan the goods again at the till as a precaution against theft.

Some supermarkets have now installed several **automatic tills** where shoppers can go at the end of their shopping, scan in their own goods and pay using either cash or a credit or debit card – there is no interaction at all with a human operator.

Activity 1

The staff at a supermarket use a large number of input and output devices. The most obvious input device is a flatbed barcode laser scanner.

Draw up a table of all the input and output devices used at a supermarket checkout, their purpose and how they are used. Use the headings below.

Device	Input or output	Purpose	How it is used

Activity 2

Barcoded product

Each number in a barcode is represented by four stripes (two black and two white). The barcode is read very quickly with very few mistakes. An article code is a unique number given to a particular product. It is often printed beneath the barcode representation of the article code. If, for some reason, the barcode reader fails to read the barcode, the operator can key in the code.

Two common numbering systems are the European Article Number (EAN) and the Universal Product Code (UPC). These numbers are structured so that each part of the code has a particular meaning. For example, an EAN product code consists of 13 digits. The first two indicate the country of origin, the next five the manufacturer and a further six identify a specific product. (The last of these six is a check digit.)

1 Read the article 'In Praise of Barcodes' by Mark Ward for BBC News that can be found at
http://news.bbc.co.uk/1/hi/sci/tech/1820532.stm
2 Describe how barcodes could be used in stores in the future.
3 Most food retail outlets sell products that are barcoded. No price is shown on the product.
   a What advantage does this have for the store?
   b How is the price determined when the product is purchased by a customer?
4 Find out more about the EAN (European Article Numbering system) at
http://www.barcode-printing.co.uk/barcode-fonts/ean-13.htm
http://electronics.howstuffworks.com/upc.htm

▶ Pricing

The **price** of a product is sent to the POS terminal from the supermarket's file server when the product's barcode is read. The barcode does not hold the price. The price is displayed to the shopper on the shelf where the product is located rather than by a sticker on the product itself. This means that, if a price changes, the value in the database is changed together with the price displayed on the shelf. There is no need for every item to have a new price sticker to cover the old one – when this used to be done it took a lot of time!

Special offers such as BOGOFF (buy one, get one for free) can easily be applied automatically by the ICT system when goods are scanned at the POS terminal.

▶ Automatic stock control

The EPOS terminal is linked to a shop file-server computer using a LAN. The file server holds a database of all stock items. For each item of stock a number of fields will be held, including:

- ▶ Product_Id_Code
- ▶ Product_Description
- ▶ Price
- ▶ Number_In_Stock (stock level)
- ▶ ReOrder_Level
- ▶ ReOrder_Quantity.

The use of ICT in shops allows **automatic stock control**. Whenever an item is sold it is identified at a POS and the **Number_In_Stock** field for that item is adjusted (downwards). At certain times during the day, the stock level is compared with the reorder level. If it is less then the ICT system will automatically instigate a reorder using the **ReOrder_Quantity** field to determine the size of the order. The shop will be linked via a WAN to suppliers and the company's distribution warehouse. Shop managers can overwrite the automatic reorder and reorder level if they notice a pattern such as a particular product needing to be reordered much more frequently than before, indicating an increase in its popularity. When goods are delivered to the shop, the **Number_In_Stock** is reset.

Very often a shop requires as much storage space for products behind the scenes as they have on the shop floor. They need to keep extra stock so that they can replenish the shelves when goods are sold. This can prove expensive as extra space has to be purchased or rented and maintained. When goods in these storage areas run low, new stock is ordered and delivered from suppliers. An approach to ordering called **just in time** uses the information from the ICT system managing the stock to minimise the amount of stock that is held.

The stock control system described above allows stock to be reordered automatically so that large amounts of backup stock do not need to be stored and the amount of warehouse space and maintenance are minimised. Fewer staff need to be employed as warehouse maintenance workers. The shop is less likely to be left with large quantities of hard-to-shift or outdated stock when using a just-in-time control system. If a product suddenly becomes popular stock levels can be increased quickly.

There are also disadvantages to just-in-time systems. Any ICT system is costly to implement and maintain; the costs incurred may outweigh the savings made. Specially trained staff will be required to run the system. If there are transportation delays then the shop will quickly run out of stock. If customer buying patterns change suddenly, the shop may find that it cannot meet customer demand. This can lead to customer dissatisfaction and loss of custom for the shop.

Many shops supply their customers with **loyalty cards** which give customers 'rewards' to encourage them to continue using the same shop or supermarket chain again and again.

See Case Study 2, page 13 for further information about loyalty cards.

▶ EFTPOS

EFTPOS is the transfer of funds electronically from the customer's bank account to the store's at a till point. By linking to an **electronic funds transfer (EFT)** system an EFTPOS till allows customers to purchase goods using credit or debit cards as their credit worthiness can be checked on line.

There are several different **payment methods** available to a customer. Traditionally, the alternative to paying in cash was to write a cheque. However, this has been phased out by many stores, who will no longer accept cheques. Instead a customer can pay using a credit or a debit card. A credit card is linked to an account where the customer can borrow money and pay later. If the full amount is not paid by the due date, interest is charged on the remaining balance. A debit card is linked to a customer's bank account and the payment is deducted from their balance at the time of purchase.

At an EFTPOS till, the customer's credit or debit card can be swiped through a card reader which reads information such as the account number and expiry date from the **magnetic strip** on the back of the card. The customer may be asked to sign their name and the signature should be checked by the shop assistant against the signature on the back of the card.

Credit card showing microchip and magnetic strip

More likely these days is the use of **chip and pin**. Here a smart card containing a microchip is placed in the reader and the customer then enters their PIN to authorise the money being debited to their account. Using a PIN provides greater security than using a signature. The account is accessed via a WAN and the transaction is authorised. A small, built-in printer is used to print out a bill which lists every item purchased together with its price.

When EFTPOS tills are widely available, the customer no longer needs to handle cash since transactions are made using cards. The tills usually provide the customer with the opportunity of receiving cashback, thus saving them a journey to an ATM.

▶ Advantages and disadvantages of computer-based shopping systems

The use of ICT in shops has brought many advantages to customers, staff and management. Just-in-time stock control can be used, saving the company money. As the system stores details of every product purchased in every transaction, far better management statistics can be produced. These allow managers to spot trends and see patterns that can result in improvement in sales through changing the layout of goods in the store, determining special offers and helping to maximise sales through stock purchase decisions. Not having to price every item on display individually saves time and brings flexibility.

On the other hand, an over-reliance on ICT can cause problems. When for some reason the technology is not available, perhaps through breakdown, normal business cannot continue. Many large stores, such as supermarkets, now use only EPOS tills that are linked to a central computer that holds a database of stock levels and prices. There have been many cases when a store has had to ask all its customers to leave because a computer failure has made all the tills inoperable. The system will also be liable to attack from viruses and hacking. The storage of large amounts of data can result in information being accessed inappropriately.

▶ Online shopping

Online shopping via the Internet (e-shopping) is taking an increasing share of the market. It is not just hi-tech and multinational companies such as Amazon that use e-commerce to sell goods. Businesses can set up their own website to market their products and make customers aware of special offers. A family-owned butchers from Yorkshire, Jack Scaife, started to use an Internet site (http://www.jackscaife.co.uk) to sell its bacon, sending deliveries all over the world. Soon e-commerce was bringing in £200000 worth of sales from a site that cost only £250 a year to maintain.

E-shopping lets the shopper make purchases without having to leave home. It allows access to products that might be hard to find in the local area. Those who have difficulty getting to shops, owing to poor health, family commitments or time constraints, are enabled by e-shopping to make the purchases they desire. Sellers are no longer limited to a local pool of potential purchasers and do not have to maintain the overhead of mailing the expensive catalogues needed for mail order.

Some people are put off e-shopping because of worries over security issues relating to the use of credit and debit cards over the Internet. Others do not like to choose items without seeing them physically.

Commercial websites

Many businesses use websites to promote themselves. Some have found that not only is this much cheaper than conventional advertising but it reaches a much larger audience. They can also include animations and videos to make the site more attractive.

It has been predicted that online shopping will account for a quarter of all sales by 2010.

When a company sells goods or services on line it can offer a customer a huge range of items. If a company such as Amazon were to sell their goods traditionally in shops they would only be able to offer limited stock in any store. If they were to set up a traditional mail-order business they would be unable to produce a catalogue of all the items they wished to sell – the catalogue would have to be massive and would be much too expensive to produce and distribute.

Selling on line is particularly appropriate for sellers of specialist goods. It allows them to locate their premises anywhere they wish and still have a worldwide potential market. They will reach a far wider audience and

E-commerce (electronic commerce) is the term used to describe the conducting of business transactions over networks and through computers. It is usually used to describe buying and selling goods over the Internet but includes other electronic business transactions such as **electronic data interchange (EDI)**, where information such as orders and invoices is exchanged electronically between two companies, electronic money exchange and use of point-of-sale (POS) terminals.

more potential shoppers than if they had a few shops in specific locations. As all sales can be made using electronic funds transfer (EFT), the seller does not need to deliver the goods until they have been paid for; this improves cash flow and reduces bad debts.

Of course, the seller will need to develop and maintain the website, which will incur costs, and staff will require some further training. Also, their pricing and marketing techniques will be easily accessed by competitors.

To sell goods on line to new customers, a company must first get them to visit the site. The Internet offers a number of facilities that the company can use to encourage use of their site by directing customers to it. The company can:

▶ register with a search engine
▶ place an advert, a pop-up window or a link on a related site
▶ add a meta tag to the web page – this will provide information such as who created the page, what the page is about and what are the keywords for the page; this can be used by a search engine
▶ add a function to their own site so that visitors can add the e-mail addresses of friends.

Case Study 2 – AquaPress

AquaPress is a company that sells specialist diving books. AquaPress was established in 1996, when they sold their books through orders placed by telephone or post. They produced catalogues of their products but these were costly and time consuming to prepare and distribute, and constantly needed updating.

They established a website which now provides information on all their products and allows customers to order on line. As they use broadband their site is available at all times. The number of orders is now at such a high level that the use of broadband technology is crucial.

Since they started selling on line using broadband technology, they have been able to improve their service to their customers in a number of ways. They now send out a weekly e-mail which describes their latest products to all their subscribers, currently around 10 000 in number.

The website also allows a customer to download sample chapters so that they can decide whether or not they wish to buy the book. This has resulted in a large increase in the sale of certain books.

1 Investigate AquaPress's website on www.aquapress.co.uk
What features can you find?
2 List the benefits to AquaPress of selling on line. Include those benefits discussed in the case study as well as any others you can think of.

Advantages of online shopping

Online shopping is particularly useful for customers who are housebound or live very busy lives. Tesco, like several other food retailers, run a successful online ordering service. Customers can choose their goods from their computer at home. They can select a convenient delivery time are therefore saved the time and bother of travelling to a store.

Advantages of online shopping include:

▶ Customers can save money as they can buy from anywhere in the world; there is a wider range of goods available to them.
▶ Twenty-four-hour shopping for any type of product is available.
▶ There is less need to travel as the buyer does not need to leave home to make a purchase.
▶ It is easier to compare prices from different sellers before making a purchase.

Not everyone is able or willing to purchase goods on line. To be able to do so they would need to have a computer with Internet access, ideally using broadband. Many people are hesitant to make payments on line as they are concerned over security issues and are unwilling to give their credit or debit card details as they fear that they might become the victim of fraud.

ICT and education

Use of computers for teaching and learning

Computers are often used by students in schools, colleges and universities to research topics and produce word-processed reports. The Internet has become a major research tool. Most students at university and college are provided with free Internet access. This means that they can access material provided by their tutors or from a wider base at any time. This makes them more independent and less reliant on their tutors. There is also less pressure on the library for books when all the students on a course are preparing for the same assignment, as they can access material stored on the Internet.

The use of **interactive whiteboards** is becoming widespread in classrooms (see Chapter 4, page 35). These can allow students to take an active part in lessons and encourage collaborative work.

If students have to miss lectures they can access the notes on line. Tutors can contact students using e-mail, which is quicker, more reliable and cheaper than sending out printed notes. Students can submit word-processed work attached to an e-mail. This is less likely to get lost and the time of submission is recorded.

▶ Computer-assisted learning (CAL)

The term **CAL** refers to a range of computer packages that allow a student to study using a computer system. This can take place either at home or within the classroom. Typical CAL packages provide information backed up with quizzes and activities that help reinforce the user's understanding. When students attempt quizzes and tests they will be given instant feedback that allows them to gauge their own progress. CAL systems allow students to work at their own pace. If they are working at home they can learn at a time that is suitable for them. They can also repeat sections of work that they found difficult to ensure that they have full understanding.

Interesting screens can be provided that use colour, animation, sound and video to stimulate the student's interest. Special adaptations can be built in to support students with learning or physical disabilities.

However, the lack of human contact that can arise from the use of CAL in the home can be a disadvantage. Its use can also restrict collaborative learning.

Authoring software is available that allows rapid development of a CAL package for a specific purpose. For example, ToolBook supplies a developer or teacher with everything they need to create a CAL package that provides interactive delivery of factual content together with quizzes, assessments and simulations as appropriate. It allows the CAL package to be created very quickly without the need for extensive technical knowledge. Standard pages with built-in interactivity can be used by adding appropriate text and images. The final product will have a professional look.

ToolBook also makes it easy to create a range of assessments that can be used to check a learner's understanding. A number of different question types are available, including true/false, multiple choice, fill in the blank, matching, and drag and drop.

▶ Computer-based training (CBT)

Computer-based training (**CBT**) is a sophisticated way of learning with help from ICT. A simulated aircraft cockpit used for pilot training is an example of CBT which is cost effective and less dangerous than the real thing. The number of CBL packages available is growing very fast because modern computers have the processing power and storage capacity to support fast-moving and realistic graphics.

▶ Distance learning

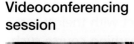

Videoconferencing session

Distance learning is learning where the provider is located away from the learner. In schools or colleges, distance learning allows students to take courses which are not viable to run in their own institution as there are not enough students wishing to study the subject. From a college viewpoint, the use of distance learning increases the potential market for their courses.

Distance learning used to be based upon traditional postal and telephone communication. Computer communications provide new opportunities for distance learning, usually referred to as **online learning** or **e-learning**. Students can send their work to their tutors by e-mail and receive back annotations and comments.

Videoconferencing allows a user to see and interact with people who are geographically distant from them. Two or more people can be connected to each other. Videoconferencing is a powerful tool in distance learning as it can be used for classes and lectures, enabling two-way communication and discussion. This is particularly useful in remote and sparsely populated areas.

apply, and had provided an increase in income for the university. Once the course had been set up and all the materials produced, it cost less to run on line than by using traditional methods.

The course was designed to take 60 hours of study. Jane was able to study in the evening at home after work. She linked to the Internet and accessed her learning materials on line. The course was divided into sections and at the end of each section there were questions to check her understanding and progress.

Jane was assigned a tutor and communicated with him through e-mail, attaching her word-processed assignments when they were completed. Of course, she was not able to have face-to-face support from her tutor.

Online study can cause students to feel isolated as they do not meet and work with fellow students. To help get around this problem, several online discussion groups were set up so that students could share ideas and help and support each other. As the students on the course were spread around the world, Jane had to choose a group whose members would be awake when she was!

Jane successfully completed the course and acquired the extra knowledge that she needed to carry out her role in the research team.

1 List other ways in which Jane could have acquired the knowledge that she needed.
2 Explain why online learning was the best option for her.
3 Identify drawbacks of online learning.
4 Discuss any health hazards that Jane might have encountered through this method of study and suggest precautions that she could have taken to protect herself.

▶ Virtual learning environments (VLEs)

Many schools and colleges have installed **virtual learning environment (VLE)** software. A VLE allows students and their teachers to interact on line and offers the following features:

▶ Access to course material and learning resources. Materials should be varied and include course content as well as quizzes and a range of exercises. Teachers can develop these materials using straightforward templates. A student can work through the material at their own pace, receiving feedback to reinforce understanding.

▶ Methods of tracking a student's progress in working through online material and assessment marks. Each student is able to check their individual progress. The teacher has access to the progress of the whole class.

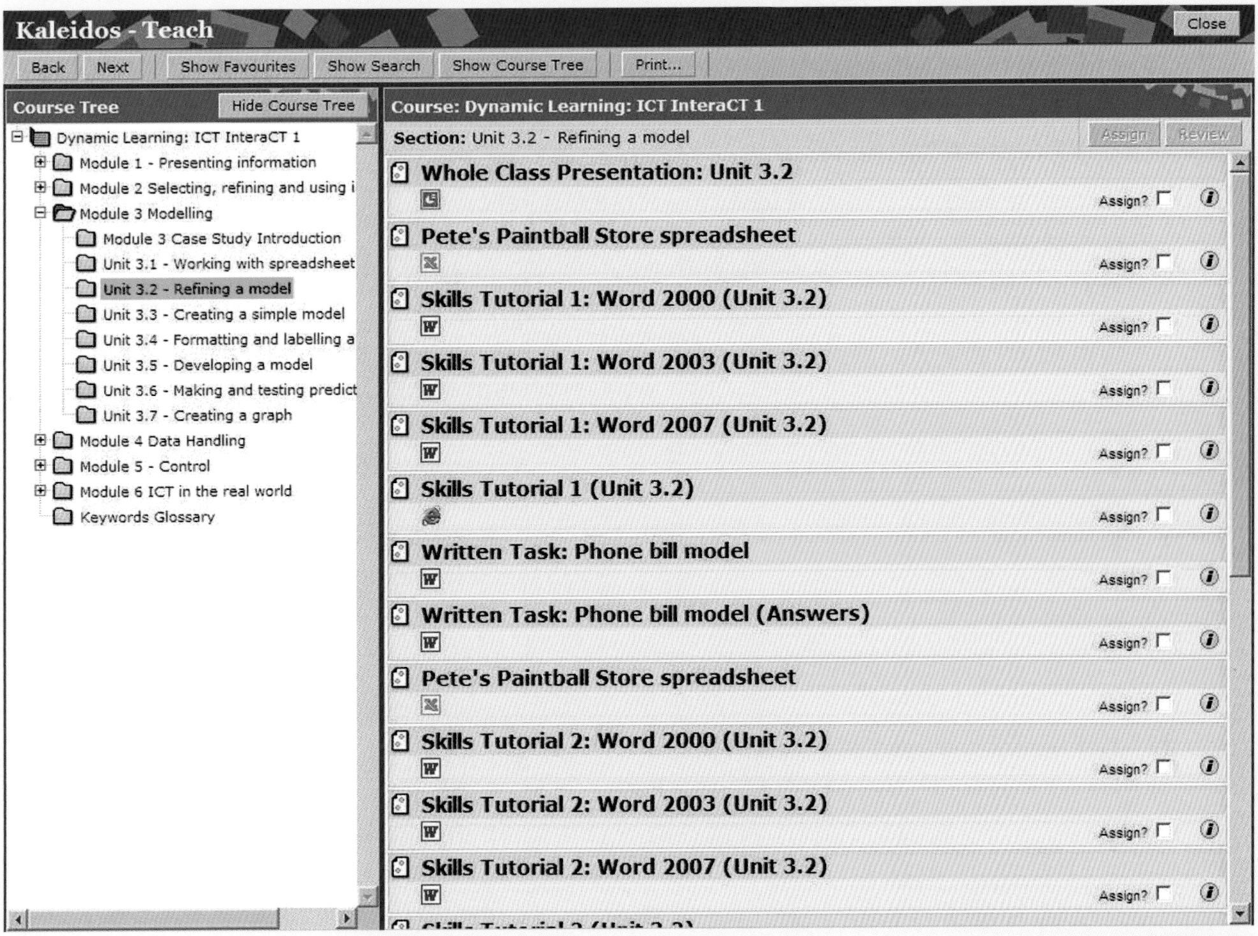

Figure 3 A VLE in use

▶ Means of communication between the student and their teacher that can provide feedback on their progress. This could be in the form of e-mail or online chat.

▶ Means of communication with other students on the course using discussion forums and chat rooms.

In most cases a VLE is an additional resource for students and teachers. It does not replace face-to-face contact in the classroom.

▶ Student record keeping

School and college administration

ICT is used extensively in schools and colleges for **student record keeping**. Data is stored in a central database which can be used by staff from numerous locations. This data is likely to include personal details for all students, such as date of birth, home contact number and critical medical details, as well as examination results and information on timetables.

Information in the form of class and year lists will be routinely produced. Standard letters to parents can be personalised using mail-merge facilities. Examination entries can be performed electronically.

The use of internal e-mail and an intranet within a school leads to improved communications.

Activity 3

In a school, student records consist of the following fields:

▶ Surname
▶ Forename
▶ Address line 1
▶ Address line 2
▶ Town
▶ Postcode
▶ Home telephone number
▶ Previous school
▶ Gender
▶ Date of birth
▶ Parent contact phone number
▶ Known medical condition
▶ Free school meals?

The data is collected when the student joins the school – the parent fills in a form.

1 Why are surname and forename stored as separate fields?
2 Why is date of birth stored rather than age?

3 What data type should be used for the following fields:
   a Town
   b Date of birth
   c Free school meals?
4 Explain why each of the following fields might have been included in the record:
   a Previous school
   b Parent contact phone number
   c Known medical condition.
5 Select a field where coding could be used and describe an appropriate coding system.
6 It is possible that there are errors in the data:
   a Explain how errors could arise.
   b Describe how these errors could be minimised.
   c Choose **two** fields and describe the possible consequences of storing erroneous data.

▶ Computer-based registration

Class registration using OMR form

Many schools use electronic means for registering their students in class. Traditionally, teachers kept paper records of attendance in school. Marks were made in a book to record whether students were present at registration at the start of the day. Attendance registers were likely to be sent to the school office.

There are a number of electronic registration systems now available to a school or college.

OMR (optical mark recognition) forms can be printed by computer. The teacher fills in a pencil mark by the name of each student to indicate that they are present. Forms from each class are then gathered into a central place for the data to be input using a special OMR reading device. This method is cheap and simple to install, but still requires someone to take the completed register to the office. Forms are usually entered as a batch when they have been collected in, hence the information is not completely up to date.

WJEC Information & Communication Technology for AS

A **wireless-based network** can be used with **folders**, special-purpose input devices. These are hand-held folders which a teacher can carry around. When the code for a class is entered, a list of students in the class is displayed and the teacher can simply mark absent or present for each student. Late arrivals can be entered. The teacher can also quickly view a student's attendance at previous lessons.

When the register is complete, the information can be sent over the wireless network to a central computer. Alternatively, if the school has a network with a computer in every classroom, registration data can be collected from the computer by use of the keyboard.

These systems are popular with teachers as they remain in control of registration.

Students can register themselves when entering a building by using a special-purpose **swipe card** or by having their **fingertip** or **retina** scanned. Cards can be misused when a student gets a friend to swipe their card for them. Fingertip and retina readers are expensive and their use requires students' permission.

A student using a fingertip reader

Electronic registration methods provide a number of benefits:

▶ Information is more accurate as lists are updated when a student comes to school late.

▶ Registration is easier to carry out more often – for every lesson rather than once or twice a day.

▶ It is not necessary to send somebody down to the office with the register.

▶ Up-to-date attendance information brought together from a number of classes is available that provides a valuable overview of an individual student's attendance as well as the opportunity to study trends in class attendance.

▶ Information can be accessed from more than one place at the same time.

▶ Reports can be produced automatically, providing better statistics for senior management.

▶ Improved tracking of attendance should reduce internal truancy.

As with all ICT systems, there will be costs involved in setting up and running an electronic registration system. If the equipment breaks down, or there is a power failure, the system cannot be used. This can result in out-of-date records with no central record of current attendance.

▶ Public examinations and university applications

Schools and colleges enter students for public examinations electronically using EDI. Files are sent to the exam boards with details of students and the modules that they are entering. Later on the results are sent in encrypted form via the Internet to the school/college, where they are imported into a local database. The results are then printed out for the students.

Students applying to university through UCAS do so electronically using EAS (electronic application system). Each student fills in an online form, entering personal details, course choice, lists of qualifications gained and examinations to be taken, and a personal statement. Once this has been completed the student's reference is added by a teacher. The application is then sent electronically to UCAS, who forward it to the chosen institutions.

Case Study 5 – Online class registration

A school uses an online registration system that allows teachers to take class registers in the classroom on a computer. Each teacher enters a unique identification code supported with a password. They then enter a code for the class they are currently teaching. The attendance data is stored centrally and links to the student database.

The teacher can view the register in two modes:

▶ as a class list which they can see as a whole
▶ student by student, with past attendance displayed.

The ICT support department manages the system, carrying out tasks such as:

▶ adding new teachers and students
▶ entering details of classes and the students in those classes
▶ making modifications to the system.

Class tutors and senior managers receive regular reports on attendance.

Students are able to access a summary of their own attendance on line through the school's intranet. Their parents can also access this information.

1 Describe **four** reports that could be produced by the registration system, stating who will use each report.
2 Explain **two** reasons why a teacher has to enter a unique identification code.
3 Give **three** reasons why the system is password protected.
4 Explain how a teacher might use each of the display modes.
5 Describe the advantages and disadvantages of this method of registration compared with the use of:
  a pupil swipe cards   b OMR forms.

Activity 4

Copy and complete the grid below, identifying **ten** ways in which ICT is used in your school or college. For each describe the benefits and limitations of using ICT.

Use of ICT	Benefits	Limitations

Summary

CAD/CAM

▶ **Computer-aided design (CAD)** software allows a user to draw accurate plans and designs.

▶ **Computer-aided manufacturing (CAM)** systems produce objects using **computer-controlled** machines.

▶ **CAD/CAM:** the output from a CAD system may be input to control a CAM process.

▶ Features of CAD/CAM packages:

a zoom	f costings
b 3D images	g calculation of stresses and strains
c rotation	h walk-through
d hatching or rendering	i clip-art.
e wire drawings	

▶ CAD packages require a computer with:

a high processor speed	d graphics tablet
b large main memory (RAM)	e high-resolution large screen
c graphics card	f plotter.

▶ Examples of use of CAD:

a product design	c house design
b garden design	d fashion design.

Computer-based shopping systems

▶ **Electronic point-of-sale (EPOS)** tills are set up to identify goods, look up prices and produce an itemised bill for the customer.

▶ Data is entered using a range of devices, including:

a hand-held barcode reader (wand)	f magnetic-strip reader
b laser flatbed scanner	g self-scan device
c keypad	h shelf-edge computers
d electronic scales	i touch screen
e smart-card reader	j automatic till.

▶ Products are identified by a unique **barcode**. The barcode represents a number.

▶ **Stock control** is carried out automatically as EPOS tills are linked by LAN to the store's file server.

▶ **Just-in-time** control systems allow fewer items of stock to be held at the shop, thus reducing storage and stock costs.

▶ Customers can be issued with **loyalty cards** that provide them with discounts based on previous purchases made.

▶ **Online shopping** allows customers to purchase goods 24 hours a day.

Use of computers for teaching and learning

▶ In education, ICT supports the Internet and encyclopedia CD-ROMs are used for research purposes.

▶ **CAL** (computer-assisted learning) refers to a range of computer packages that allow a student to study using a computer system.

▶ **Authoring software** allows the rapid creation of targeted CAL packages.

▶ **CBT** (computer-based training) refers to the use of simulation to teach a skill.

▶ **Distance learning** allows learners to follow courses remotely – the courses may not be available locally. It can include:

  a videoconferencing, which allows a learner to join a 'class' remotely

  b online learning – using learning materials over the Internet at a time and place that suits the learner

  c discussion with a tutor or other course members using chat rooms.

▶ **Revision programs** are available to students to help support their learning.

▶ **Interactive whiteboards** are frequently used in classrooms.

School and college administration

▶ ICT plays a major role in educational administration.

▶ Computer-based student registration uses a variety of methods:

  a OMR forms

  b student swipe cards

  c wireless networks with hand-held registration folders

  d classroom computers linked to LAN

  e student identification using retina or fingertip scanning.

▶ ICT is used in student record keeping.

Questions Chapter 5

1 Explain how each of the following is used in a supermarket:
  a EFTPOS (3)
  b just-in-time stock control systems (3)
  c loyalty card. (3)

2 CAD/CAM systems have a number of features. Describe how the following features can be of benefit in the design process:
  a rotation (3)
  b hatching or rendering (3)
  c calculation of stresses and strains. (3)

3 A design team uses computer-aided design (CAD) and computer-aided manufacture (CAM) software in designing its products.

  a Describe, using a suitable example, the role of CAD and CAM in design. (3)

  b One advantage of using CAD software to design products is the ability to have a 3D view of the product. Discuss **other** advantages and disadvantages to the design team of using CAD software. **(3) WJEC June 2006**

4 Discuss the benefits and limitations of online shopping to retailers and their customers. (9)

5 Advances in technology have led to schools and colleges making greater use of ICT systems for administration.

  a i Name and describe **three** different ICT systems schools or colleges are now using to register students. (6)
  ii One advantage of using ICT systems to register students is that it is faster for students and teachers. Discuss the other main advantages to a school or college of using ICT systems to register students. (4)
  b Schools and colleges now use ICT systems for student record keeping. Give **three** distinct fields **other than** name, address, postcode and telephone numbers, and discuss why they are needed. (6) WJEC Jan 2006

6 Many schools now make increasing use of distance/online learning and computer-assisted learning (CAL) programs.

  a Give **two** advantages and **one** disadvantage of distance/online learning. (3)
  b Give **two** advantages and **one** disadvantage of CAL for students with learning difficulties. Your answers must be different to those for part **a**. (3) WJEC Jan 2005

7 A large supermarket company has many shops throughout the country. The company uses both a local area network (LAN) and a wide area network (WAN).

  a Explain the difference between a LAN and a WAN. (2)
  b Describe a suitable role for a LAN in the supermarket stock control system. (2)
  c Describe a suitable role for a WAN in the supermarket stock control system. (2)
  d Discuss, using specific examples, the advantages of using LANs and WANs:
   i for the supermarket customer (3)
   ii for the supermarket manager. (3)
   Use **distinctly different** examples in **each** case.
  e The company also makes use of e-commerce. Discuss **two** advantages and **two** disadvantages of using e-commerce for the company. Use **distinctly different** examples in **each** case. (4) WJEC June 2006

8 Discuss in detail the use of ICT in computer-based shopping systems. Your answer should make reference to:
  a the input, output and storage devices used at the point of sale (5)
  b the processes involved in automatic stock control (3)
  c the benefits to the company of automatic stock control (3)
  d the benefits to the customer of e-commerce systems (3)
  e potential disadvantages to the company of using computer-based shopping systems. (2) WJEC Jan 2005

6

Uses of ICT in Health and the Home 4.1.6 (Part 2)

ICT and health

ICT plays a big role in the health sector. Computers are used in the administration of hospitals and doctors' surgeries for purposes such as storing patients' records. Computers are also widely used to monitor patients' health. For example, scanning devices are used to aid diagnosis. Computer-controlled equipment can provide instant feedback and can free nurses to carry out other duties. Artificial intelligence and expert systems help health professionals to treat and support their patients.

Scanners and computer-controlled life-support equipment

▶ Sensors

When patients visit a doctor, stay in hospital for care or undergo an operation, they can have one or more of their body functions monitored. These monitoring systems use sensors to collect the data. A **sensor** is a device that measures a physical quantity, such as blood pressure, and converts it into a form than can be read by a computer or a human. The information can be output in the form of a graph or as a series of readings. These sensors can be **analogue** or **digital**. The output gives the medical professionals vital information on the current state of the patient which they can use to determine the treatment they should be giving.

The intensive treatment unit (ITU) in a hospital admits patients who have undergone trauma such as a severe road traffic accident, who have just undergone major surgery or who are suffering from a very serious illness. The patient may be linked to a number of sensors that measure such functions as:

▶ temperature
▶ blood pressure
▶ central venous pressure
▶ blood gases (for example, the level of oxygen in the blood)
▶ breath gases (used to monitor lung function)
▶ brainwave pattern
▶ electrical activity of the heart (recorded as an electrocardiogram – ECG)
▶ fluid level
▶ intercranial pressure (the pressure in the skull)
▶ heart rate
▶ pulse.

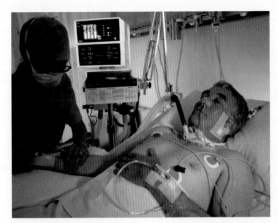

The use of sensors in this situation allows a patient to be constantly monitored (24/7). If the patient's condition gets worse an alarm can be sounded. For example, if the heart or brain function stops the doctors are warned. This allows medical staff to leave the patient without continuous supervision thus freeing up time for other tasks. Doctors can study the information produced and spot trends in the patient's body functions that could determine a new course of treatment.

Computers are used for control in other situations in a hospital. Newborn babies are each given a wristband

Patient in an ITU linked to monitoring devices

containing a sensor that activates an alarm if the band is removed from the baby's wrist. Certain types of surgery can be performed using a robotic device. Sometimes patients need to have a steady flow of medication or fluids administered. These can be given using a drip whose rate of flow is automatically monitored.

Activity 1

1 Find out how an ECG works.
2 Find out what a sphygmomanometer is used for.

▶ Scanning devices

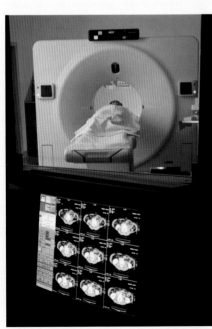

CAT scanner in use

MRI (magnetic resonance image) and **CAT (computerised axial tomography)** scanners are devices that provide vital information in the diagnosis of many illnesses.

CAT scan machines produce X-rays. A conventional X-ray image is rather like a shadow. The X-ray beam is directed at one side of the body and a piece of film on the other side shows the shape of the bones. This two-dimensional (2D) image provides an incomplete picture. A CAT scanner produces a complete three-dimensional (3D) computer model of a patient's bones and internal organs.

In a CAT scan machine, the X-ray beam is moved all round the patient. It carries out many scans, each from a slightly different angle. The information from all the scans is combined to form a 3D image of the body. CAT scanners are used to investigate many conditions, including head injuries, osteoporosis and cancer.

An **MRI** scanner is a radiological device that uses a combination of magnetism, radio waves and a computer to produce images of body structure. The scanner looks like a very large tube with a hole at one end into which a patient, lying on their back on a trolley, can be inserted.

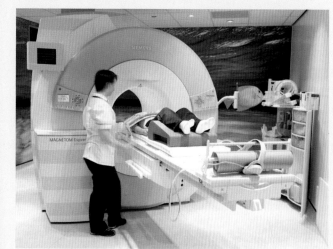

An MRI scanner in use

The tube is surrounded by a very large magnet. The scanner can explore different parts of the body – the patient can be moved in head or feet first either fully or partially within the magnetic field.

The MRI scanner can isolate a very small point inside the patient's body and determine what type of tissue it is. As this is repeated throughout the area being investigated 2D or 3D maps of tissue types are built up. The maps are used to create 2D images or 3D models. These images and models provide a tremendous level of detail and assist medical professionals considerably in their diagnosis of a wide range of conditions such as brain tumours and multiple sclerosis (MS) and injuries such as torn ligaments.

MRI examinations take some time to complete – typically from 20 to 90 minutes. A patient must lie very still during the scan as movement can cause distortion of the image.

Scans produced by CAT and MRI scanners are made up of a number of slices through the patient which can be put together to produce a 3D image. This allows doctors to investigate problems that could previously be looked at only using surgery. For example, the inner part of the brain can be examined, a doctor can see inside joints, and blockages in veins can be identified. CAT and MRI scans allow doctors to provide a more accurate diagnosis. The ability to see inside the body without using surgery also removes the danger of postoperation infections.

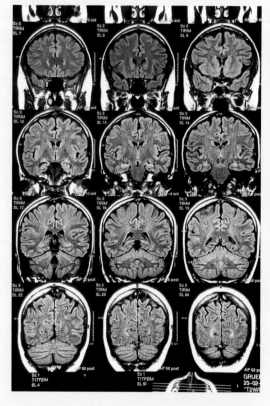

Image from an MRI scanner

The X-rays used in a CAT scanner can cause side effects. An MRI scanner has few side effects and is more flexible as it can produce images in any plane.

People who have pacemakers, plates or artificial joints cannot be scanned using an MRI device. Patients can find MRI scanners very claustrophobic and frightening as they have to lie still in a very confined space, often for long periods. An MRI scanner is very noisy.

These scanners are very expensive and thus scanning a patient is very costly. Over-reliance on their use may result in the loss of traditional diagnostic skills.

Case Study 1 – How bones can be tailor-made

Advances in technology mean that surgeons will soon be able to create made-to-measure titanium bone replacements within hours.

The irreparably damaged bone will be scanned, a titanium copy created and then surgically inserted into the body.

The technique is being developed by an engineer, Siavash Mahdavi, who studied robotics at University College London. He used artificial intelligence to produce the software that would create the 3D image needed. Recently machines capable of printing in high-quality titanium have been developed. This means that the new software can be applied to create made-to-measure orthopaedic implants.

'Imagine a hip-bone replacement,' says Mahdavi. 'A surgeon will have the existing bone MRI scanned. This information is passed via a CAD program to the 3D printer. By the time the patient gets to the operating theatre, we will have printed out a medical-grade titanium bone which is an identical match to the one being replaced.'

But will these titanium bones be as reliable as existing implants? Mahdavi insists that they will not only be just as reliable but have advantages over traditional implants: 'They are much lighter as, like human bone, they are porous rather than solid. And having an internal mesh means you can fuse the implant to the bone, so the natural bone will grow into the holes and lock itself in. Because it's a porous structure, you can X-ray the implant and see how the natural bone is melding with the implant.'

Implants manufactured using this e-technology also have several features that could appeal to the health service. 'Firstly the method is cheaper than both custom-made and off-the-peg prostheses,' says Mahdavi. 'It should be particularly helpful in complicated surgical cases, where an expensive custom-built orthopaedic implant, which currently takes three weeks to prepare, could be replaced by a cheaper one made in two hours.'

1 Why would the surgeon use an MRI scan rather than an X-ray?
2 List the potential advantages of the titanium bones:
   a to the patient
   b to the health service.
3 Explain, in your own words, what takes place in an MRI scan.
4 Find out what is meant by *artificial intelligence.*

Activity 2

The following web links are to video clips showing applications of an MRI scanner.

http://videos.howstuffworks.com/sciencentral/2877-brain-scan-of-adhd-children-video.htm

http://videos.howstuffworks.com/reuters/919-mri-may-catch-cancer-earlier-video.htm

Write a brief summary of each clip.

▶ Backup and recovery procedures

Intensive care units rely very heavily on ICT equipment. Any major equipment failure would have very severe consequences for the patients as there would not be adequate staffing to monitor all the functions. If the equipment was being used for life support, carrying out functions such as performing the breathing for the patient, they would die. It is therefore vital to have power-supply and computer backup. These need to be periodically checked to ensure that they will work when needed.

▶ Recent and future developments and limitations

New techniques and devices are being developed that will increase the scope of scanning and computer-controlled medical equipment. Breakthroughs have been made in facial reconstruction which can be of great benefit to burns victims.

Using a network link, doctors can view a scan from far away and make a diagnosis. This allows optimum use of scarce expertise around the world.

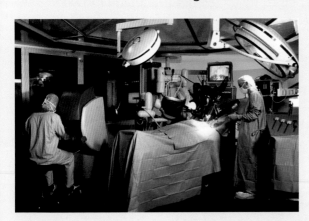

Surgeon (on left of picture) operating a robotic device

Robotic surgery is a fast-developing field. Although robots cannot yet carry out surgery alone, they allow a surgeon to carry out intricate surgery without physical contact with the patient. Robots provide greater control and precision for the surgeon and surgery can be carried out that is less invasive. The robots are activated by remote control and voice recognition. The da Vinci Surgical System is already in use in the USA for procedures such as heart bypass surgery. The following web link is to a video clip that shows the procedure in action:

http://videos.howstuffworks.com/multivu/3378-heart-bypass-surgery-using-only-4-holes-video.htm

Sensors that pick up vibrations can be used to reproduce hearing for a deaf person. These take the form of **cochlear implants** that consist of two parts. One part is implanted into the bone surrounding the ear. It receives, decodes and transmits an electrical signal to the brain. The second part is an external device that receives the sound, converts it into an electrical signal and transmits it to the internal portion of the implant.

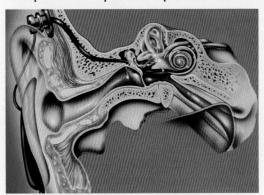

Figure 1 Diagram of a cochlear implant

Laser eye surgery is becoming commonplace and is generally available in a hospital's outpatient department. The laser, which is

Doctor carrying out laser surgery on a patient's eye

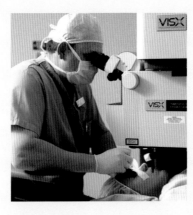

operated remotely by the surgeon, can be used to repair tears in the eye's retina.

However, computer-controlled support systems may lead to an over-reliance on technology so that insufficient trained staff will be available in the future. The equipment is expensive to buy and uses up considerable amounts of the limited resources available. Specialist staff are needed to maintain the equipment.

Medical databases

Filing paper medical records

Traditionally patient notes were stored in paper files. This meant that they could be in only one place at a time. Hospitals stored them in vast rooms and if they were misfiled they were quite likely not to be found again!

Many hospitals and GP surgeries now keep all, or partial, online patient records. When GPs see a patient they will display the patient's record on their computer screen and add information gained from the visit. Some hospitals use a computer database to record details of a patient's inpatient and outpatient treatments as well as test results from departments such Haematology and Pathology. Data on medicines that have been prescribed will also be stored.

Some hospitals are now experimenting with storing medical records on a smart card kept by the patient and taken with them every time they visit a doctor, dentist, pharmacist or hospital. The smart card can store a complete medical history and can be updated at the end of each visit.

▶ Electronic patient record keeping

A system of **electronic patient records (EPR)** is being developed by the National Health Service. The idea behind it is simple – the health records of all NHS patients would be stored on line and accessible to appropriate health professionals anywhere in the UK. This means that if a patient needed treatment at a hospital anywhere in the UK, perhaps after sustaining an accident whilst on holiday, for example, then the medical professionals would have instant access to information about former treatments elsewhere as well as details of any medication being used by the patient. Thus patient information would be shared between hospitals, GPs and the health authority.

A number of different medical personnel would use the system, for example:

▶ A clerk would record details of appointments and visits to hospital outpatient clinics.
▶ The ward clerk would enter details of a patient's stay in a hospital ward.
▶ The radiographer would store details of X-rays.
▶ Laboratory staff would enter results of blood and other pathology tests.

▶ Ward nurses and doctors would enter details of medication issued and treatments undertaken in hospital.

There would be a number of advantages of such a system:

▶ Patients would not have to give the same information over and over again.
▶ Paper records can get lost and can be in only one place at a time. Computerised records would be available at any time to any authorised user. They could be updated immediately.
▶ Access to a patient's previous medical treatment would improve diagnosis.
▶ The computerising of patient records would also create a huge database that could be used by an epidemiologist. Epidemiology is the scientific method used to track population health and to find causes of disease in groups of people. Records could be searched to find out which treatments for a medical condition were the most effective.

The EPR system has already fallen well behind schedule and is costing considerably more than its original budget.

Case Study 2 – NHS 'Choose and Book'

'Choose and Book' is a national Internet booking system for NHS services. It aims to provide patients with a choice of time, date and place for their first appointment as an outpatient. This new system is designed to give patients much greater involvement in decisions about their treatment.

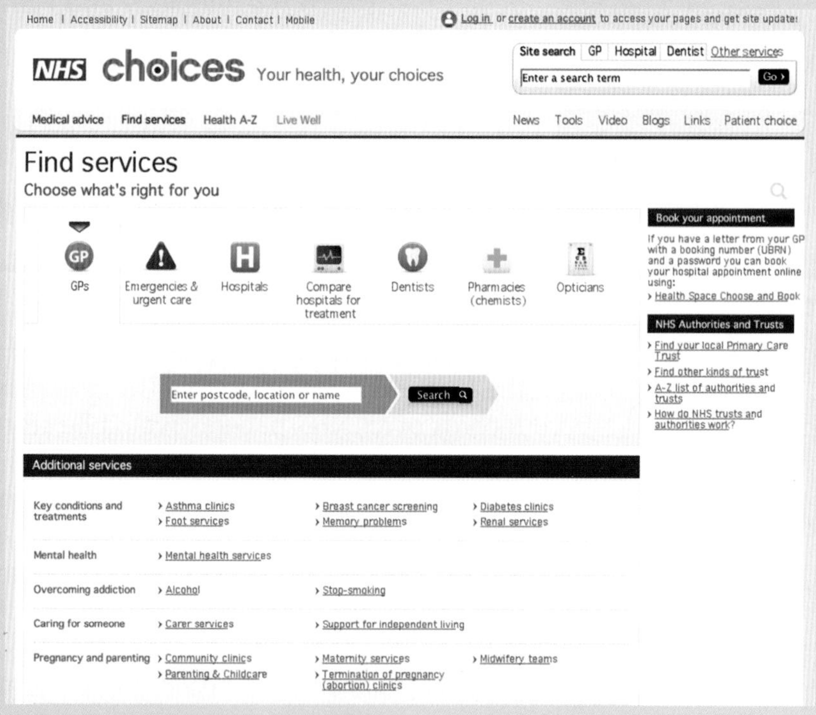

Patients can choose one of four or five hospitals and information on these hospitals should be available to GPs and other staff, as well as patients, on http://www.nhs.uk (see Figure 2). Patients can either

Figure 2 'Choose and Book' on the NHS Choices website

book their hospital appointment electronically when they are at the doctor's surgery, with the help of the GP, or they can book later by themselves using the Internet.

1 Find out more about the new system on http://www.chooseandbook.nhs.uk
2 Explain the main benefits of the 'Choose and Book' system.
3 What factors should be considered when designing an interface for the patient?

Activity 3

Find out about the current progress of the EPR system by accessing the BBC website or the website of a national newspaper.

1 When is the system due to 'go live'?
2 How much will the system have cost to implement?
3 Describe the concerns that some people have about the system.

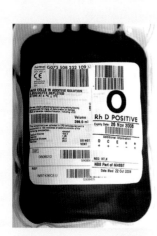

Example of an ISBT 128 label

▶ Blood barcoding and tracking systems

ISBT (International Society of Blood Transfusion) **128** is a barcoding system for the identification, labelling and processing of blood. It is an internationally standardised system. A unique barcode is attached to blood which can, if any problem occurs, be used to trace the blood from who gave it to the patient who received it. This need for tracking arose a few years ago when problems occurred with the possible spread by transfusion of disease, especially CJD (Creutzfeldt-Jakob or 'Mad Cow' disease).

Any patient who is to receive a blood transfusion is given a barcoded bracelet that holds details of their blood type. The barcode on the patient's bracelet and the barcode on the unit of blood both have to be scanned to check that the blood groups match before the blood can be administered as a part of a treatment or operation. This ensures that the correct blood is given to the patient and cuts down the chance of a mistake, which could have very serious health consequences. Barcoding the blood makes it easy to check that out-of-date blood is not used. It also cuts down the chance of cross-contamination.

▶ Use of the Internet, intranets and extranets

Medical professionals have fast online access to medical journals and other resources which can provide them with up-to-date information on the latest research findings. Sites can be used to aid in medical diagnosis.

▶ Distributed medical databases

The data in a hospital's database may be distributed around a number of computers in different departments. Records relating to blood tests might be held on a computer in the haematology department, records of outpatient visits might be stored on a computer in that department. However, all records for a patient can be linked using their unique patient identity number. All the computers are part of a local area network. Data on a different computer can be accessed as long as the user has authorisation.

Using a distributed database improves security and speeds up data access as much of the information required is available locally.

▶ Backup and recovery procedures

Medical records are vital to a patient's treatment, so it is of utmost importance that they are available whenever needed. It is therefore crucial that adequate backup and recovery procedures are in place.

Backup refers to making copies of data so that these additional copies may be used to restore the original if a loss of data occurs. The purpose of backup is to ensure that if anything happens to the original file, the backup copy can be used to restore the file without loss of data and within a reasonable timescale. Restoring files to their original state before failure occurred is called **recovery**.

A hospital needs to put procedures in place that will allow lost or corrupted files to be restored by making use of backup copies. These procedures need to be carefully planned and personnel made aware of them. The methods of recovery should be practised so that, when they are needed, they will run smoothly.

Backup is used to avoid permanent data loss and ensure the integrity of the data. It needs to be undertaken on a regular and systematic basis.

▶ New and future developments and limitations

The national EPR system has, at the time of writing, not yet been implemented. When it is functioning, all patient records across the UK will be linked so that any hospital will be able to see a full record of a patient's medical history. This should lead to improved patient care.

It is already possible to book some appointments over the Internet (see Case Study 2, page 72). It is likely that this facility will become more extensive – in a few years it may become the normal way to arrange to see a GP.

The use of patient bracelets with embedded chips could allow information to be stored so that it is linked to the patient, thus removing chances of error in administering drugs or performing surgical operations.

Artificial intelligence

Artificial intelligence refers to the use of a computer system that behaves in the same way as a human. Computers are good at carrying out prescribed tasks (written in a program) again and again, very rapidly,

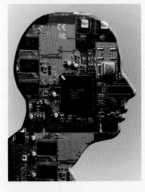

without making mistakes. Some things that humans are good at – recognising objects and people, understanding speech and making decisions in real-life situations – are very hard to replicate using a computer.

Advances have been made in a number of fields of artificial intelligence, but any system is limited to a very narrow field.

Systems exist that can understand natural

languages such as English, although no computer can perform as well as a human in this field. Natural-language processing allows people to interact with a computer simply by talking to it. However, programming computers to understand natural languages is very hard. Programming languages such as **Prolog** are used for artificial-intelligence applications.

A **neural network** is a system that simulates human intelligence by attempting to reproduce the types of physical connections that occur in human brains. Currently work on neural networks is being carried out in fields such as image analysis, pattern analysis and financial trends. As neural networks require huge amounts of computer processing, parallel processors are used. A special-purpose programming language, **Asprin**, is used to develop neural networks.

Traditional processors carry out only one operation at a time – they operate sequentially. Although these operations are carried out very fast, they are still too slow for the tasks required for a neural network. A **parallel processor** allows a number of operations to be carried out at the same time and in this way can mimic the operation of a human brain.

To help understand how parallel processing works, imagine that you want to knit a jumper in a hurry. You will need to knit a front and a back, two arms and a collar. The front, back and arms can all be knitted at the same time, each by a different person. They are produced in **parallel**. The jumper cannot be put together and the collar knitted until all the other parts are complete. This is known as a **sequence**. Special programming languages such as **OCCAM** have been developed to write programs that can exploit parallel capabilities.

▶ Expert systems

Expert systems, often referred to as a branch of artificial intelligence, are computer systems which mimic the decision-making ability of a human expert. Expert systems can be set up to help in medical diagnosis by asking questions about symptoms and using the answers to draw conclusions.

An expert system for medical diagnosis would have information about diseases and their symptoms as well as the drugs used in treatments. The expertise of the system is gathered from human experts but it can store far more information on a specific field than an individual doctor would have at their fingertips. It can draw on a wide variety of sources such as stored knowledge from books and case studies to help in diagnosis and advice on treatments. Unlike a human doctor, a computer does not 'forget' or make mistakes: it will remember obscure cases of a condition such as heart disease. Data can also be kept up to date.

The computer does not take the place of the doctor but can be used to help the doctor make decisions. An expert system can provide accurate predictions with probabilities of all possible problems and can thus be used to give more accurate advice, especially for obscure illnesses.

An expert system can free up a doctor's time to deal with more serious cases as the patient can provide initial information to the system. An expert system is often used to give doctors a second opinion, which can be helpful in diagnosis.

An expert system can be built using **expert system shell** software. An expert system shell consists of:

▶ a **knowledge base** where the facts and rules gathered from the human experts are stored
▶ an **inference engine**, the program that analyses the knowledge
▶ a **user interface** that allows the user to interact by asking and answering questions.

In a typical medical expert system, a patient is asked questions about their symptoms. The inference engine searches the knowledge base, using its rules, and makes suggestions about possible diseases and treatments. Often probabilities are assigned to diagnoses.

Mycin was an expert system designed to diagnose and recommend treatment for certain blood infections. Doctors have to make quick judgements about the likely problems from the available data and decide on treatment. The knowledge required to make good judgements grows with experience. Mycin provided junior or non-specialised doctors with an expert tool to help them make a correct decision.

Advantages of using an expert system

▶ Cheaper to update than to train doctors.
▶ Always available 24 hours a day and will never retire – it is useful to ensure that expertise is not lost.
▶ Can be made available over a network to people, perhaps in rural or third-world locations, who do not have access to a human expert.
▶ Some people prefer the privacy of 'talking' to a computer rather than to a GP.
▶ Gives the doctor more time to deal with other patients.
▶ Can provide a second opinion.
▶ Can store far more information than a human, drawing on a wide variety of sources such as stored knowledge from books and case studies to help in diagnosis and advice.
▶ Does not forget or make mistakes.
▶ Data can be kept up to date.
▶ Provides more accurate predictions with probabilities of all possible problems.

Disadvantages of using an expert system

▶ Lack of personal contact.
▶ Dependent upon the correct information being stored – if the data or the rules are wrong the wrong advice could be given.
▶ If incorrect data is mistakenly entered, the expert system will output incorrect findings, perhaps prescribing an incorrect dosage of a drug.

IT in the home

Access to the Internet provides a wide range of leisure opportunities to the home user, such as chat rooms, applications such as Friends Re-united and online games. Many home users use software to trace and record their family tree, to plan a journey by accessing route planning and mapping software, or to find information from an encyclopedia held on a CD-ROM.

Home users can also book holidays, carry out their personal banking and order goods from a supermarket that will be delivered to their door. Such e-commerce facilities save time and people can carry out these tasks whenever it suits them.

Of course, there are dangers as well as benefits from such a wealth of facilities. Extensive use of computers can lead to health problems such as RSI, back trouble, eye strain, headaches or epileptic fits (see Chapter 10). Particularly in children, too much time sitting at a computer or games console can lead to obesity and poor social development. There are also many websites, such as those displaying pornography, that are unsuitable for children.

Entertainment

Television **pay-to-view** services are available from providers such as Sky. These services are not part of the normal subscriptions. For example, users can pay to watch a new film, a world-title boxing match or music concert.

 Games

A high percentage of households use a home computer for game playing as well as having a games console. Games can either be purchased on a CD-ROM or downloaded from the Internet. Many games require a subscription. Online games can be played individually or in collaboration with other remote players.

Many games have fast-moving, high-quality graphics and sound. To play such games successfully, a computer is needed that has a fast video card with extra RAM (memory), a large monitor, speakers and a good sound card. Specialist input devices, such as joysticks, are often used.

There are a number of fears regarding computer games. There is some evidence that violent games can have a harmful effect on the behaviour of players. There are also concerns that playing games for too many hours in the day can stunt a young person's social development.

Activity 4

A wide range of input and output devices can be used with modern computer games. Some are listed in the grid below.

Copy the grid and add **three** more devices. Find out how each device works then fill in the rest of the grid.

Device	Description	Use
Joystick		
Steering wheel		
Voice recognition		
Wireless 3D glasses		

Case Study 3 – Ministers plan clampdown on 'unsuitable' video games

In an effort to stop children playing video games unsuitable for their age, government ministers are planning to introduce a system for classifying games similar to the system already used for films. The new system would make it illegal for shops to sell classified video games to children younger than the age recommended for each category.

Child playing a video game

Government sources suggest that guidelines for parents on use of games in the home will also be issued. Advice will include keeping computers and games consoles out children's bedrooms and encouraging children to play games in living rooms or kitchens.

Screens and other devices should be positioned so that adults can see which games children in their care are playing.

Internet and computer games can be highly profitable for business and are a valuable source of entertainment, knowledge and pleasure for children, but this must be balanced, ministers believe, against growing concerns about lack of regulation of games and overuse by children.

1 Explain the classification system currently used for films.
2 Discuss potential dangers to children when using the Internet.
3 Describe useful skills and knowledge that games can provide for children, giving specific examples.
4 Why would it be difficult to police such a system?

▶ Photography

Transferring photos from a digital camera to a computer

Digital photography is increasing in popularity. Digital cameras can take movies or still photographs and the move away from cameras using film has been very rapid.

Photographs taken using digital cameras can be stored and printed using a home computer system. To transfer image data from camera to computer, the digital camera can be connected to the computer via its USB port or the memory card can be removed from the camera and inserted into a card reader connected to the computer.

Image-processing software packages such as Adobe Photoshop, Windows Media Player or Windows Movie Maker can be used to modify an image, perhaps by cropping, altering the brightness or contrast, or removing the 'red eye' effect caused by the use of flash. Photographs can then be printed out to a particular size, kept on storage media (such as CD-R) or displayed as slide shows on the screen. There is no need to print out every photograph as the images can be stored in an electronic album rather than a paper-based one. Printers that are of photograph quality allow the user to adjust the paper feed size and use high-quality printing on photographic-quality paper. Printers which are dedicated to printing photographs are also available.

Case Study 4 – Showing photographs

There are many companies that will print digital photographs for home users who do not wish to print them themselves. Such a company is PhotoBox. As well as offering standard photo-printing services, PhotoBox offer an ever-increasing range of printed products such as calendars made up of images of the customer's photographs and customised to include special text for certain dates.

1 Go to PhotoBox's website at http://www.photobox.co.uk/shop/prints/standard-prints List **six** different services offered by PhotoBox.

Another service offered to photographers is sharing photographs on line with friends. Flickr is a website where a user can store their photographs, tag them then share them with others either through a link to the site or by embedding them in their blog or web page.

2 a Explain what is meant by tagging a photograph.
  b What are the benefits of tagging?
  c Uploading photographs can be time consuming. The process can be speeded up if data compression is used. Describe data compression.

▶ Listening to music

See Chapter 10, page 150 for details of the Copyright, Designs and Patents Act 1988.

For many years people bought their music records from a shop on vinyl, then on CD. Nowadays more and more people are downloading music via the Internet. There are many sites where you can listen to samples of music of all types, including the latest releases, and then download those that you wish to purchase, paying by debit or credit card. There are also websites that allow illegal downloading of music without payment. Obtaining music in this way breaks the law.

To reproduce music well a high-quality sound card is required. Sound data, like all data, is stored within a computer in digital form. The sound we hear is in wave or analogue form, so the digital data has to be converted into analogue form, amplified and output via a loudspeaker. Conversely, when music is recorded and stored as digital data, the sound has to be converted from analogue to digital form.

Conversion from analogue to digital form (or from digital to analogue) is carried out by the sound card. The quality of the sound is determined by the sample rate (the number of times per second that a measurement of the sound wave is made and stored as a number) – the higher the sample rate the better the quality of the sound that can be played back. The greater the resolution of the sound card the greater the accuracy of the sound that is stored.

Case Study 5 – Tom's music

Tom enjoys listening to music both at home and on the move. He downloads the music of his favourite artists from the iTunes website – often as soon as the album becomes available. He pays either using his credit card or with vouchers that he has received as a present. He stores all the tracks on his PC's hard drive.

Tom can listen to music in a number of different locations around his house and garden. He has a several amplifier/speaker systems that are connected wirelessly to his PC. He can play different music at different locations at the same time! He has a hand-held remote controller that allows him to transfer any music from his computer or directly from the Internet onto a device at any location.

When he is away from the house, Tom uses his iPod. This has its own hard disk which he can load with music from his computer.

1 Describe the advantages and disadvantages to Tom of having a computerised music system.
2 Explore what iTunes offers on http://www.apple.com/uk/itunes/
3 Describe the type of interface that is provided on an iPod or similar device.
4 What problems might arise from buying music on line using a credit card?

▶ Making music

As well as storing and reproducing music obtained from CD or downloaded over the Internet, ICT can be used to create, edit and play music. In addition to the hardware described in the previous section, input devices such as microphones are required. A standard interface, **MIDI (musical instrument digital interface),** is universally used. MIDI is a format for data that gives information about the music created. It does not reproduce actual sounds as a digital music file but contains a list of events or messages that tell an electronic device, such as a musical instrument or computer sound card, how to generate a certain sound. The use of MIDI with a powerful computer allows a musician to make music at home using virtual instruments.

Sequencer software will also be needed. A **sequencer** is software that is designed to create and manage computer-generated music. It builds up complex files by layering them with simpler ones.

Another form of software used in musical composition is the **notator**. This allows a musician to write musical scores in the traditional way but using a computer. The computer can then 'play' the music by outputting the sounds that the score notation represents. A score can be edited in many ways, including changing notes or tempo, extracting parts for individual instruments or adding lyrics.

A further type of software lets a musician **edit sound waves** – it allows the digitised sound-wave pattern to be edited. Such software is used to remove extraneous sound known as 'noise'.

Interactive services

A range of interactive services are available via the Internet. The HM Revenue and Customs website, as well as providing a great deal of information, provides a tax payer with the opportunity of filling in their self-assessment **tax return** on line.

Some people lead such busy lives, working very long hours, that they find it hard to meet potential partners. There has been a tremendous growth in **online dating**. Subscribers share details and select people to meet up with.

▶ Online shopping

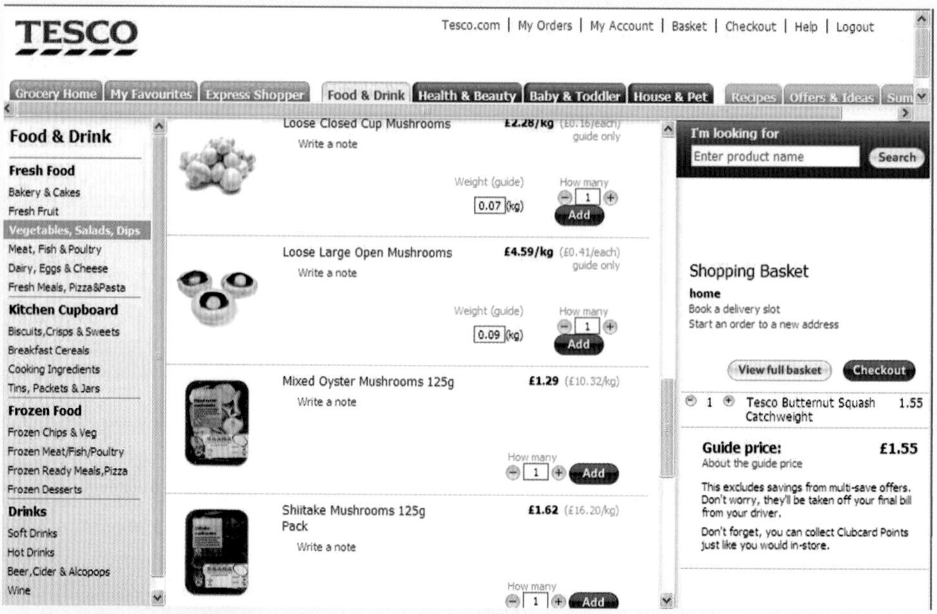

Figure 3 Online shopping with Tesco

Online shopping is particularly useful for customers who are housebound or live very busy lives. Tesco, like several other food retailers, run a successful online ordering service. Customers can choose their goods from their computer at home. They can select a convenient delivery time and are therefore saved the time and bother of travelling to a store.

Not everyone is able or willing to purchase goods on line. To do so they need to have a computer with Internet access, ideally using broadband. Many people are hesitant to make payments on line as they are concerned over security issues. They may be unwilling to give their credit/debit-card details as they fear that they might become the victim of fraud.

For more on online shopping, see Chapter 5, page 52.

Activity 5

Explore **four** different e-shopping sites on the Internet. Try a variety of sites – include a small specialist site as well as a large food retailer.

1 Describe the common features that you find.
2 A member of your family is trying to decide whether or not to become an e-shopper. To make sure that they make a reasoned decision, list **three** benefits of e-shopping and **three** drawbacks.

▶ Booking on line

As well as purchasing goods, users can use the Internet to make a range of bookings by accessing remote databases, including booking:

For more on booking flights, see Chapter 4, Case Study 4, page 36.

▶ flights
▶ train and coach journeys
▶ hotels

▶ holidays
▶ theatre and cinema performances
▶ concerts.

Websites provide up-to-date details of availability and prices that allow users to make a choice and book very quickly. They can search for holidays, trains or flights to suit their requirements and make provisional or firm bookings.

Airlines produce e-tickets that are issued at the time of booking. The customer must provide all necessary personal details on line and will be issued with a unique identifying code. Upon arrival at the airport, all the information will be available to the check-in clerk's computer. Payment is made by credit or debit card at the time of booking.

Booking on line has advantages:

▶ Bookings can be made from home.
▶ There is access to a very wide range of providers.
▶ Services are available 24 hours a day, 365 days a year.
▶ Bookings take place immediately so there is little possibility of overbooking as the database will be updated.

Case Study 6 – Booking a seat at a cinema

everyman

Online Reservations
Entertainment
Food & Drink
My Venue
Venue Hire
Join the Club
Get in Touch
E-Store
Everyman Media Group

We indulge you.
Please indulge us by not bringing food & drink from other outlets into the venue

Search

Change Cinema
Screen at Winchester
Submit

You have selected

Venue	The Screen Winchester
Event	Easy Virtue (PG)
Date	Mon 17 Nov
Time	6:00PM

Please choose the number of seats you require below. Some performances are allocated and you may be asked to select your preferred seats on the following screen. Please note that certain venues have sofas available and may seat more than one person.

Please remember to bring your debit/credit card upon collection of your tickets.

SEAT TYPE:	QTY:	COST:	SUBTOTAL:
CHILD TICKET:	0	6.00	0.00
SENIOR TICKET:	0	6.00	0.00
STANDARD TICKET:	0	7.50	0.00
STUDENT TICKET:	0	6.00	0.00
		TOTAL:	0.00

including VAT
* Service and Systems Surcharge to be applied

Change Session

Figure 4 Booking screen for cinema tickets

A cinema sells tickets for numbered seats and maintains an ICT system to deal with all bookings. A customer can buy tickets either in person just before the film is shown or in advance by telephone or via the Internet. When an Internet booking is made, the customer selects the film and date and time of performance. A layout of the cinema is then displayed on the screen showing which seats are still available for booking. The customer can then select the seat or seats required and the system records the booking. The customer can either have the tickets sent to them or pick them up from the box office when they arrive at the cinema.

1 A key requirement of a seat booking system is that seats cannot be double booked. Explain why this is important and describe how the system can make sure that this requirement is met.
2 For what reasons might a customer choose to make a booking:
   a in person   b by telephone   c on line?
3 What kinds of information could the seat booking system provide for the manager of a cinema?

▶ E-mail

E-mail is discussed in detail in Chapter 8, pages 115–116. See Case Study 4, page 113, for more on VoIP and Skype.

The use of **e-mail** to keep in touch with family and friends around the world is becoming increasingly popular. E-mail is replacing the standard postal service as the main method of written communication for many people. More and more e-cards are being sent for birthdays and to mark other special days and events. **VoIP** systems such as Skype are also growing in popularity.

▶ Social networking sites

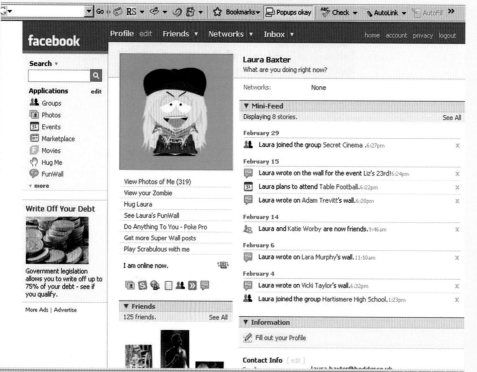

A **social networking site** such as Facebook allows a user to create online links with friends or colleagues. These links build up to create communities as a small initial group of users invite their friends to become part of their own personal network. These friends then invite others, and so on. There are now hundreds of social networking sites worldwide; millions of users have accounts.

Figure 5 **Facebook in use**

Users share basic personal information, including a photograph and details such as their favourite music, books and films, to establish their identity. They keep in touch with friends, exchange information and share links.

Software can be added that offers a peer-to-peer service allowing a user to share or stream media such as music to their friends.

Activity 6

1 Using presentation software, prepare a tutorial on the use of networking software.
2 Discuss the benefits and problems of the growth of social networking software.

▶ Gambling

There are many online **betting sites** where an individual can place bets on a wide range of events such as the outcome of football matches or television programmes such as *Big Brother*. There is a trend for continuing to make bets during a match with the odds shifting as the game progresses.

In the 5 years from 2001 to 2006 the amount gambled in the UK rose from about £7 billion per year to £40 billion. This is thought to be due partly to the removal of betting tax and partly to the growth of online betting. During the same period, there has been a rapid growth in the use of an online gambling advice service. The average amount owed by people seeking advice was £25 000.

Online gambling using betting sites can create a particular problem for isolated and lonely people, who may find interacting with people difficult. They can find themselves spending more on gambling than they can afford.

Case Study 7 – US online gambling ban

In October 2006, US Congress passed a bill outlawing online gambling. A Republican congressman described online gambling as: 'you just click the mouse and lose your house', adding that people could even lose money on their BlackBerrys while waiting in line at the movies.

But soon after the ban an online petition opposing it was started with a goal of attracting 400 000 signatures. A congressman who was trying to repeal the ban stated, 'The existing legislation is an inappropriate interference on the personal freedom of Americans and this interference should be undone.'

The chief executive of an online betting company had been unexpectedly arrested while he changed planes in the US the previous summer. Six months after the ban he was still under house arrest at a hotel in Missouri.

1 Find out about the current state of the law relating to online gambling in the USA.
2 Summarise the arguments for and against online gambling.

▶ Voting

Online voting is now used in a variety of situations. It is commonplace in organisations such as universities, where it is often used to elect members of the student union.

Some countries have allowed online voting in national elections. Many people in the UK believe that online voting would be good for democracy here. Current turnout for local and general elections is poor, particularly amongst young people. Recent research has shown that 66% of the British citizens who did not vote in the 2005 election would have been more likely to have voted if online voting had been available.

Online voting can be used in many other situations. In 2005 a competition was held for a £50 million National Lottery grant. The grant was to be awarded to a special project that would inspire a community to revitalise the area in which they lived. There were 33 entries to the competition. Four projects were chosen to go through to the final. These were put to a public vote which was carried out on line and by telephone. A total of 286 285 votes were received.

Activity 7

1 Find **five** further examples of online voting.
2 Many people have concerns about the use of online voting in a national election. Describe what these concerns are likely to be.

▶ Teletext services

Teletext is an electronic information service which can be viewed on most televisions using the remote control. It can be used to view information such as news, weather forecasts, TV schedules, traffic information and sports results provided by TV companies. Teletext is free and

Figure 6 Teletext page

is easy to use. Eighty per cent of UK households have a teletext TV, with an average of 20 million people using the service each week. Pages are numbered and transmitted in sequence. When a particular page is requested the viewer must wait until it is next transmitted.

Teletext services are offered by the BBC, ITV, Channel 4 and Channel 5. Viewers can access over 3200 pages, with around 50 000 daily updates. However, pages can be slow to load and restricted by the format of the page. Few colours are used and the graphics are poor.

▶ Mobile phones

Mobile phones have become part of everyday life in the UK and can be used wherever there is a signal. A mobile phone runs on a battery which has to be recharged. A user may find that the battery runs out just when they need to use the phone.

Calls can be paid for by subscription account, where the customer is sent a bill every month for calls made, or through 'pay as you go' schemes. Advance credit for 'pay as you go' can be bought on line or from shops. The owner of the phone is issued with a card with a magnetic strip that holds a unique identifying number for their account. When payment is made, the account for their phone is credited.

Call charges are usually lower for subscription accounts. However, if the phone is stolen a large bill can be run up, whereas the money that can be lost on a 'pay as you go' is limited to the amount of unused credit that has already been paid for.

Activity 8

Many mobile phones allow the user to do much more than simply make a voice call. Make a list of features that are available on some mobile phones, such the ability to take photographs. Think of as many as you can.

Ask **ten** members of the class (or your friends) whether they have each feature. If they have a feature, do they make regular use of it? If they do not have a feature, would they like to have that feature?

Count up the responses that you collect and present them in a table with the headings below.

Feature	Number having feature	Number regularly using feature	Number who would like feature
Ability to take photos			

Banking

The number of transactions carried out by banks has grown so rapidly that they could not now operate without computers. Banks transfer money electronically. Most workers' wages or salaries are paid directly

EFTPOS is the transfer of funds electronically between a customer's bank account and a retailer's at a till point. See Chapter 5, page 51.

into their bank account by computer. Many regular payments such as mortgages, utilities and insurance premiums are transferred electronically from an individual's bank account to the company's bank account as a direct debit or a standing order. This means that an individual does not have to worry about remembering to pay bills, thus avoiding the risk of extra charges if they forget to pay.

Cash is not as important as it used to be. Most individuals do not need to carry as much cash as before thanks to credit and debit cards.

Case Study 8 – The cashless society

There have been many developments in ICT that are leading to a society without cash. These include:

▶ credit cards where computers store financial details

▶ cheques which are processed by computers using MICR (magnetic ink character recognition)

▶ direct debits used to pay regular bills that are generated by computer

▶ wages and salaries being paid by electronic transfer and not in cash

▶ phone cards that can be used for telephone calls

▶ smart cards containing a microchip that are used for automatic debit and credit

▶ electronic funds transfer connecting shops with banks' computers.

1 Many people welcome the fact that they do not have to carry around large amounts of currency. Why do you think this is so?

2 Other members of society feel 'left out' of the move towards a cashless society as they cannot have, or do not want to have, credit and debit cards. Identify the categories of the population who might feel this way and give reasons why they might do so.

3 Make a list of all the transactions that you think will continue to require cash in the future – for example, giving pocket money to young children.

4 Describe the benefits and drawbacks of a cashless society. When preparing your answer consider different categories of people – the young, those on a low income, the elderly.

Credit cards can be obtained from a number of companies. Essentially a cardholder borrows money from the company, which pays for goods purchased. The company keeps detailed records of purchases made by a cardholder using their card. The cardholder is sent a list of all transactions every month and can either pay the amount owing in full or make a smaller payment. If they do not pay in full, they will be charged interest on any amount outstanding. Every adult has a credit rating that is used to determine whether or not they will be allowed a card and, if they are, their credit limit – the maximum amount they can owe the credit-card company at any particular time.

A **debit card** is linked to the holder's bank account. When transactions are made using a debit card, money is transferred immediately from the customer's account.

If a person runs out of cash, they can visit an **automated teller machine (ATM)** at any time. Before banks introduced ATMs, they had to employ more staff to act as tellers who worked at a desk and dispensed money to customers. The customers had to queue until a teller was free, write a cheque or fill in a withdrawal form and show identification before they were given cash by the teller.

The development of ATMs has brought benefits to both customers and banks. Customers now have access to cash at any time of the day or night, which is much more convenient. ATMs save time for the customers, who no longer need to queue at the bank counter behind someone who is depositing 20 bags of small coins! The bank needs fewer staff or can use its tellers for other tasks. It can close some branches and just provide an ATM device, which reduces costs. Many banks have used the space and staffing freed up by the installation of ATMs to develop new services which are useful to customers and increase profits.

There are also drawbacks to the use of ATMs. There has been a growth in fraud and card theft as well as attacks on customers who have just withdrawn money. Many customers preferred the more personal approach when human tellers were used. There have also been occasions when computer failure has occurred, putting many ATMs out of action.

► Home online banking

Home online banking means that users with access to the Internet can check their account balances, transfer money between accounts and pay bills from home. This can be much more convenient than having to visit a bank in person and transactions can be carried out more quickly than by using the normal postal service. Money is saved on postal and travel costs. Online banking has the added convenience of its services being available at any time from anywhere in the world.

Customers can organise their accounts to make the best use of interest rates as it is very easy to transfer money between a current account, used to carry out day-to-day transactions, and a savings account that accrues interest. In fact online savings accounts often offer better rates of interest than traditional ones. It is very easy for a customer to look at their bank statement to check whether certain transactions have been carried out and money taken from their account.

There are some disadvantages to using online banking. It is necessary for the user to have Internet access, which can be too costly for those on a low income. If the user has problems with their computer or Internet access they will not be able to carry out their banking activities in their normal way. Internet banking does not provide access to physical cash, which may still be needed for certain transactions. As more people use online banking, there will be less custom at local bank branches, which may result in their closure.

The most common reason why some people do not use online banking is fear of fraud. It is possible that others could see a person's bank information either accidentally or by hacking. The details of a credit or debit card could be used fraudulently to spend money.

It is important that a user of home online banking maintains sensible **security** precautions. They should ensure that any password used to access the computer is kept secret. The bank will provide a secure interface. The user is likely to be asked for another password as well as a number of questions that have been set up in advance – for example, mother's maiden name, name of first school or first pet. These are questions that a stranger is unlikely to be able to answer correctly.

Some customers are provided with a special device called a **dongle**. This is a small wireless device that generates a random number. This is read by the computer. The user also types it in and access is denied if the two numbers do not match exactly.

▶ Card crime and methods of prevention

The newspapers are full of articles about credit and debit card crime. There a number of different ways that cards can be used for fraudulent purposes.

The card can be physically stolen – taken from a pocket, handbag or wallet, or from home when a thief breaks in. The card is then used by an impostor, who pretends it is their own, to obtain goods or services. Very often the person who steals the card is not the person who uses it – the card is sold to a third party.

A card can be copied: this is often referred to as **cloning** or **skimming**. When the card is handed to an employee of a shop, restaurant or petrol station, they put it into a special electronic reading device without the owner's knowledge and steal the card details. These are then used to make a counterfeit card. The cardholder will be unaware that anything has happened until they receive the next statement of their credit-card account.

Phishing is another technique used to get the details of a credit or debit card illegally. An e-mail is sent to the cardholder, falsely claiming to be from a legitimate enterprise and asking them to send private information that will then be used for identity theft. It works by the e-mail supplying a link to a bogus website masquerading as a legitimate one. At the false site the cardholder is asked to update personal information, such as credit-card number and password.

Card details can also be found by going through a cardholder's receipts. These details can be used without a physical card to order goods or services fraudulently over the Internet.

A number of measures are being considered to help prevent card crime, some of which have already been implemented. In many places users insert their card into a reader themselves and enter a secret PIN number. Cards used to be verified by comparing the user's signature with the one on the back of the card. These signatures were easy to forge and very often the seller did not bother to check for a match.

Bank and credit-card-company computers check accounts for irregular or unusual spending patterns. If such a pattern is detected, the account is frozen and the bank will contact the account holder to check that the transactions were legitimate.

What you can do to prevent card fraud
Based on a BBC article

▶ Keep your cards safe at all times.
▶ Don't let anyone know your PIN number – even if they phone you and say that they are from the police or the credit-card company!
▶ When using your card to make a payment, don't let it out of your sight.
▶ Only use secure, well-known Internet sites when shopping on line.
▶ Always check bank and credit-card statements carefully, and query anything you don't recognise immediately.
▶ Take care when disposing of bank statements and credit-card receipts. Criminals search dustbins. Use a shredder.

The use of stolen credit and debit cards could be reduced by including a photograph of the holder on the card. To reduce credit-card fraud on the Internet, it is sensible for the cardholder to use a secure service such as PAYPAL. Cloning has been made harder by introduction of programmable smart cards with holograms, which make the cards more difficult to copy.

Summary

ICT is used in the **health** sector in many ways:

▶ Scanning devices, such as CAT and MRI scanners, are used as a powerful diagnostic tool.

▶ A wide range of sensors are used to monitor bodily functions.

▶ Electronic patient record keeping is widespread in hospitals and doctors' surgeries. A national scheme is currently being developed.

▶ ISBT 128 is a barcoding scheme for tracking blood from donor to transfusion recipient.

▶ Artificial-intelligence systems behave in the way that a human would behave.

▶ Neural networks are systems than mimic the working of the human brain.

▶ Neural networking requires parallel processing.

▶ Expert systems take on the expertise of humans in a specific field such as an aspect of medical diagnosis.

▶ An expert system shell is software with which an expert system can be built.

▶ An expert system is made up of a knowledge base, an inference engine and a human/computer interface.

In the **home** ICT is used for:

▶ games
▶ photography
▶ listening to music
▶ creating music
▶ pay-to-view services
▶ online shopping
▶ booking services
▶ e-mail
▶ interactive services such as betting, voting and dating
▶ teletext
▶ mobile phones.

In **banks**, computers are replacing human workers. Most people's wages or salaries are paid directly into their bank account by computer. An increasing number of other financial transactions take place electronically:

▶ Some people predict a cashless society.

▶ Debit and credit cards are widely used but are subject to fraud.

▶ Many people now carry out their banking transactions on line.

Questions Chapter 6

1 Discuss the benefits and limitations of online banking. (8)

2 Describe **three** ways in which ICT is used in the home for entertainment. (6)

3 Most health authorities now use medical databases and expert systems. Describe in detail the main advantages and disadvantages these give a doctor in the diagnosis and treatment of patients. (6)
WJEC Jan 2005

4 Modern hospitals make extensive use of ICT to help them deliver a better service.

   a Intensive treatment units (ITUs) use sensors to monitor patients. Other than temperature, name **two** other sensors that could be used in the care of an ITU patient. (2)

b Using sensors allows a patient to be constantly monitored (24/7). Give **two** other benefits of using sensors in patient care. (2)

c Explain why hospitals have adopted a system for barcoding blood. (2) WJEC June 2005

5 Expert system shells are important in the development of medical expert systems.

a Describe the **three** main parts of every expert system shell. (3)

b Describe, using examples, **two** advantages of using an expert system in medicine. (2) WJEC Jan 2006

6 The use of ICT systems in the home is growing daily.

a The HCI (human/computer interface) in software used to help young children learn is important. With reference to appropriate examples, discuss **two** factors that should be taken into account when designing such an interface. (4)

b Discuss the health issues raised by the increased use of ICT systems in the home. (2)

7 ICT is widely used in medicine.

a Doctors use spreadsheet software to process patient data. Define **each** of the following features of spreadsheet software and give an appropriate example of how it can be used in processing patient data:
   i statistics (2)
   ii graph. (2)

b Describe how the following are used for patient care in medicine:
   i computer control (2)
   ii barcode systems. (2) WJEC June 2006

Chapter

7

Presenting Information 4.1.7

Formats, media and audience

Information itself is very important but the way in which it is presented is also important. There are a range of different formats that can be used, via different media. The **format** and **medium** chosen should be the most appropriate for the intended **audience** (the person or group of people at whom the information aimed).

Within an organisation there are likely to be a number of different kinds of audience for whom information might be required. For example:

▶ Company shareholders want to be given information summarising the performance of the company over the last year.

▶ A group of salespeople may need to be briefed about the prices and specifications of new products.

▶ An operations manager needs to be informed of the performance and output of each factory.

▶ Output format

A sales manager writing a sales report can use different formats to present the same information depending on who will read the report.

Graphs and charts

A director may want to see sales figures at a glance, probably including last year's figures for comparison. Graphs make it easier to detect trends and patterns. They can enhance information, making it easier to understand – as the saying goes, 'A picture is worth 1000 words.' Figure 1 is a column graph showing sales figures for this year and last year month by month.

Different types of graph, such as pie charts (both 2D and 3D), can be used to show the relative size of figures, as in Figure 2.

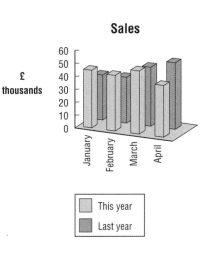

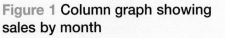

Figure 1 Column graph showing sales by month

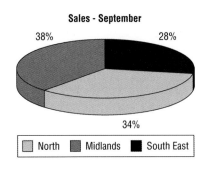

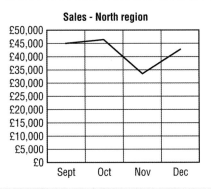

Figure 2 Pie chart showing sales by area

Figure 3 Line graph showing sales by month

Line graphs are used to show trends in figures, as in Figure 3.

Tables

An accountant may want to see more information, possibly broken down by area, by month and compared with previous figures. Such information can be presented in a table and studied in depth. It could be printed out on paper (hard copy) or presented on screen (soft copy). Part of it might look like the table in Figure 4.

	A	B	C	D	E	F
1	2006	Sept	Oct	Nov	Dec	Sept - Dec
2	North	£ 56,934	£ 53,192	£ 48,923	£ 59,204	£ 218,253
3	Midlands	£ 35,880	£ 32,901	£ 30,120	£ 41,245	£ 140,146
4	South East	£ 43,901	£ 38,103	£ 47,399	£ 58,104	£ 187,507
5	Total	£ 136,715	£ 124,196	£126,442	£ 158,553	£ 545,906
6						
7	2005	Sept	Oct	Nov	Dec	Sept - Dec
8	North	£ 56,191	£ 54,012	£ 49,231	£ 60,123	£ 219,557
9	Midlands	£ 26,712	£ 23,431	£ 29,012	£ 37,371	£ 116,526
10	South East	£ 41,021	£ 40,159	£ 46,912	£ 60,932	£ 189,024
11	Total	£ 123,924	£ 117,602	£125,155	£ 158,426	£ 525,107
12						
13	Increase	Sept	Oct	Nov	Dec	Sept - Dec
14	North	1%	-2%	-1%	-2%	-1%
15	Midlands	34%	40%	4%	10%	20%
16	South East	7%	-5%	1%	-5%	-1%
17	Total	10%	6%	1%	0%	4%

Figure 4 Part of a table comparing monthly sales by area for different years

Sales have risen year on year but an overall increase in sales of 4 per cent masks exceptionally good performance in the Midlands, where sales rose by 20 per cent compared with last year, while in other areas sales actually fell. The good performance in the Midlands is the result of excellent work by our sales staff and an intensive advertising campaign in the region.

Figure 5 Extract from a full text report

Reports

The manager's immediate superior may want even more information. They may require an exception report including details of where the company has done exceptionally well or exceptionally badly. Reasons for good and bad performance may be included. A full text report may be necessary (see Figure 5).

Spreadsheet software such as Microsoft Excel enables users to present information in a variety of chart formats. These charts can be copied and pasted into other software and then embedded into files in other programs such as Microsoft PowerPoint using OLE (see page 98). This means that if the spreadsheet is updated, the graphs are updated both in the spreadsheet software and in the presentation.

▶ Output media

All the output formats described above can be produced on **paper** for distribution to the appropriate people. However, there are times when information needs to be presented to a group of people at a meeting.

A report to a group of directors could be presented on a **screen** using an LCD data projector and presentation software such as Microsoft PowerPoint. Such a presentation could include graphs, tables and text.

PowerPoint gives the option of printing out a presentation in a variety of formats. A hard copy of all the slides with additional notes can be printed for the presenter. A hard copy of all the slides with additional space to make notes can be printed for the audience to take away for later reference.

Electronic whiteboard in use at a business meeting

Using an electronic **whiteboard** offers even more facilities for presenters. For example, an on-screen keyboard allows data to be entered at the whiteboard.

Information can also be presented on the **Web**.

For more on PowerPoint presentations and electronic whiteboards, see Chapter 4, pages 34–35.

▶ What is the best way to present information?

This will depend on a number of factors:

- ▶ the nature of the information
- ▶ its complexity
- ▶ needs of the recipient
- ▶ time available to study the information
- ▶ its life span.

The **nature** of information can be very varied. For example, information produced within a school could include a summary of examination results in all subjects, the attendance record of a particular student during the previous week, the total number of employees on the payroll and an inventory of stationery items in stock. Each of these will need to be presented in a different way.

Complex data can be hard to interpret and may be best displayed in pictorial or graphical form. For example, sales figures over a period of time for a number of products in a number of regions can be hard to understand when displayed just as numbers. The use of graphs can highlight important features and trends in the information.

Different **recipients** require information in different forms depending upon their individual needs. Some people find numerical information hard to digest and prefer a pictorial representation, whilst others require the precision and detail provided by actual numbers. The **time** that the recipient of the information has to study it will also be a factor in deciding how it should be presented. A picture gives a quick impression but tables of information might have to be studied to get the true picture of what is happening.

All information has a **life span.** How long it is useful will vary from situation to situation. For example, information needed to determine how much stock to order will no longer be required once the order has been submitted and the goods delivered. Ensuring that all output information is **date stamped** (giving the date and sometimes the time when the information was produced) can prevent old information from being used in error.

Activity 1

Copy and fill in the grid below, giving the most appropriate output format and medium for each example.

Information	Audience	Output format	Output medium
AS-level module results	Jo Bloggs, a student		
The school's AS-level performance in each subject	The school governors at a governors' meeting		
The overall A-level performance by all schools in Wales	The general public		

Word processing/DTP

Word-processing packages are used to produce documents such as letters and reports. Text can be formatted in a variety of ways to improve the look of a document. Parts such as headings can be made to stand out by using different fonts, text sizes, bold or italics. Bullet points can usefully highlight important points. Text can be edited using facilities such as copy and paste, find and replace, insert or delete a word, line or paragraph or through the use of spell check.

Faster processing speeds and increased computer memory have allowed modern packages to include many extra features such as mail merge, text wrapping around imported graphics, e-mail, spelling and grammar checks, and displaying text in tables and columns.

Text written by one person can be reviewed by another and comments added. This book has been written by two authors. When one completed a chapter they sent it to the other, as an e-mail attachment, for checking and comments. The word-processing package we used can show all edited changes made by the reviewer. Deleted text is highlighted and added text displayed in another colour. Comments can be added as well. When the reviewed chapter is returned to the author they can accept or reject each change (see Figure 6).

> Text written by ~~someone~~ <u>one person</u> can be reviewed by another and comments can be added. This book is written by two authors. When one author completed a chapter he[IS1] sent it to the other, for checking and commenting. The word-processing package has the facility to show all edited changes made by the reviewer. Deleted text is highlighted and added text displayed in another colour[IS2]. When the reviewed chapter is returned to the author he can accept or reject each change.

Figure 6 Reviewing a document

A **template** is a master document which is stored. It has a pre-defined layout and can be used as a basis for other documents. It could be a master document in which standard opening and closing parts are already filled in. An example would be a template for memos where the title and headings are provided. A memo document would be created based on the template and the message added.

Templates provide the user with the benefit of not having to design a whole document from scratch when a similar one has been produced before. The use of templates also encourages the use of a common 'house' layout for documents within an organisation. A template for a company's letterhead would contain the logo as well as information about the company.

In DTP (desktop publishing) templates consist of prepared pages with pictures and words that are going to be reused repeatedly. For example, the pages of this book are built on templates with a pre-determined layout.

Mail merge merges text from one file into another file. It can incorporate data automatically from a database into an outline document, such as a letter, to produce a set of personalised documents. This is particularly useful for generating large numbers of files that have the same format but different data. For example, an outline letter can be created with a number of merge fields, such as the recipient's name, which are copied from selected records from a database. Each letter will then have a different name added to it. A bank could use data from their client database, importing relevant fields from each record into a personalised document. In this way they could send a letter to all clients informing them of changes in fees.

A **style sheet** is a file that can be used to define the format and layout of a section of a document. The user sets up a style sheet by selecting parameters such as font style and size, page size, number of columns or margins. The same style sheet can be used any number of times. For example, a style can be set for headings with a font of 14 point Arial in bold italics.

A word processor allows the user to **import** objects from other software. These objects are then incorporated into the document that is created. Examples of objects that can be imported are a graphical image, part of a spreadsheet or database fields. Imports can be made in such a way that when updates are made to the original object they will also be made in the document to which it was imported. This is known as **OLE (object linking and embedding)**. For example, if a section of a spreadsheet is copied into a word-processed document using 'cut and paste', the values in the cells at the time of pasting will be copied into the document and will stay as they are. If OLE is used any subsequent changes made to the cells of the spreadsheet will be reflected in the document.

A sequence of keystrokes and menu choices can be saved as a **macro** then repeated simply by running the macro. Macros can speed up common operations by automating them so that one keystroke is used instead of many or by customising a package for a particular use. They also allow a complex operation to be set up by an experienced user and used by those less experienced. For example, in an office a macro can be set up that allows the user to select an icon from a tool bar (or an entry from a menu) that calls up the template for a particular type of document. The macro can then move the cursor to different positions in the document where data needs to be entered.

Although word-processing software is essentially a package that allows processing of text, modern packages provide many of the features traditionally only found in **DTP** (desktop publishing) software. The functions provided are usually sufficient for a home user who wishes to produce posters, newsletters or flyers. Examples of these functions include the use of columns, mixing text and graphical images, flowing text around images and producing banner headlines.

Large-scale, professional DTP software that is used commercially, such as QuarkXpress, has many more features and requires the user to have extensive training. A professional package gives the experienced user much greater control over the layout of pages. The design is based around frames – blocks within a page – into which text or graphical images can be dropped. Much greater precision with layout is possible and a very wide range of fonts are available. Such software has been used in the production of this book.

Functions provided in a DTP package such as QuarkXpress include:
▶ use of layers to organise items
▶ rotation of lines or boxes with their content in 0.001 degree increments
▶ scaling, cropping, rotating and skewing pictures
▶ scaling a picture to fit its box or a box to fit a picture

For more on using **DTP** software, see Unit 2, Task 1, page 188. For more on using **mail merge** and creating **macros**, see Task 2, pages 210 and 225.

►grouping items so they can be selected, moved, rotated, resized or modified as a single item.

Presentation software

Presentation software such as Microsoft PowerPoint is used to produce slide shows. A slide show consists of a number of screens that can be shown automatically in sequence.

A designer will create a **show** using a variety of elements. Presentations can include text and graphics, displays can be animated to attract the audience's attention or show part of a page at a time. Sound files can be added for extra effect. **Animated transitions** relate to the way that text and graphics appear on the screen. A range of methods are available such as flyin and chequerboard. These can be used to liven up a presentation – for example, as one slide fades the next can fly in. A timing can be added for each slide and the presentation set to autorun. This allows a show to be delivered without a human presenter. Files of many types can be **imported** into a slide show, including tables, graphs, images, sound and video clips.

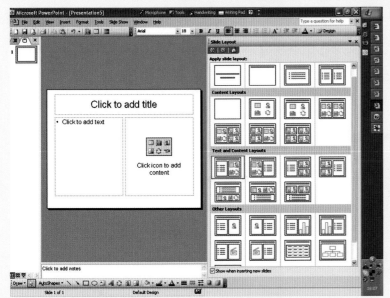

Figure 7 Select design layout of slide

Templates are used in presentation software in a similar way to those used in word-processing and DTP software. Microsoft PowerPoint provides a large selection of templates. A designer can modify these and add their own elements to create their own design template, which will then be available in the Slide Design task pane. A template can be applied to all the slides in a show or to selected slides only. More than one design template can be used within a presentation.

When a design template is used, an extra slide called a slide master that stores information about the design template (such as font styles, background design and colour schemes) is added to the presentation. If a different template is applied to all the slides, the old slide

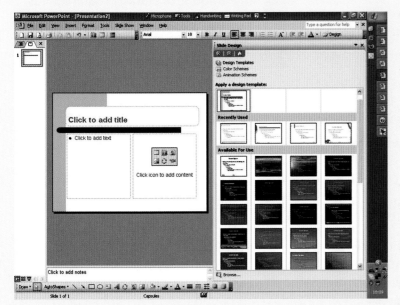

Figure 8 Select slide design

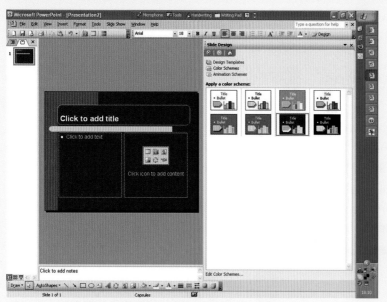

Figure 9 **Select colour scheme for slide**

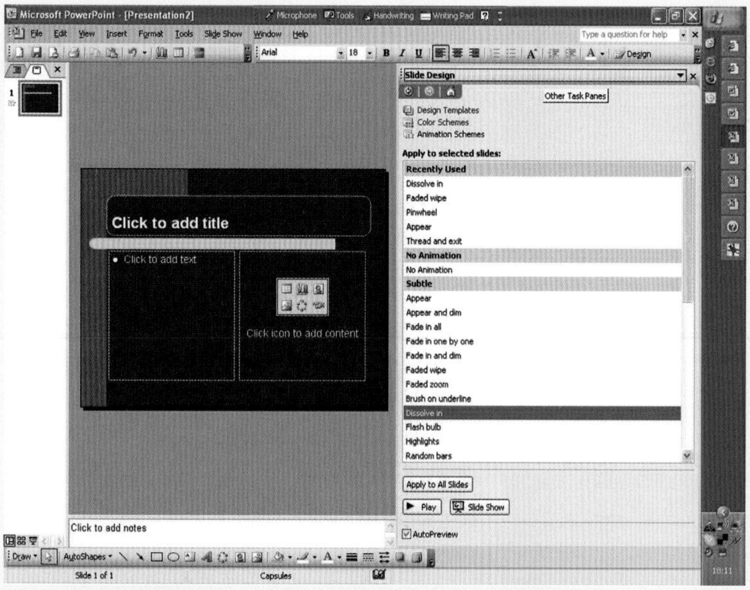

Figure 10 **Select animation for slide transition**

Figure 11 **Save the selections as a template**

master is replaced by the master in the new template.

Figures 7–11 show the stages in the creation of a template. The layout of the slide can be selected from a large number of possibilities. These allow different objects such as title, text, images, charts or media clips to be included in the chosen layout (Figure 7). Next the design of the slide can be chosen from a standard selection (Figure 8) or a new design can be created that is specifically tailored to the slide show. For example, each slide could incorporate the company logo or have a relevant image as a backdrop. The colour scheme for standard designs can be chosen (Figure 9) then the appropriate animation for slide transition (Figure 10). This newly created template can then be named and saved for reuse (Figure 11). Note that a template is stored as a **.pot** file rather than a standard **.ppt** PowerPoint file.

Presentation files that include images, sound or video clips are likely to be large, requiring considerable memory to store. **Data compression** techniques are often used to minimise the amount of storage required.

The use of presentation software has become increasingly common with the development of data projectors. These devices can project a computer display onto a large screen and are ideal for a presentation to an audience, usually replacing an old OHP (overhead projector).

Presentation software might be used by the head of a sales team who wishes to present information during talks to groups of salespeople in different parts of the country before the launch of a new range of products.

Using presentation software together with a data projector has a number of advantages not available with an OHP:

▶ Animation can be used so that the contents of a slide can be built up bit by bit to tie in with what the presenter is saying.

▶ A presentation can be automated and require no physical intervention as would be required for slides. Animation can be set to occur automatically after a certain time delay.

See Unit 2, pages 185–186 for examples of data compression.

See Chapter 4, page 35 for more on LCD **data projectors**.

For more on creating PowerPoint presentations see Unit 2, Task 3, page 240.

▶ Clip-art, sound and video clips can be added to the presentation – these can increase impact.

▶ Links can be added so that it is possible to go through the presentation in a different order or to miss out slides, depending on the audience.

▶ The speaker can easily go back to the previous slide to review information.

▶ The package will print out hard copies of the slides in a variety of formats so that members of the audience of a presentation can have a copy on which to add notes. Such presentations appear much more professional than those based on standard acetates.

▶ The speaker can use a remote-control mouse to move the slides on, so can stand anywhere in the room.

▶ Changes can be easily made, even at the last minute, which would be more difficult with acetate slides.

Potential problems with presentations

Using presentation software and a data projector will not make a boring presentation interesting. Cluttered screens, small fonts, too much text, poor colour choice and overuse of animations are symptoms of poor presentations.

Activity 2

Many presentations are ineffective because the creator has focused more on the visual effects than on the content. Some people call this 'Death by PowerPoint'.

1 On the Internet, use a search engine to search for 'Death by PowerPoint'.
2 Produce your own slide show that demonstrates points to consider when creating an effective presentation.

Databases

The **query** feature in a DBMS (database management system) allows the database to be searched so that records that meet certain criteria can be selected. It is a very powerful feature. For example, a supermarket may maintain a database that contains records of all customer purchases. A query could select the records of all customers who have purchased luxury ready-made meals in the last few weeks. These customers could then be targeted with promotional material about a new range of meals.

A **report** is information that is output from the system, such as a list of all the customers who buy dog food more than twice a week. An example of a report is given in Figure 12, which shows a list of exam results for students in a school.

Exam Results

Surname	Forename	Subject	Teacher	Result
Ambreen	Aisha	French	Miss Knight	E
Ambreen	Aisha	Art	Mr Hill	C
Davis	Gareth	Physics	Mrs Edwards	A
Davis	Gareth	French	Miss Knight	B
Hunt	Fay	History	Mr Galloway	D
Hunt	Fay	French	Miss Knight	B
Hunt	Fay	English	Ms Cornwell	B
Hunt	Fay	Art	Mr Hill	C
Smith	Jamie	Art	Mr Hill	E

Figure 12 Student results using data from more than one database table

Data can be **imported** into or **exported** from a database program. This simply means that data can be transferred from or to another program, such as another database, a spreadsheet or word-processing software.

For example, a supermarket could export a file consisting of a list of customers who buy luxury goods to another company (and charge them for this information). Exam boards create a file of A-level results for each school which is exported to the school's own database software.

Web authoring

The global nature of the Internet and easy accessibility mean that it is used for distributing information.

Many public bodies such as local councils use the Internet to publish agendas of meetings and their minutes. Anyone can simply go to a search engine on the organisation's website and type in 'online minutes'. This is much easier for the organisation than printing several copies and posting them. It is also a way of giving the public easy access to information. Reports can also be made available to subscribers only, such as the law reports at http://www.lloydslawreports.com

Web pages are created using **hypertext mark-up language (HTML)**, which is an authoring language specifically designed to create documents on the World Wide Web. The language defines the layout and structure of a web document by using a variety of tags and attributes.

Web authoring involves the use of navigational tools that allow users to select further pages. A **hyperlink** is a connection to another related page or a different section on the current page. When a hyperlink is activated the software sends a request for another web page, specified by the hyperlink, to be downloaded. A **hot spot** is a part of a piece of text or a graphic that, when selected by a pointing device, activates another function such as playing a video or displaying a picture.

Web pages can include **animated images** produced using **Flash programming**. A **frame** is a section of a web page in which semi-independent activities can take place – for example, an area with a menu or group of links.

Web pages can include an option to be formatted by the user to fit their specific requirements. For example, a user may wish to display text in a larger than normal font: this facility would be particularly useful to the partially sighted.

Web authoring provides a range of options and techniques that can be used to make a web page clear and easy to understand and navigate. These include:

- choice of text colour and background colour
- use of white space to make sure the page is not cluttered
- use of **marquee** – text scrolling across the screen
- sound
- **animated gifs** – apparently moving pictures
- animations using **JavaScript** coding or special software such as Macromedia **Flash**
- video.

Activity 3

Explore the subject of web animation by accessing 'How Web Animation Works' on the HowStuffWorks website http://computer.howstuffworks.com/

1 What is a plug-in?
2 Explain the difference between an animated gif and a Flash animation.

Case Study 1 – A web page

Figure 13 (on the following page) shows a web page that can be accessed by entering http://www.totaltravel.co.uk/travel/Wales/north-wales-coast/rhyll-prestatyn
Certain web authoring features are shown.

1 Explain the use of:
  a hyperlink   d animation
  b hot spot   e keyword search.
  c frame

2 Other methods of web navigation include:
  a bookmarks – these are saved web-page

addresses (URLs) that allow the user to revisit a saved page without having to re-enter the URL
  b pull-down menus
  c graphics buttons.

Describe an example of the use of **each** of the above.

3 Access a further website such as http://www.bbc.co.uk/wales/programmes/
Describe the web authoring features that are present.

Animation

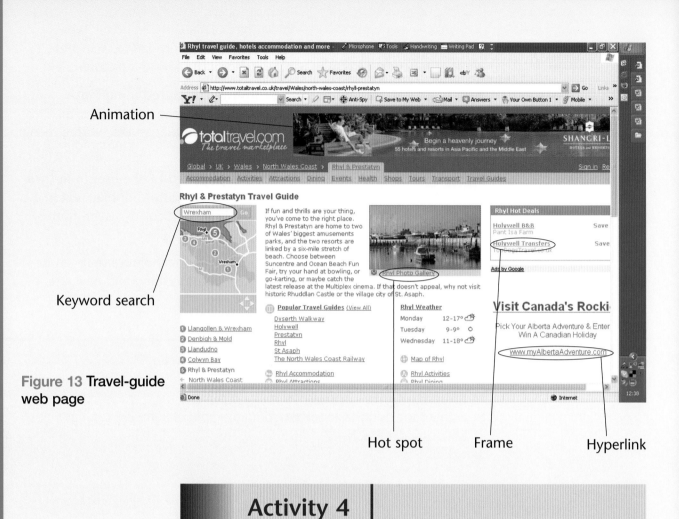

Keyword search

Figure 13 Travel-guide web page

Hot spot   Frame   Hyperlink

Activity 4

Visit these two websites:

▶ http://www.bbc.co.uk/radio1/
▶ http://www.antique-furniture.co.uk/

They obviously have very different audiences.

1 Write down **five** differences between the designs of these two sites. Then write down **five** similarities. For example, a similarity might be that they both have a search facility. A difference might be the position of the search facility.

2 For each site, identify **three** different web-page features. Explain the function of each feature.

Web design disasters

Not all websites are well designed. Garish colours, poor contrast, unreadable fonts, too much animation and huge images that take a long time to load are some of the symptoms of bad web design.

http://www.webpagesthatsuck.com/ is a website that gives awards for poor web design. Every day it selects its daily sucker – another website that in its eyes is terrible.

For more on creating web pages, see Unit 2, Task 3, page 240.

Activity 5

Visit http://www.webpagesthatsuck.com/ and go to its daily sucker page. Do you agree that the site is not very good? Give reasons why you think the site is good or bad.

If a web page is not attractively presented then nobody will want to read it. When designing a web page it is important not to forget that its purpose is to communicate information to its audience. It is crucial that the design, layout and text are suitable for that audience.

Summary

- ▶ Information can be presented in a range of different **formats** and via different **media**.
- ▶ The way in which information is presented will depend on the target **audience**.
- ▶ Different formats are available such as text, graphs and tables.
- ▶ Information can be disseminated to a larger audience in one place by creating a **slide show** using presentation software and presenting it via a data projector.
- ▶ Different techniques are used on the Internet to attract and hold our attention.
- ▶ Key features of **word-processing** and **DTP** software are:
  - a templates
  - b style sheets
  - c importation of objects
  - d mail merge
  - e macros.

- ▶ Key features of **presentation** software are:
  - a templates
  - b creating a show
  - c animated transitions
  - d importing files (including video and sound)
  - e exporting files
  - f data compression techniques.
- ▶ Key features of **database** software are:
  - a import/export function
  - b queries
  - c reports.
- ▶ Key features of **web authoring** software are:
  - a hyperlinks
  - b formatting
  - c animation
  - d frames
  - e HTML.

Chapter 7 Questions

1 A headteacher and the school's governing body want to consider the school's recent exam results at AS and A level at their next meeting. You have been asked for your advice on how the results could be presented.

   a Describe **three** different possible format options. (6)

   The headteacher decides to develop a computer-based presentation to be displayed using an LCD (data) projector rather than creating OHP transparencies.

   b State **three** functions of presentation software that are available for use with an LCD projector but not with OHP transparencies. (3)

c Give **four** factors that should be considered when designing an effective presentation. (4)

2 A manager of a stationery-supplies company says, 'I haven't got time to read lots of figures. I want the facts in an easy-to-read format.'

a State which information format is likely to be the most appropriate for the manager. (1)

b Describe **two other** factors that can determine the way that information should be presented. (4)

3 A national firm of accountants makes extensive use of ICT software. The firm employs an ICT expert to design their web pages. Give **three** features of a web authoring program the expert could use in the creation of the web pages. (3) WJEC Jan 05

4 A tourist information office has prepared a presentation to be run in all of its information centres and from the council website.

a Define **each** of the following functions of the presentation software and give an appropriate example of how each could be used:

i templates (2)

ii animated transitions. (2)

b Give **two different** methods a tourist could use to find this information on the council website. (2) WJEC June 05

5 A large national supermarket company uses a database to store customers' records. Define **each** of the following functions of the database software and give an appropriate example of how each can be used in this context:

a import/export (2)

b query (2)

c report. (2) WJEC Jan 06

6 A design company uses word-processing and DTP software to produce documents. Define **each** of the following functions of the software and give an appropriate example of how each could be used by the design company:

a templates

b style sheets

c mail merge. (6) WJEC June 07

7 A large number of people are now involved in producing web pages. Explain the following terms in relation to web authoring, giving suitable examples in each case:

a hyperlinks

b frames. (4) WJEC Jan 08

Chapter

8

Networks 4.1.8

A **computer network** consists of two or more computers and peripherals that are linked together.

A **stand-alone** computer is one that is not part of a network. Stand-alone computers can only access data files that are stored on a backing storage device that is linked directly to that computer. Any peripheral device used, such as a printer or scanner, will also need to be directly linked to the computer. Typically such a computer would have a number of backing storage devices such as a hard disk, floppy-disk drive and a CD-ROM or DVD drive attached directly to it. All modern computers have a USB port that allows devices such as printers, digital cameras and USB flash memory devices (memory sticks) to be attached. A user of a stand-alone computer has sole use of the data stored on the hard disk – no one else can access it. The computer and installed software can be customised to meet the user's needs exactly.

Data files stored on a **networked computer** can be accessed by different network users. Networked computers can share hardware (such as printers) and software. Very often a networked computer will not have a dedicated printer directly attached. A network will have extra hardware installed to allow each computer to link in to the network. Extra cabling may be necessary although the use of wireless networking is quite widespread.

To provide the security necessary to prevent unauthorised access, it is usual to present the user with a log-in screen when the computer is turned on. When several people use the same stand-alone computer, they must each enter a unique code to identify them to the network operating system, together with a secret password to confirm their identity.

A network user has access to a greater range of disk drives. Some of these are called logical drives as they are merely part of a shared central file server that is used by many users. A user can be allocated their own private space on such a disk (often referred to as the **f:** drive). Other drives, each identified by a different letter, may be shared by a group of users.

It is necessary to plan a network with great care. The number of computers in the network will be an important factor in deciding how it should be set up. It will also be crucial to work out the potential usage at peak times and any likely future expansion of the network.

► Advantages of networking computers

►**Hardware can be shared.** Resources such as printers, scanners and modems can be shared, so saving costs. A common Internet gateway can be used, which can make it easier to maintain security.

►**Data can be shared** rather than each user having their own copy. Shared data could be a centralised database containing details of stock prices and sales data. A standardised template for a word-processing package could be stored centrally to allow all users to produce documents in the same format.

►**Improved communication between users**. This is particularly useful for e-mail and sending data accurately so that it does not have to be typed into a computer again (for example, examination-board entries, newspaper stories and National Lottery ticket sales). Intranets can be used for publishing company information. Team members can work collaboratively on projects since everyone can access common files.

►**Software can be shared**. For a network of, say, 20 machines, you can buy a network licence to run a program such as Microsoft Office. This will be cheaper than buying 20 copies of Microsoft Office, which you would need to do if you had 20 stand-alone machines. You will need to install the software only once and it will be available to all network stations. With 20 stand-alone machines the software would need to be installed 20 times.

►**Security.** Access to the network can be restricted to registered users who have an individual user ID which can only be used with a password. Different users can have different access privileges to control the data they can access. There can also be greater control over the software that is loaded and stored, especially if the networked computers do not have individual floppy-disk and CD-ROM drives.

►**Backup can be controlled centrally**. One person can be given the responsibility for backing up files rather than relying on individuals to carry out the process.

► Advantages of a stand-alone system

►**Fewer hardware requirements.** A network requires extra hardware. Unless wireless connections are used, cables are needed to link computers together, and may be difficult and expensive to install. Each computer on the network requires a network card. Extra devices such as switches or bridges may also be needed.

►**Reliability of performance.** A stand-alone computer should always work at the same speed, whereas a user working at a network computer may notice a slowing down in response time caused by high network traffic or the speed of connection. If the network server fails then every computer in the network will be unable to access the network resources.

▶ **Security.** A virus introduced on one network computer may quickly spread to the rest of the network. A stand-alone computer (with no e-mail or Internet access) is only susceptible to viruses through software or files loaded through media such as CD-ROM or floppy disk. The only way for someone else to access your data if it is stored on a stand-alone computer is to physically use that computer.

▶ **Less ICT knowledge needed.** Any problems occurring will be local to the computer. With a network problems are harder to trace.

Case Study 1 – A graphic design studio

Three graphic designers, Adrian, Helen and Sanjit, have decided to set up a new business together. They will be employing two assistants. They have to decide on the IT equipment to buy for the business. One of the decisions they need to make is whether to install a small network or to have stand-alone computers.

If each designer were to have their own computer they would each need specialist peripherals: a scanner and high-quality printer. This would be expensive. However, there would be no need for one of them to wait while a device was in use by someone else, as might occur with a network.

If they chose to install a network the designers and assistants would be able to share data. This would allow two or more of the team to work on the same project.

A network would allow the team to communicate with each other through e-mail, to share online diaries and to access each other's documents for proofreading.

1 The team have to decide whether to install a network. Discuss the issues involved. Add ideas not included above.
2 Discuss the benefits and disadvantages to the designers of having Internet access.

⬤ LANs and WANs

For more on small home networks where several computers are linked using a wireless router, see Chapter 6, Case Study 5, page 80.

A network may be restricted to one room or one building or cover a small geographical area. Such a network is called a **local area network** or **LAN**. It was traditionally connected via direct lines – physical links using its own dedicated cables. These could be twisted wire, coaxial or fibre-optic cables. The development of wireless networks means that many small LANs now operate without physical cables. Many small businesses use a peer-to-peer LAN where resources can be shared very easily.

Alternatively, a network may be spread over a wide geographical area, possibly covering different countries. Such a network is called a **wide area network** or **WAN**. It can be linked by public telecommunications systems such as telephone lines, satellite links and microwave signals.

Large international companies such as IBM or Unilever maintain their own WANs which are independent of the Internet. They have their own secure links between sites. This means that sensitive data is not transferred over the public network and is therefore easier to keep secure.

Examples of the use of WANs include:

► airline, theatre and hotel booking systems
► home banking
► bank ATMs
► the National Lottery
► e-mail
► videoconferencing
► stock control.

The Internet is a very large WAN, so a home user who accesses the Internet is using a WAN.

For more on the use of LANs and WANs by supermarkets, see Chapter 5, page 50.

Many larger organisations have their own server-based LANs linked into a WAN. A supermarket company that has many shops throughout the country would use a WAN as well as shop-based LANs. At each shop a LAN would be used to control the POS system. Each POS would be linked to the shop's server so that when a barcode is scanned at a POS, the appropriate price can be found from the database stored on the server. The WAN could be used to order stock from a warehouse or suppliers.

Case Study 2 – The National Lottery

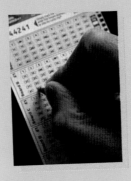

The National Lottery, run by Camelot, sells tickets in around 35000 retail outlets. Tills in all the retailers are connected to Camelot's WAN either by cable or by satellite. As lottery tickets are sold, details of the numbers chosen are entered by optical mark reading (OMR).

The data is transmitted to Camelot's computer centre in Rickmansworth, Hertfordshire. The network needs to be very sophisticated to cope with the large volumes of sales (particularly early in the evening before the draw is made), which have reached over 50000 transactions a minute. Camelot say that the network has been designed to cope with considerably more traffic than this.

1 What data needs to be transmitted from a lottery network station to the central computer?
2 Discuss the reasons why Camelot use their own WAN for collecting data from shops rather than linking into the Internet.
3 Describe the hardware that would be needed to enable lottery sales in a new store.

Case Study 3 – Networking in an FE college

Faxton College is based on two sites, a mile and a half apart. All the students on the main site are full-time students aged 16–19; the second site is used for part-time adult courses. All financial, examination-support and personnel functions are carried out at the main site. Each site has had its own LAN for several years and both have been managed by a shared IT team. Software has been installed and maintained on two servers, one for each site. Computers within each site are connected by cable.

A few years ago, the IT manager decided to link the two LANs with a WAN. The link between the two LANs was established using a dedicated telephone line. Central file servers at one site hold the database files and management information software for the whole college. This means that the IT support team have to maintain the software in only one place: when upgrades are issued they need to be applied only once.

Members of staff on either site can now share the software and access common information. Staff who work on both sites can easily access all the files stored on their personal network drive. One further benefit of having installed a WAN is that files can be backed up in a different location.

1 What is the difference between a LAN and a WAN?
2 Why is the ability to back up files on a separate site seen to be an advantage?
3 If you wished to link the two LANs today, in what other ways could you provide the link?

The Internet

The **Internet** (international network) is a very large number of computer networks that are linked together world wide via telecommunications systems. Messages and data are sent from the source computer through a number of other computers until the destination computer is reached.

The **World Wide Web (WWW)** is a vast collection of pages of information in multimedia form held on the Internet. Pages can contain images, videos, animations and sounds. An organisation or individual can set up a website consisting of stored pages that are made available to other users. Much of the material on the Web is freely available to anyone. Websites have a home page which provides links to other pages within the site.

Some web pages are **password protected** and available only to subscribers. Businesses may password protect some of their information pages so that they are available to their employees but not to the general public.

Web pages are written in a language called **HTML** (hypertext mark-up language). Web pages can be created and websites built using web design software such as Microsoft FrontPage or Macromedia DreamWeaver or just written in HTML using a text editor such as Notepad. The user can create, edit or delete pages and set up or edit links between pages to allow easy navigation of the site.

For more on ISPs, see page 114.

► Services available

Once connected to the Internet via an ISP (Internet service provider), the user can:

- ► access pages of information on the World Wide Web, including text, images, sound and video
- ► save these pages and images locally for later reference
- ► leave messages on bulletin boards and join discussion forums
- ► share user videos (on sites such as YouTube)
- ► talk to friends on a social networking website (such as Facebook)
- ► send and receive e-mail, which is stored on the ISP's computer.

The ISP may also provide:

- ► free web space to set up and edit your own web pages
- ► additional e-mail addresses for family members
- ► up-to-date news, weather, TV and radio information
- ► its own search engine for searching the Web
- ► its own Internet shopping facility
- ► bulletin boards for newsgroups (special storage space used for messages relating to a particular interest group – for example, *Star Trek*, old computers, coarse fishing or teaching ICT).

Activity 1

1 Write down the facilities listed above that you have used.
2 Compare you answers with other members of your class.
3 List any further features of the Internet that you have used.

► Development and uses of the Internet

Through the Internet, to which users can connect from even remote parts of the world, millions of computers can be linked together. This means that users can:

- ► communicate with each other quickly – for example, by VoIP and e-mail
- ► share data
- ► use browser software to access web pages
- ► search for information.

All organisations and individuals need to **communicate**, to send information to and receive information from each other. The Internet has transformed the way we communicate. New methods of communication have been developed, each with its own features and advantages. E-mail is widely used by millions of people. Growing in use is **VoIP** (voice-over Internet protocol), which allows a more personal form of contact and supports Internet conferencing.

Case Study 4 – Use of VoIP (voice-over Internet protocol)

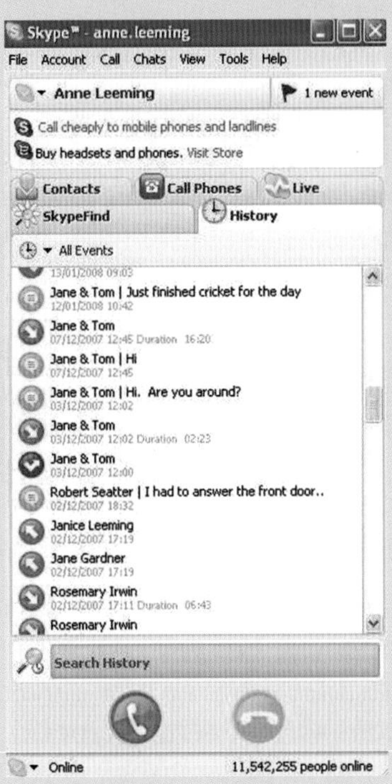

Figure 1 Skype in use

Skype provides a free VoIP service that allows people to talk to other users anywhere in the world. To use the service, you simply need to download the software from the Skype website onto your computer and (if there isn't one built in) plug a microphone into the USB port. If you want the person you are calling to see you during the call, you will need a webcam as well.

Anne has two sons – Tom lives in Australia and Dave in a different town in Britain from Anne. All three of them have Skype installed on their home computer. Anne is able to talk to Tom very regularly and appreciates being able to see him as they chat.

Dave has three young children, Anne's grandchildren. They all enjoy chatting on the phone and showing their grandmother their latest toys and paintings.

1 Describe the benefits of using VoIP.
2 What does a user need to be able to communicate with someone using VoIP?
3 Access the Skype website www.skype.com and list other features that are offered by Skype.

The Internet also allows users to share data. This can be done by sending attachments to e-mails, sharing photo, video or music files with other users or by transferring files. The website http://www.flickr.com/tour/ explains how to use Internet photo sharing and management software.

Thousands of academic papers and articles on a huge range of subjects are stored on the Web and available for access over the Internet, allowing users to share ideas.

Activity 2

A fast-growing use of the Internet is the creation of **wiki** websites. Follow the web links below to find out more about them:

▶ http://computer.howstuffworks.com/wiki.htm
▶ http://pbwiki.com/content/casestudy-financialtimes
▶ http://www.wetpaint.com/

1 What is a wiki?
2 Describe, in your own words, how a wiki could be used by fans of a band.
3 Describe, in your own words, how a wiki could be used in project management.

▶ Accessing the Internet

A **browser program** is needed to view web pages (written in HTML) in a form humans can understand. Some examples are Microsoft Internet Explorer, Netscape Navigator and Mozilla Firefox.

The browser allows users to retrieve information from the Web interactively over the Internet. It provides facilities for a user to store the addresses of commonly visited sites as bookmarks or favourites. It stores pages locally on the computer so that pages load quickly if they are revisited.

A home user may subscribe to an **Internet service provider (ISP)** such as AOL, Tiscali or Wanadoo. The ISP will normally provide an e-mail address, to enable the user to send and receive e-mail, and a limited amount of web space, so that the user can set up their own website. The ISP has a host computer that deals with communications and also stores data such as e-mail messages and web pages for the user.

A user's ISP will provide them with a software package that they will need to install on their computer. This will enable them to log on to the Internet and use facilities such as the Web and e-mail. The software may allow the user to set up filters so that certain types of website are blocked. Many parents do this to prevent their children accessing undesirable sites.

Activity 3 | Comparison websites

A number of websites exist that provide users with the opportunity to compare prices of goods or services from different suppliers. Uswitch.com is one example and states:

> USwitch.com is a free, impartial online and phone based comparison and switching service that helps customers compare prices on a range of services including gas, electricity, home phone, broadband providers and personal finance products. Our aim is to help customers take advantage of the best prices and services on offer from suppliers.

1 Explore Uswitch.com on http://www.www-uswitch.co.uk/
2 Find out how much your family pay for one or more of the services. Using the website, find out if your family could save money by switching to a different provider.
3 Another price comparison site is http://www.kelkoo.co.uk It allows a user to find out the prices of a product such as a DVD from a large number of online suppliers. Explore the range of prices for an item of your choice.

▶ Electronic mail (e-mail)

With e-mail software, it is very easy for any individual or organisation to send and receive electronic mail anywhere in the world for the same cost as accessing the Internet. Senders and recipients simply require an e-mail address, known as a mailbox. Most businesses now advertise their e-mail addresses.

E-mail addresses are usually of the form:
sally.miggins@computerland.co.uk

Addresses are in lower-case letters. Words may be separated by full stops. No spaces are allowed. The 'uk' at the end is the only indication of the geographical location of the address above.

E-mail is almost instantaneous, so provides a very efficient means of communication. It saves time and the cost of postage. If the recipient of an e-mail is not in at their desk, the e-mail is stored until they are ready to read it. An e-mail can be **forwarded** to a third person or a user can send the same message to a group of people just by listing all their e-mail addresses. A user can build up an **address book** of contacts that allows them to quickly select a recipient for a message rather than having to type in the address every time.

Internal e-mail is suitable for memos within a business using an internal network. E-mail does not allow a two-way conversation of the kind possible in a telephone call. Overuse of e-mail can lead to a lack of social interaction. In some organisations it is not unusual for employees sitting at nearby desks to communicate by e-mail rather than by talking. Generally, an e-mail message is written in a more informal manner than a memo or a letter. There can be a tendency to abruptness, which may cause misunderstanding in a way that would not occur in face-to-face conversation. However there are times when sending an e-mail has a substantial advantage – an e-mail that has been sent and replied to will contain an accurate transcript (written copy) of the exchange. This is not the case for a telephone or face-to-face conversation.

E-mails can include **attachments** – computer files that are sent with the e-mail. For example, it is possible to send word-processed documents and images as attachments. The person receiving the e-mail can then store and use these files in the normal way. There is a danger that an attachment from an unreliable source could have a virus that transfers to the recipient's computer when the attachment is opened.

Many people complain that they receive too many e-mails and consequently have to spend a considerable amount of time reading and following them up. Some senders use the carbon-copy facility (cc) to circulate an e-mail to many people who are not directly concerned with the message, thus clogging up the network with mail messages and increasing the amount of unwanted mail. Junk e-mail (spam) can also fill up a user's mailbox. Some employees waste considerable amounts of working time sending and reading personal e-mails.

E-mails for a home user are stored on the ISP's computer whether or not the recipient's own computer is switched on. Users have to check their mailbox to see if they have any mail. If they forget to check, e-mail isn't very quick! E-mail can also be sent within an organisation on a local area network.

Activity 4

E-mail software such as Microsoft Outlook Express enables users to:

▶ click on a reply icon to reply to an e-mail without having to type in the e-mail address of whoever sent it
▶ create a carbon copy of an e-mail to send to a third person
▶ forward an e-mail to another e-mail address without retyping it
▶ set up an address book of e-mail addresses so that an e-mail address does not have to be typed in full every time it is used
▶ set up a group of several e-mail users to whom the same e-mail can be sent
▶ set the priority for an e-mail
▶ store all e-mails sent and received
▶ attach files to be sent with an e-mail.

Using e-mail software, carry out each of the operations listed above.

Case Study 5 – Group e-mail

Charlie Moffat is the secretary of his local Civic Society. The society's executive committee meets four times a year. The committee has ten members.

Whenever there was a meeting, Charlie used to type out an agenda, photocopy it ten times, place each copy in an envelope, write a name and address on each envelope, stick on stamps and post the letters.

Now Charlie sends out the agendas by e-mail and has set up a group consisting of all the committee members in his e-mail address book.

When he writes to all the committee members, he creates a new e-mail. Then he only has to select the group name in his address book and the e-mail will be sent to all ten people.

1 Describe **five** other features of e-mail.
2 Summarise the benefits and limitations to an organisation of using e-mail.

FTP (file transfer protocol)

FTP (file transfer protocol) is a standard set of rules that have been established to allow the exchange of files over the Internet. FTP uses the Internet's protocols to enable data transfer. FTP is most commonly used to download a file from a website. It can also be used to upload a file.

Discussion groups

A **forum** is an online discussion group. Users with common interests can exchange messages that can be read by everyone who is currently accessing the forum. Within a company, a forum can be set up for discussions between employees, who can share views on important issues. It enables many people to be involved, even if they work in different locations or even countries.

On the Internet a forum is often called a **newsgroup**. There are thousands of newsgroups covering every interest you can think of. To view and post messages to a newsgroup, a user needs a **news reader**, a program that runs on their computer and connects to a news server on the Internet. Web browsers such as Microsoft Internet Explorer and Netscape Navigator include a news reader.

A **chat room** is a website where a number of users can communicate on a particular topic in real time – the users take part in a text-based conversation. A number of users can join in the conversation. Many such sites allow the use of file sharing and the displaying of photos. Chat rooms usually have rules that users must follow in order to participate. Most chat rooms do not allow users to use offensive language.

Search engines

A **search engine** is a program that searches for documents on the World Wide Web that have the **keyword** or keywords that the user has specified. The program produces a list of the documents which contain the keyword(s). There are many search engines available and it is important that an appropriate one is chosen for the task. For example, some search engines provide links to academic sites, others to music sites or for images. The web page http://www.internettutorials.net/choose.html provides a useful table of different types of search engine.

Activity 5

Search engines such as Google and Lycos enable users to search the Internet using keywords. A search engine is a program that allows a user to enter a query and will search a very large database to find matching items. Google is the world's most popular search engine.

If you want to attract visitors to your site, it is a good idea to put keywords into the HTML script for a web page so that they are picked up by search engines.

1 Go to a search engine like Google. Type in **diy online**. What do you get? Do you get a link to www.diy.com?

```
<meta name="keywords" content="kodak home page, kodak.com, www.kodak.com,
kodak, eastman kodak, kodac, kodack, kodak united states, digital cameras,
kodak.com, photography">
```

Figure 2 The keywords from the Kodak site

2 Visit a commercial site like http://www.cadbury.co.uk Click on **View > Source**. Scroll down to the line beginning **<meta name="keywords"** to find the keywords for the site. Then go to a search engine and search on **three** of the keywords. Is the site listed?

3 Search engines such as Google allow companies to set up sponsored links related to specified keywords. The links are displayed prominently on the page – see Figure 3. The company is charged at an agreed rate every time a user clicks on their link.
   a Where are the sponsored links to be found?
   b Investigate the use and costs of sponsored links.

Figure 3 Google displaying links

Intranets and extranets

▶ Intranets

An **intranet** is a communication system providing similar services to the Internet, but solely within a company or organisation. It is made up of web pages which can be accessed by standard Internet browser software such as Microsoft Explorer or Mozilla Firefox. The intranet is accessible only to employees of the organisation and must be accessed using an identity code backed up with a password.

An intranet website looks and behaves in the same way as any other website. It can be used across a local area network (LAN), a wide area network (WAN) or across normal Internet lines when it is protected from unauthorised access by a firewall.

An organisation uses its intranet to provide employees with information. For example, letters, documents, schedules for the day, stock information, orders due for delivery and weekly sales figures could be made available. The web pages can be accessed by authorised users over the Internet, so an intranet allows employees based at different locations around the world

WJEC Information & Communication Technology for AS

to share a wide range of private data without the need to establish a private network. Developing an intranet is a much cheaper option.

An intranet can also provide a shared diary system as well as an internal e-mail system.

When the use of an intranet is well established in an organisation, the volume of paper documents that need to be distributed can be greatly reduced. An in-house phone book or health-and-safety manual will no longer need to be printed and distributed to every employee but can be made accessible on the intranet. Not only is money saved but these documents can be kept up to date. Changes can easily be made when they occur – it is not necessary to print out a new version of the document.

As the intranet web pages can be accessed using a standard Internet browser, the intranet can be accessed by users with any type of computer hardware. An intranet is easy to install and easy to use as the user is able to access its pages using familiar browser software.

Software is readily available to build an intranet without requiring a large team of programmers to create bespoke software for the organisation.

An intranet can be of great use to teachers in a school. It could provide access to staff manuals that would be easy to keep up to date. It could provide daily briefing information for teachers without the need for a physical staff meeting. It could provide access to staff rotas and allow teachers to pick up a colleague's work so that they could cover a class in case of absence.

Case Study 6 – The Bullring intranet

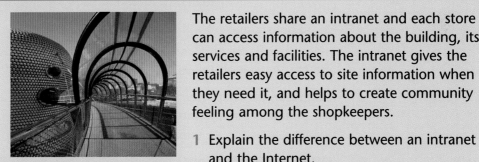

The Bullring shopping centre in Birmingham

The Bullring shopping centre in Birmingham is one of the most popular shopping centres in Europe.

The retailers share an intranet and each store can access information about the building, its services and facilities. The intranet gives the retailers easy access to site information when they need it, and helps to create community feeling among the shopkeepers.

1 Explain the difference between an intranet and the Internet.
2 Explain how an intranet could be used by a school or college, and describe the information that could be stored on it.

Setting up an intranet

There are a number of issues relating to the establishment of an intranet within an organisation. How well these issues are met will determine its success and volume of use:

▶ Care must be taken when devising a new intranet to develop an appropriate house style that will provide a consistent look and feel to all pages.

▶ Considerable thought must be given to the structure of the intranet and how specific information can be accessed.

▶ The task of keeping the information up to date must be assigned to the appropriate person or people. Out-of-date or incomplete information will quickly result in dissatisfaction in the user.

▶ Adequate training must be given both to users and to those who have been allocated the task of updating information.

▶ Extranets

An **extranet** is an intranet that is made partially accessible to people outside an organisation. These people must be authorised. An extranet can be accessed only by someone who has a valid user name and password. The user identity will establish exactly which parts of the intranet can be viewed by that user.

Extranets are widely used and provide an effective and secure way for businesses to exchange information. Typically, a business might share parts of its information with suppliers, customers or other businesses. If a supplier was allowed to access sales information for their products, this up-to-date information could help them plan their production schedules. Customers could have access to details of their past and current orders, or they might be able to track the progress of any outstanding orders.

Two companies could use an extranet to exchange large volumes of data using electronic data interchange (EDI). For example, stock orders could be transferred in this way to suppliers.

Online catalogues of products could be shared with selected customers. For example, a clothing manufacturer may make their catalogue of current items available to the wholesalers with whom they trade.

A school or college could set up an extranet by making part of their intranet available to parents so that they can access selected pages to obtain information relevant to their son or daughter.

It is important that information is kept secure when accessed. When extranet links use the Internet, data can be encrypted. Alternatively, private leased secure lines can be used.

Case Study 7 – WHSmith extranet saves £1 million

WHSmith News uses an extranet to allow key customers such as Tesco, Asda and its own retail arm, WHSmith, to access sales data to improve their efficiency and help spot trends.

Richard Webb, business systems manager at WHSmith News, said that the reports enable the company to react to sales trends and to help customers with their internal reporting to support decisions about production quantities:

'It also shows how we're performing. It's much more of a collaborative approach.'

WHSmith News saved £1 million in costs in its first year by using ICT to streamline its supply-chain processes and reduce waste of the magazines it sends out to retailers.

1 What advantages, other than cost savings, could use of the extranet bring?
2 In what other ways could the extranet be used?
3 What information could be made accessible to employees of WHSmith on a company-wide intranet?

Summary

▶ A **network** consists of two or more computers and peripherals that are linked together.

▶ A **stand**-alone computer is a computer that has no connection to any other computer.

▶ A **local area network (LAN)** is a number of computers that are linked together. Direct physical connection using cables is possible. A LAN may be restricted to one room or one building or cover a small geographical area.

▶ A **wide area network (WAN)** is a number of computers and/or LANs that are linked together and spread over a wide geographical area, possibly covering different countries using a range of telecommunications links.

▶ The **Internet** (international network) is a very large number of computer networks that are linked together world wide via telecommunications systems.

▶ The **World Wide Web (WWW)** is a vast collection of pages of information in multimedia form held on the Internet.

▶ **E-mail** is a commonly used method of sending messages from one computer user to another.

▶ An **intranet** is a network based on Internet protocols that belongs to an organisation.

▶ An **extranet** is an intranet that is partially accessible to people outside an organisation.

Chapter 8 Questions

1 Explain the difference between the Internet and the World Wide Web. (4)

2 A British company has offices in California and New Zealand. Describe **three** ways in which the company can use the Internet to communicate with its offices abroad. (6)

3 A company that makes squash racquets intends to set up a website to advertise its range of products, and to take orders on line.
   a Describe **two** ways in which the company could use the facilities available on the Internet to encourage visitors to use their site. (4)
   b Describe the benefits to the company of taking orders on line. (4)

4 A retail company has decided to set up an intranet for the use of its employees and to enable certain information to be available on an extranet.
   a Explain what is meant by the term *extranet*. (2)

b Discuss the advantages to the company of installing an intranet and the issues that must be considered. (10)

5 Describe advantages and disadvantages of e-mail in the workplace. (6)

6 Three colleges in a large city are to merge and become a single college spread across the three sites. Each college has a LAN and these networks are to be joined together to form a WAN.

    a Explain **two** differences between a LAN and a WAN. (4)

    b Give **two** advantages to the merged college of using the new WAN. (2)

7 A small company that develops games software employs several program developers as well as administrative staff. The company has installed a local area network. The developers sometimes use their computers in stand-alone mode rather than as part of the network.

    a Explain **one** advantage to the developers of using their computers in stand-alone mode. (2)

    b Describe **two** advantages to the company of installing the network. (4)

8 At the central office of a large landscape-gardening company there are ten employees. Each employee has their own stand-alone computer system and printer. The chief executive realises that it would be beneficial to network these computers.

    a State **three** benefits that the company would gain from networking the computers. (3)

    b The company has an extranet for its employees and a website for its customers. Describe, with examples, **three** benefits these facilities bring to the company or its customers. (3) WJEC Jan 06

9 An organisation has decided that its ICT system needs upgrading and a network installed.

    a With reference to appropriate examples, **other than** sharing peripherals and e-mail, describe **three** benefits that networking would give the organisation in dealing with its administration needs. (3)

    b The organisation also realises that it needs an intranet. Define the term *intranet* and describe **one** advantage to the organisation of having an intranet. (2) WJEC June 07

The Human/Computer Interface
4.1.9

Characteristics of users

There is no such person as a 'standard ICT user'. Different users have differing requirements which depend on a number of factors:

- experience of user
- needs of user
- preferences of user
- environment of use
- task to be undertaken
- resources available.

▶ Experience

Some people use a particular ICT system on a regular basis. They will become familiar with the system and will want to be able to carry out tasks as quickly as possible. They are likely to be irritated by operations that slow them down, such as having to make selections from numerous submenus before reaching the function they require, having to wait while introductory screens with music are displayed when the system is loaded or having to carry out the same actions repeatedly without the facility to save entries for later use.

Other people will use an ICT system infrequently. For example, they may order goods from a particular website just once or twice. They will not build up any expertise in using the system and would become frustrated if it was not made very clear how the system should be used.

Those who rarely use any ICT systems generally find it much harder to use a new system than those who have worked extensively with a range of other systems.

Activity 1

1 Identify **three** ICT systems that you use on a regular basis. For each, list features that are appropriate for you as a regular user and those things that irritate you.

2 Identify **three** ICT systems that you have used only a few times. For each, describe how easy the system was to use and identify the features that made it so. Suggest any improvements that could be made to help an inexperienced user.

▶ Needs of user

Users have different needs owing to different physical characteristics. Some users have poor eyesight, others may lack manual dexterity and be unable to use a standard keyboard.

ICT offers many opportunities for people with disabilities, particularly those who have difficulty communicating. There are various computer adaptations available for people who cannot use a mouse or keyboard or who cannot see a normal monitor too well.

Someone who can operate a pointing device like a mouse but not a standard keyboard can use an on-screen keyboard. This provides point-and-click access to standard keyboard letters, whole words and communication phrases.

A person who is unable to operate a keyboard or a mouse may use a computer system with **speech recognition**.

To assist those with poor eyesight, output can be to large screens, spoken using speech synthesis, or in the form of Braille via a special printer.

Software and websites should be designed to make then **accessible** to as many users as possible.

Young children have specific needs that are different from those of a typical adult. Pictures should be used rather than text to make it easy for the child to choose the correct option. When text is used, it should have a large, clear font. Specialist, simplified keyboards are most appropriate for a young child.

Case Study 1 – Microsoft Vista accessibility

The operating system Microsoft Vista offers a range of features that can make the computer accessible to a wider number of users. The software provides a location where a user can adjust accessibility settings such as magnification or use of special keys, as well as manage special accessibility programs that are included.

The user can enlarge a part of the screen image in a separate window using a magnification program called Magnifier.

Another program, Narrator, converts on-screen text into speech using a natural-sounding voice.

An on-screen keyboard can be displayed in one of several layouts. The keyboard can be configured to a suitable font.

A speech-recognition program is also included.

A user can also replace system sounds with visual images such as a flash on the screen.

1 A user with poor eyesight might wish to use the magnification program. What other methods of input and output could be suitable for a partially sighted person?
2 Explain the circumstances when a user might decide to use the speech-recognition software and describe the uses to which this software could be put.
3 Find out more about the accessibility features of Microsoft Vista.
4 Produce a presentation on one or both of the following:
   a ICT systems for users with visual impairment
   b ICT systems for users with physical disabilities.
   Search the Web for information.

▶ Preferences of user

When an interface is chosen for a system, what the user wants is an important factor to be taken into consideration. For example, some users prefer to enter their own text using a keyboard, whilst others might consider using voice-recognition software to perform the same task. A user of Microsoft Windows is able to modify their desktop according to their own requirements. A range of features such as screen saver, size of icons and layout can be individually configured.

▶ Environment of use

While many computer systems are used by people sitting at a desk, this is not true of all ICT systems. Consider a system that allows a train passenger to buy their ticket at a booth. They require a system that is quick to use, is robust and has clear instructions. An ICT system using a touch screen would be appropriate.

When a person is on the move, they may wish to access their e-mails using a mobile phone. As the display screen will be small, the interface will need to be very simple and clear to use.

Users who are working in a noisy area may not be able to hear sounds used as a method of highlighting alarms or events that need attention. Instead of beeps they will need a flashing light.

▶ Task to be undertaken

If an application requires large amounts of text to be entered then the most appropriate form of interface will probably involve a keyboard. However, human/computer communication is not just entering data at the keyboard and reading text on the screen. A voice-recognition system may be more appropriate.

Adventure games have video-quality graphics and CD-quality sound. A keyboard or mouse would not be quick or precise enough as an input device – a joystick is needed.

Some tasks require occasional computer use whilst others require repetitive data entry, such as a travel agent entering holiday bookings.

▶ Resources available

Resources, in terms of input and output devices, memory, backing storage and processor speed, will help to determine the nature of the interface. In some situations, input devices are limited to a keyboard with no pointing device available. Memory and processor-speed limitations will restrict the opportunity to use extensive graphics in displays as these require a fast processor and extensive memory. A microphone is needed to input speech.

If a touch screen or concept keyboard is available in a supermarket, then loose products which are not barcoded can be identified by touching an image that represents them. If no touch screen or concept keyboard is available, the operator may have to look up the item code from a list and type it in.

▶ How users interact with ICT systems

Most ICT systems involve human interaction at some point. For example:

▶ a shopper ordering goods on line needs to select items and fill in a form, probably using a keyboard and a mouse
▶ a passenger may purchase a ticket for a train journeys at a ticket booth using a touch screen to make selections from a set of menus
▶ a garden designer may create or modify an idea for a garden layout using a CAD package on a computer with a large screen and a graphics tablet
▶ a sales assistant in a supermarket may process a customer's purchases using a POS (point-of-sale) till with a flatbed barcode scanner.

The **human/computer interface (HCI)** is the point of interaction between people and computer systems. The HCI should be designed to make it as easy as possible for humans to communicate with the computer. In particular, creating an appropriate HCI requires:

▶ choosing hardware devices (both input and output devices)
▶ designing the 'look and feel' of the software, including screen layout design.

Types of interface

There are a number of types of user interface:

▶ command-line interfaces
▶ graphical user interfaces
▶ voice interfaces
▶ graphical devices

▶ game-playing devices
▶ touch-sensitive screens
▶ biometric devices.

Command-line interfaces

A **command-line interface (CLI)** is an interface where the user types in commands for the computer to interpret and carry out. For example, to run a word-processing program the user may have to type in **WORD**.

As the command is typed in, it appears on the screen. The user has to know the commands and there are no clues to help a user guess them.

The MS-DOS operating system uses a command-line interface. The screen is usually blank and **C:>** (called the C prompt) appears on the left of the screen. This means that the computer is looking at drive C – its internal hard drive. Any file references typed in refer to that drive.

Some operating systems, such as Unix and Linux, use both command-line interfaces and graphical user interfaces.

Figure 1 shows a typical command line in the Unix operating system.

The **1s** command lists the files in the current, or specified, directory. It has many options: **-1** produces a long (detailed) listing.

Many commands are complex. There may be additional parameters, usually extra letters at the end of the command, that modify its meaning.

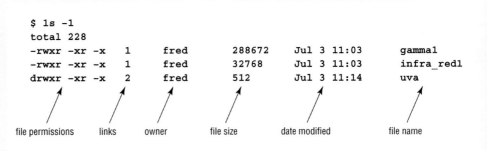

Figure 1 Unix command-line interface

Little computer memory is required for command-line interfaces. Complex commands can be entered quickly in one line. Precise sequences of instructions can be entered, allowing complex tasks to be performed. The first computers, with tiny memory and limited processing power, used a CLI.

The user has to learn all the commands. As a result, CLIs are normally used only by experienced and expert users. A computer programmer or network manager is likely to use a CLI, but for someone with little experience, a CLI can be very frustrating and frequent reference to manuals may be needed.

Case Study 2 – Ping: a command-line interface

When network developers are installing a new network, they use a utility program called **ping** to test whether one computer on the network is connected to another.

Ping sends a small packet of information to a specified computer, which then sends a reply packet in return. From this reply, the ping program can check whether the other computer can be reached and how long it takes to get the reply.

Ping uses a command-line interface as users can do a variety of different tests by typing in different commands.

You can use the MS-DOS prompt on a PC to experiment with ping.

1 Click on **Start, Run**. This may be disabled on your college/school computers but should work on a home computer.
2 Type in **command** (Windows 98) or **cmd** (Windows Vista). The MS-DOS prompt screen opens as in Figure 2.

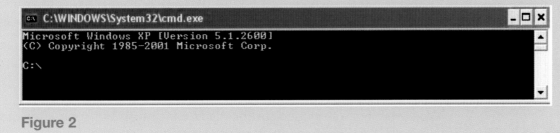

Figure 2

3 a To test a connection to another station on a local area network (LAN), type in **ping** followed by the IP address of the other station, e.g. **ping 192.168.0.2**. Figure 3 shows that a connection has been found.

```
C:\WINDOWS\System32\cmd.exe                              _ □ ×

C:\>ping 192.168.0.2

Pinging 192.168.0.2 with 32 bytes of data:

Reply from 192.168.0.2: bytes=32 time<1ms TTL=128
Reply from 192.168.0.2: bytes=32 time<1ms TTL=128
Reply from 192.168.0.2: bytes=32 time<1ms TTL=128
Reply from 192.168.0.2: bytes=32 time<1ms TTL=128

Ping statistics for 192.168.0.2:
    Packets: Sent = 4, Received = 4, Lost = 0 (0% loss),
Approximate round trip times in milli-seconds:
    Minimum = 0ms, Maximum = 0ms, Average = 0ms

C:\>
```

Figure 3

b If you are not connected to a LAN but are connected to the Internet, try **ping** followed by a known Internet URL, e.g. **ping www.google.co.uk**.

```
C:\WINDOWS\System32\cmd.exe                              _ □ ×

C:\>ping www.google.co.uk

Pinging www.google.akadns.net [66.102.11.99] with 32 bytes of data:

Reply from 66.102.11.99: bytes=32 time=78ms TTL=246
Reply from 66.102.11.99: bytes=32 time=76ms TTL=246
Reply from 66.102.11.99: bytes=32 time=70ms TTL=246
Reply from 66.102.11.99: bytes=32 time=77ms TTL=246

Ping statistics for 66.102.11.99:
    Packets: Sent = 4, Received = 4, Lost = 0 (0% loss),
Approximate round trip times in milli-seconds:
    Minimum = 70ms, Maximum = 78ms, Average = 75ms

C:\>
```

Figure 4

Graphical user interfaces

A **graphical user interface (GUI)** is a form of interface that employs high-resolution graphics, icons and pointers to make the operation of the computer as user friendly as possible. The aim of the interface is to make it intuitive for a user. This is often achieved by building on real-life ideas such as a window or a desktop where different documents or tasks are displayed on the screen in the form of icons in a similar way to work on a real desk. Sound and video are also used in many GUIs. Options can be chosen easily with a pointing device – usually a mouse.

A GUI is sometimes called a WIMP environment as it uses:

► windows ► icons ► menus ► pointers.

GUIs were first developed for the Apple Macintosh but soon afterwards Microsoft Windows was developed as a GUI for the PC.

GUIs tend to need a lot of memory and disk space and take time to load because of the large number of graphical images used. However, today's computers are more than powerful enough to cope with a GUI. The main operating systems used nowadays all offer the user a GUI.

Case Study 3 – Railway ticket machines

Automatic ticket machines are common at many railway and underground stations. These machines use a GUI to allow customers to purchase a ticket quickly and easily without having to queue in a ticket office. Customers use a touch screen to choose their destination from a list and to choose the type of ticket, such as single or return. Payment is by credit/debit card: the ticket machine can automatically read the card details from the magnetic strip on the back.

A touch screen is used because:

▶ it is more durable than other pointing devices such as a mouse

▶ it is easy to operate, even for an inexperienced user.

The instructions for use are printed on the screen and are very simple to follow. The user has few decisions to make. The HCI is thus robust and very easy to use.

1 List **five** other situations when it would be appropriate to use a touch screen, justifying your choice in each case.

2 Design the screen layout for one of the situations you have listed.

▶ Features of GUIs

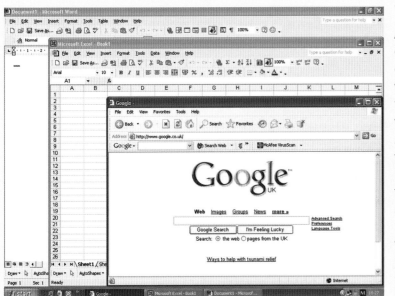

Figure 5 Three windows on one screen (Microsoft Vista).

Windows

A **window** is a rectangular division of the screen that holds the activity of a program. There can be several windows on the screen at the same time. The user can switch between windows and change the size and shape of the windows. The active window – the one in which the user is currently working – appears at the front. In Figure 5, Google is the active window.

A **dialogue box** (spelt **dialog box** in the USA) is a window that appears on the screen when information is wanted from the user. For example, a wizard can be used

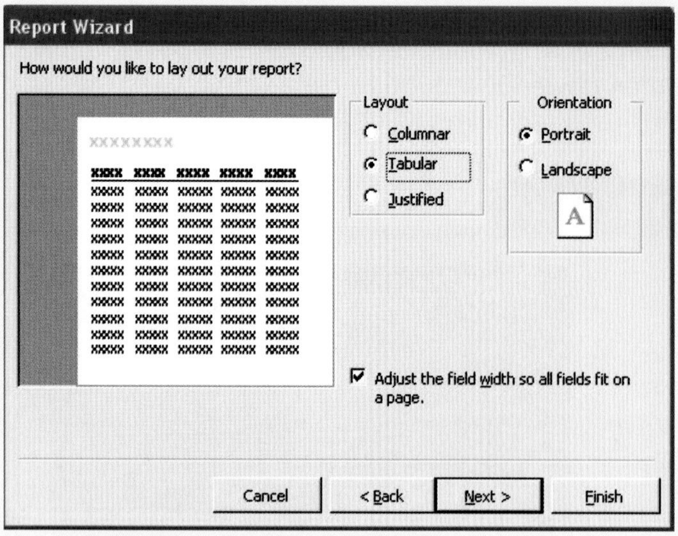

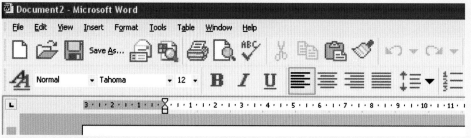

Figure 6 **Dialogue box in the Microsoft Access report wizard**

in Microsoft Access to create a report. Several dialogue boxes appear on the screen, one after the other, asking the user to choose settings so that the report appears as the user wants.

Icons

An **icon** is a small picture on the screen. Clicking on an icon performs an action such as saving a file. The same action can be performed using the menu system but the icon is used as a shortcut. The action performed when you click on an icon should be easily recognisable from the image.

Today icons are used in nearly all software. Different programs often use icons that are very similar, as most software uses icons to open files, save files, etc.

Icons can be grouped together in toolbars on the screen. In many applications packages, icons and toolbars can be customised to suit the user. Icons can be added or removed. The image on an icon can be edited.

Software like Microsoft Word offers the facility to display icons in a large format. This is useful for people with a visual impairment or who find it difficult to click on a small icon.

Figure 7 **Large icons in Microsoft Word**

Menus

A **pull-down menu** is a menu that expands downward when selected with a mouse or other pointer. The user then scrolls through the options and clicks a second time to make a selection. Windows software typically has a menu bar of pull-down menus across the top of the screen.

A **pop-up menu** is a similar menu that expands upward when clicked with the pointing device. In Microsoft Excel and Microsoft Word, the drawing toolbar typically appears at the bottom of the screen. When you click on an item on this toolbar, a pop-up menu appears.

In most Windows software, if you click the right mouse button, a shortcut menu appears. If you right click near the top of the screen, a pull-down menu appears. If you click near the bottom of the screen, a pop-up menu is displayed.

Figure 8 **Pull-down menu**

In many applications packages, menus can be customised to suit the user. Options can be removed, new options added, whole menus removed or new menus added.

Pointers

A mouse is a very common pointing device. It can move a cursor around the screen to select a choice from a menu or to point to any place on the screen. However, there are other pointing devices associated with GUIs. A laptop computer usually has a built-in touch pad. A PDA (personal digital assistant) has a stylus. If a computer is to be used by members of the public, a mouse may not be robust enough. In this case a touch screen is often used. A tracker ball may be used in a similar way.

Voice interfaces

▶ Speech-recognition systems

A speech-recognition system can recognise spoken words. Such a system consists of **artificial-intelligence** software that learns the difference in the pronunciation of words. It does not interpret or understand what is being said. Such interpretation is carried out by natural-language processing (see page 133).

Speech recognition is a complex process. Different people say the same word in different ways as they have different accents and voices. We naturally slur words together as we speak and do not differentiate between words clearly. Some words with different meanings sound the same, but are spelled differently. For example, *there* and *their* or *hair* and *hare*.

There are a number of speech-recognition systems available. The most powerful are able to recognise thousands of words. Most such systems require the user to undergo interactive sessions where the computer system is trained to recognise their particular voice and accent. Although progress has been made in producing systems that can follow normal speech, many systems still need the user to speak slowly, separating each word with a short pause. Background noise can interfere with the interpretation of the speech. If the speaker has a cold it could affect the way they sound their words – the software may not recognise what they are saying.

A high-specification computer, with a fast processor and large main memory (RAM), is required if a speech-recognition system is to run effectively.

The speech-recognition software turns the user's voice into an input device. Just by speaking the user can, as well as enter text, open a program such a spreadsheet and perform complicated commands.

Doctors and other medical professionals are becoming users of speech-recognition systems to dictate their notes directly.

Case Study 4 – Using speech-recognition software to write a book

An author suffering from repetitive strain injury (RSI) was unable to use a keyboard for her work. She purchased Dragon NaturallySpeaking software and was able to write her book by speaking to her computer. This process was painless and she completed her book more quickly than she had previous books.

She stated: 'From now on, I plan to author every future book using Dragon NaturallySpeaking software. It was a very personal and effective way to write a book in record time. I use it heavily to write articles, create press campaigns, draft speech outlines, and otherwise make myself more productive.'

The software provided her with a way to create her book with speed and accuracy without the need to pay someone to transcribe her dictation.

1 Describe other situations when the use of speech-recognition software would be appropriate.
2 Windows Speech Recognition, which is installed with Windows Vista, enables a user to interact using their voice. Explore how to use Windows Speech Recognition by visiting http://www.microsoft.com/enable/products/windowsvista/speech.aspx

▶ Natural-language interfaces

In the real world humans communicate in natural languages such as English. A natural-language computer interface, where humans and computers could communicate in normal English, would be enormously advantageous. A natural-language interface would be appropriate for use by a search engine.

Natural language is extremely flexible and powerful. However, to interpret natural language easily, a computer needs it to be precise, with a limited number of commands and strict syntax rules.

English is not like this. It is not precise and has a huge vocabulary. New words appear and the meanings of other words change over time. Sentences can be ambiguous. It is often only when the context and tone are taken into account that the meaning is clear.

It is not yet possible to develop systems that accept a natural language but systems have been developed using a subset of a natural language by restricting instructions to a limited number of commands. Commands are usually typed in at a keyboard, but if such a system is combined with speech recognition, there is potential for humans and computers to have a limited dialogue.

Pure natural-language interfaces may still be the stuff of science fiction but there are many research projects exploring the possibilities of talking to computers. The SLS (Spoken Language Systems) Group at the MIT (Massachusetts Institute of Technology) Laboratory of Computer Science has been trying to get computers to communicate in the same way as humans since 1989. Progress has been made, as can be seen from the following excerpt from a conversation between a user and JUPITER, an SLS-based weather-forecasting system.

User Yes I would like the weather forecast for London, England, please.

JUPITER In London in England Wednesday partly cloudy skies with periods of sunshine. High 82 and low 63. Is there something else?

User What is that in degrees Celsius, please?

JUPITER In London in England Wednesday partly cloudy skies with periods of sunshine. High 28 and low 17. What else?

You can check out the SLS Group's progress at their website: http://www.sls.lcs.mit.edu/sls/whatwedo

The search engine Ask Jeeves (http://ask.com/) uses a system called Natural Language Processing (NLP) that allows the user to ask questions in natural language. It builds up a bank of questions and uses these to help interpret new ones.

With NLP, Jeeves appears to be able to understand the context of the question and so can offer answers and suggestions in the same human terms in which we all communicate.

In Microsoft Office software, such as Microsoft Word, if you press F1 a help dialogue box appears. You can type in a natural-language question to get help.

One of the problems in creating a natural-language interface is the fact that natural languages like English can be ambiguous. For example, the word 'lead' has several meanings. It can mean the leash for a dog. It can mean the person in front in a race. Pronounced differently, it can mean the writing part of a pencil. The written sentence 'I want the lead' could mean:

▶ I want the leash for my dog.
▶ I want to be in front.
▶ I want the lead to put in my pencil.

The word 'by' is interpreted in different ways in different contexts:

▶ The lost children were found by the searchers [who].
▶ The lost children were found by the mountain [where].
▶ The lost children were found by nightfall [when].

The structure of a sentence can also be ambiguous. If you were to say: 'My car needs oiling badly', would you really want someone to make a bad job of oiling your car? What do you make of the sentence: 'Fruit flies like a banana'?

▶ Speech synthesis

Speech synthesis is the production of human-like speech by a device such as a computer. Many systems can read text files and output them in an understandable voice, but the voice can lack variety and appear flat and dull. In some systems the user can choose the type of voice, perhaps a male or female one.

Synthesised speech can be created by joining pieces of prerecorded

Summary

▶ The **human/computer interface (HCI)** refers to how people communicate with computer systems. The choice of HCI will depend on the application and the needs of the user.

▶ Different users have differing requirements which depend on a number of factors:
  a experience of user
  b needs of user
  c preferences of user
  d environment of use
  e task to be undertaken
  f resources available.

▶ There are a number of types of HCI:
  a command-line interfaces (CLIs)
  b graphical user interfaces (GUIs)
  c voice interfaces:
    i speech-recognition systems
    ii natural-language interfaces
    iii speech synthesis
  d graphical devices
  e game-playing devices
  f touch-sensitive screens
  g biometric devices.

▶ A **command-line interface (CLI)** is a user interface where the user responds to a screen prompt by typing in a command. The system displays a response on screen and the user then enters another command, and so on.

▶ A **graphical user interface (GUI)** is a form of user interface that does not rely on text. It requires high-resolution graphics.

  GUIs usually have the following features:
  a windows
  b icons
  c pull-down/pop-up menus
  d use of pointers.

  A GUI is easy and intuitive to use but demands fast processing speeds and a large computer memory.

▶ It is very difficult to enter instructions into a computer system in a **natural language** like English. This is because computer instructions need to be very precise and English has a large vocabulary which can be ambiguous.

  Benefits of a natural-language interface:
  a uses the natural language of humans, who can express themselves freely without constraint
  b no need for special training
  c extremely flexible.

  Limitations of a natural-language interface:
  a natural language is ambiguous and imprecise
  b natural language is always changing
  c the same word can have different meanings.

Chapter 9 Questions

1 Most modern PCs use a GUI (graphical user interface). Describe **four** characteristics of a GUI. (8)

2 Explain what is meant by the term *command-line interface*. (2)

3 An Internet search engine is said to have a natural-language interface. Discuss the benefits and limitations of using a natural-language interface. (8)

4 WIMP (windows, icons, menus and pointers) interfaces are used in many software packages on personal computers. Name **two other** types of interface and discuss the benefits and limitations of each. (12)

5 Good human/computer interfaces (HCIs) are designed so that they have features suitable for the intended user.

   a Graphical user interfaces (GUIs) are suitable for the non-expert user. Give **two** features of GUIs which make them suitable for the non-expert user. (2)

   b Name a **different** suitable HCI for each of the following:
     i a computer programmer (1)
     ii a person with special needs. (1) WJEC June 06

Social Issues 4.1.10

Health and safety issues associated with ICT

Many computer users have blamed computers for various problems with their health. In some cases the effects can be long term and prevent the user from working in the future. Many of these problems are avoidable. The Health and Safety (Display Screen Equipment) Regulations of 1992 made it a legal requirement for employers to take various measures to protect the health of workers using computers.

▶ Repetitive strain injury (RSI)

It is widely accepted that prolonged work on a computer can cause **repetitive strain injury (RSI)**. Using a keyboard which is positioned so that hands have to be held at an awkward angle can cause this injury, as can sitting for long periods at a poorly organised workstation. Squeezing a mouse over long periods can lead to stiffness. RSI affects the shoulders, fingers and particularly the wrists of those typing all the working day. The symptoms are stiffness, pain and swelling. Permanent injury can be caused, preventing the employee from working.

A young graphic designer took her employers, Shell UK, to court and won. She claimed that she was never shown how to use a computer mouse. She was awarded £25 000 damages for RSI that she began to suffer two years after joining the firm at the age of 20.

The risk of RSI can be reduced by using specially designed, 'ergonomic' keyboards. These should be tiltable and have well sprung keys. It can help to use wrist supports while typing. Desks should have sufficient space on them to allow users to rest their wrists when not typing.

Managers should ensure that work is varied during the day so that no user spends all the working day at the keyboard. Users should take regular breaks from working with a computer. They should maintain a good posture and ensure that they do not press the keys too hard.

Case Study 1 – Industrial injuries

At a recent tribunal a city-council employee won her case and claimed £250 000 in compensation for office injuries.

The employee, an accountant, is suffering from a form of RSI called tenosynovitis, an inflammation of the tendon sheaths of the wrist, caused by, among another things, excessive use of keyboards. Tenosynovitis is commonly found among data inputters and journalists.

Tenosynovitis is the best known form of RSI because it is a glaring medical condition and was the first type to be recognised by the courts. The employee's illness began when her employer computerised the office.

She was issued with a chair that was so high her feet didn't reach the floor. She got into the habit of leaning forward to compensate, which aggravated a latent back complaint. When she started to take time off sick, she was expected to clear the backlog on her return, which meant more time in her chair, and so on. These problems were aggravated by cramped working conditions and the stress of having to report to two different managers. She was refused a new chair.

She won her case on the grounds that she had been discriminated against as a disabled person. Recently, the ceiling on compensation for such claims was removed, opening the way for huge damages.

▶ Produce a report outlining the steps that the accountant's employers could have taken to prevent her from suffering from RSI.

▶ Eye strain

Looking at a screen for a long time can lead to eye strain, particularly if the screen is of a poor quality and flickers or has the wrong contrast setting. Problems also occur if the lighting in the room is at the wrong level, or the screen is poorly sited, causing glare or reflection on the screen. The symptoms are headaches and sore eyes.

The risk of eye strain can be reduced by having suitable lighting, using non-flickering screens and fitting screen filters to prevent glare and reflection. Appropriate blinds (rather than curtains) should be fitted to windows to reduce glare and prevent sunshine reflection. If necessary, appropriate spectacles should be worn when using a computer. The eyeline should be approximately level with the top of the screen and the screen slightly tilted.

Employers are obliged to pay for any employee who works long hours in front of a computer screen to have a free eye test. Users should take regular breaks from working with a computer and should refocus their eyes every ten minutes.

▶ Back problems

Sitting in an uncomfortable position at a computer or bad posture can lead to serious back problems. This is likely to be the case if chairs are an incorrect height. The symptoms are back pain or stiffness, possibly a stiff neck and shoulders and sore ankles.

The risk of back problems can be reduced by having an ergonomically designed, adjustable swivel chair that supports the lower back, and can be adjusted to the right height and tilt. Chairs should also have a five-point base, as this is more stable than just four legs. Screens that tilt and turn can be adjusted to the correct position so that the back is not twisted or bent. Document holders next to the screen can reduce the neck movement that would otherwise occur – frequent neck movement can create back problems.

Users should take regular breaks from working with a computer. The use of a footrest can also help prevent back damage.

▶ ELF (extremely low frequency) radiation

In the USA research has revealed that an unusually high percentage of pregnant computer users have abnormal pregnancies or suffer miscarriages. This may be pure coincidence but it has been suggested that it is caused by electromagnetic radiation from monitors.

Low-emission monitors give off less radiation. Screen filters can also cut down radiation.

▶ Stress

Using computers can be frustrating and repeated frustration can lead to stress. Frustration can occur if:

- ▶ a user has inadequate training in the use of a piece of software
- ▶ the response time is very slow
- ▶ the human/computer interface is inappropriate – perhaps too cluttered
- ▶ there are too many stages or keystrokes required to carry out a simple task
- ▶ hardware failure is a common occurrence – for example, the printer gets jammed or the computer crashes several times a day.

Frustration can be removed by providing users with adequate support and training, choosing well-designed software that has an interface appropriate for the user and installing hardware that is capable of meeting the demands of the tasks.

Activity 1

Find out more about health hazards and ICT at the Health and Safety Executive's website: http://www.hse.gov.uk/

List the services that the site provides for:

1 an employer   2 an employee.

The Trades Union Congress (TUC) health and safety newsletter site http://www.hazards.org/ is worth exploring too.

Activity 2

Produce an induction booklet for new employees that provides them with guidelines on how to use the organisation's computer equipment safely. You should include a description of the organisation's responsibilities to them.

Acceptable use of ICT equipment and services

Every user has responsibilities relating to the appropriate use of ICT equipment, networks and the Internet. Organisations should draw up an ICT code of practice for all employees. A **code of practice** is a behaviour code for ICT users describing their responsibilities, rules for maintaining security and the penalties for misuse.

The responsibilities of the ICT user relate to the use of hardware, software and data. Such responsibilities might include:

▶ using hard-disk space sensibly – deleting old files and e-mails to save space
▶ handling all data according to laid-down procedures
▶ not installing unauthorised software on the company's computers even if it complies with copyright laws
▶ not copying software for personal use
▶ not using the company's computers for personal gain
▶ not sending or receiving personal e-mails
▶ not overusing network resources through actions such as playing games or downloading music from the Internet
▶ not harassing workmates using e-mail
▶ not visiting pornographic websites or Internet chat rooms
▶ always keeping to the requirements of legislation such as the Data Protection Act and the Computer Misuse Act.

The code of practice is likely to cover all aspects of ICT security. These would include:

▶ only using your own user ID and not letting others use it
▶ how often passwords should be changed
▶ what possible passwords are acceptable – for example, only combinations of letters and numbers, not dictionary words or names
▶ not writing down passwords
▶ logging off or locking the workstation if leaving it for even a short while
▶ taking care to keep a laptop safe when away from the organisation's premises
▶ taking every precaution to prevent the introduction of viruses
▶ using appropriate encryption procedures when data is transmitted across public networks.

Activity 3

Read through the story of Tom's day at work then highlight as many examples of unacceptable practices as you can before reading the suggestions given on page 156.

Tom's day at work

Tom arrives in his office and immediately switches on his desktop workstation. He has a network user account and when he logs on he is asked for his password. He types it in – 'TOMRULES' – and waits for the system to load.

First he checks his e-mails. He has 20 waiting for him. Eight of these relate to work, six are from friends and six are SPAM (unsolicited messages – the junk of e-mail). He opens the messages from his friends. One contains photo images of the friend's holiday that take a while to download.

After 20 minutes spent dealing with social e-mails, Tom opens a SPAM message that has the headline 'Earn £5000 without working'. The message has an attached document. When Tom opens it he realises that the message is a hoax and immediately deletes the message.

Now Tom gets down to work. He has to access a database for which he needs another password. He uses the one that was originally assigned to him by the database administrator and, as it is UZ682GH7J, he keeps it on a post-it note stuck on his computer screen.

During the morning Tom feels ready for a break so, without logging off, he walks out to the water cooler in the corridor, where he meets up with some colleagues from a different department. They stay talking for ten minutes, discussing a new computer game that one of his colleagues has recently bought. Tom borrows the game CD-ROM and returns to his desk. He is keen to try the new game so he installs it on the local hard disk of his workstation and plays the game for half an hour. He is not very good at first but quickly improves.

When it is lunchtime, Tom logs off his workstation and goes to a sandwich bar with a friend. A colleague comes in and asks Tom if he could go back to work as he has forgotten to print out a report that is urgently needed. Tom has not finished his lunch so he tells his colleague where to find the file so that she can print it out for herself. 'You'll need to log on as me: my password is TOMRULES,' he says.

In the afternoon, while he is working Tom downloads ten songs from a website so that he can listen to them later on his iPod. He plays his new game again, but he doesn't seem to be getting any better so he surfs the Internet for a while instead, visiting a couple of his favourite 'porno' sites and downloading a couple of images that he stores on the hard drive of his workstation.

Case Study 2 – Misuse of the Internet in the workplace

A few years ago, mobile-phone company Orange sacked 40 members of staff for the 'distribution of inappropriate material'. Employees have also been sacked or disciplined at insurance company Royal and Sun Alliance, and bank Merrill Lynch, following the sending of pornographic images and e-mails.

In a recent survey, Internet and e-mail abuse were found to be the main instances of office work misconduct. Twenty per cent of companies in the survey said that they monitored staff usage of online facilities, although only half of them had informed the staff of the monitoring.

▶ Describe **four** ways in which an employee could use e-mail or the Internet inappropriately in an office environment.

Legislation covering the use of computers

A number of laws have been passed over the last 20 years as the use of ICT has grown. These laws protect computer data and systems in various ways.

▶ Computer Misuse Act 1990

The **Computer Misuse Act 1990** was introduced as a result of concerns about people misusing the data and programs held on computers. It allows unauthorised access to be prosecuted and aims to discourage the misuse or modification of data or programs.

The Act aims to protect computer users against malicious vandalism and information theft. Hacking and knowingly spreading viruses were made crimes under the Act.

The Act has three sections:

1 unauthorised access to computer material
2 unauthorised access with intent to commit or facilitate commission of further offences
3 unauthorised modification of computer material.

The penalties for the three categories are increasingly severe.

Section 1 – Unauthorised access to computer material
In this category, a person commits an offence if they try to access any program or data held in any computer without permission and know at the time that this is the case.

The maximum penalty is six months in prison and a £5000 fine.

This category applies to people who are 'just messing around', 'exploring the system', 'getting into the system just for the sake of it' and have no intention of doing anything to the programs or data once they have gained access. It covers guessing passwords to gain access to a system and have a look at the data that is stored.

An authorised user of a system may still be in breach of this category of the Act if they access files in the system that have a higher level of access than the level to which they have been allocated rights. A student who gains access to a fellow student's area, or breaks into the college administrative system, is breaking this category of the Act. It is an offence even if no files are deleted or changed.

Section 2 – Unauthorised access with intent to commit or facilitate commission of further offences

This category covers offenders who carry out unauthorised access with a more serious criminal intent. The access may be made with an intention to carry out fraud.

For example, breaking into a personnel or medical system with the intention of finding out details about a person that could be used for blackmail falls into this category. Another example of an offence would be breaking into a company's system with the intention of finding out secret financial information that could be used when carrying out stock-market transactions. The information obtained in this way could be used by a rival company. A further example of an offence in this category would be guessing or stealing a password, using it to access another person's online bank account and transferring their money to another account.

Persistent offences under Section 1 are also included in this second category.

Prosecution under this category can lead to a maximum of five years in prison.

Section 3 – Unauthorised modification of computer material

This third category concerns the alteration of data or programs within a computer system rather than simply viewing or using the data or program. This could involve deleting files or changing the desktop set-up. However, the deleting or changing has to be done deliberately and not just by mistake. If the program code was deliberately changed, this could stop a program from running or make it act in an unexpected manner. Alternatively, data could be changed: the balance of a bank account altered, details of driving offences deleted or an examination mark altered.

This category includes using a computer to damage other computers linked through a network even though the computer used to do the damage is not modified in any way. It also includes the deliberate distribution of computer viruses.

Prosecution under this category can lead to up to five years in prison.

Case Study 3 – Computer Misuse Act cases

A temporary employee at British Telecom gained access to a computer database containing the telephone numbers and addresses of top-secret government installations. The employee, who had worked at BT for two months, found passwords written down and left lying around offices and used them to call up information on a screen. The employee was guilty under Section 1 of the Act as he accessed the data but made no use of it, nor did he tamper with it in any way.

Christopher Pile, who called himself the Black Baron, was the first person convicted under the Computer Misuse Act. Pile created two viruses named Pathogen and Queeg after characters in the BBC sci-fi comedy *Red Dwarf*. The viruses wiped data from a computer's hard drive and left a Red Dwarf joke on the screen which read: 'Smoke me a kipper, I'll be back for breakfast ... unfortunately some of your data won't'. The Black Baron was guilty under Section 3 of the Act as data was altered on a computer's hard disk.

Two 18-year-olds arrested in Wales were alleged to be computer hackers involved in a million-dollar global Internet fraud that involved hacking into businesses around the world and stealing credit-card details. A home PC was supposedly used for the crime. Apparently the youths had accessed the credit-card databases of nine e-commerce companies, and had published the details of thousands of credit-card accounts on the Internet. They were prosecuted under Section 2 of the Act as they used the data they obtained to facilitate fraud.

For each of the cases described below, explain which category (or categories) of offence under the Computer Misuse Act has been committed.

1 A student at a college plays around with the desktop settings of a computer in the IT centre.
2 An employee, having used a computer to order some books over the Internet, leaves their credit-card details, written on a piece of paper, next to the computer. Someone else finds the paper and uses the details to order some books for him/herself, changing the delivery address.
3 In January 2003, Simon Vallor was jailed for two years having been convicted of writing and distributing three computer viruses. He apparently infected 27 000 PCs in 42 countries.
4 An 18-year-old man hacked into a major newspaper's database and made changes which cost the newspaper £25 000.
5 In 2004, John Thornley pleaded guilty to four offences contrary to the Computer Misuse Act. He had mounted a hack attack on a rival site, introducing a Trojan-type virus to bring it down on several occasions.

Activity 4

Research prosecutions under the Computer Misuse Act. The website http://www.computerevidence.co.uk/Cases/CMA.htm provides some useful cases.

Summarise your findings under the headings below:

Description of crime	Which section of Act	Details of sentence

▶ Data Protection Act 1998

What is personal data?

Personal data covers both facts and opinions about a living person. Facts include date of birth, marital status or current bank balance. Results in examinations, details of driving offences, records of medications prescribed and financial credit rating are further examples of facts that could relate to an individual. Personal opinions such as political or religious views are also deemed to be personal data.

Lists of names and addresses are **not** classed as personal data. Organisations are able to sell lists of names and addresses without permission and without breaking any law.

The increase in personal data stored on computer has worried many people. Their main concerns are:

▶ **Who will be able to access this data?** There is a fear that personal data could be accessed by unauthorised people who could use it to defraud an individual. Will information about me be available remotely over a network and therefore vulnerable to being accessed and result in identity theft, for example? Could my medical records be examined by a potential employer?

▶ **Is the data accurate?** If data is stored, processed and transmitted by computer, who will check that it is accurate? People often think something must be true if 'it says so on the computer'. Inaccurate personal data could have an adverse effect for an individual. For example, if inaccurate data is stored regarding payment of bills, an individual might be refused a credit card or a loan.

▶ **Will the data be sold on to another company?** For example, could my health records be sold to a company where I have applied for a job? Could my school records be sold on to someone else? Could my personal details, collected by my employer, be used by a commercial company for targeting junk mail?

▶ **How long will the data be kept?** It is very easy to store vast amounts of data. Will data about me be stored even if it is not needed? For example, if I apply for a job but don't get it, will data from my application form be deleted?

'Think before you give away personal information, you never know where it will end up!' (Advertising campaign slogan)

It was these concerns about the use of personal data that led to the Data Protection Act 1984. The 1984 Act is a law that sets out regulations for storing personal data that is processed automatically. The Data Protection Act 1998 strengthened the 1984 Act and enshrined the European Union directive on data protection into UK law. This means that UK law is in line with the data protection laws in all the other countries in the European Union.

What the Act says

The Data Protection Act 1998 sets rules for the electronic processing of personal information. The Act also applies to paper records from 23 October 2007.

The Act refers to:

▶ **data subjects** – people whose personal data is being processed
▶ **data controllers** – people or organisations who process personal data.

The Act works in two ways:

▶ data subjects have certain rights
▶ data controllers must follow good information handling practices.

What data controllers must do

Data controllers must follow eight data protection principles.

Data controllers must register the fact that they are storing personal data with a government official called the Information Commissioner. The following information must be registered:

▶ the data controller's name and address
▶ a description of the data being processed
▶ the purpose for which the data will be used
▶ from whom the data was obtained
▶ to whom the data will be disclosed and countries where the data may be transferred.

The eight data protection principles

The data protection principles say that data must be:

1 fairly and lawfully processed
2 processed for registered purposes
3 adequate, relevant and not excessive
4 accurate and up to date
5 not kept for longer than is necessary
6 processed in line with the data subject's rights
7 secure
8 not transferred to countries without adequate protection.

Principle 1 means that you cannot collect data for one purpose and then use it for another purpose (even if the purpose is registered) without the permission of the data subject.

Principle 2 means that if a company intends to sell data on to another company it must register this with the Information Commissioner. (It will need the permission of the data subjects to do this.)

Principle 3 means that any irrelevant data should be deleted. For example, data about unsuccessful job applicants should not be kept.

Principle 4 means that the organisation must take steps to ensure that its data is accurate. Once a year, for example, a school may provide each student (the data subject) with a printout of their personal details for checking purposes.

Principle 6 means that data subjects have the right to inspect the data held on them, for payment of a small fee. They have the right to require that inaccurate data is corrected. They have the right to compensation for any distress caused if the Act has been broken.

Principle 7 means that appropriate technological security measures must be taken to prevent unauthorised access. Information must be kept safe from hackers and employees who don't have the right to see it. Your data can only be passed on to someone else with your permission. Backup copies should be taken so that data is also safeguarded against accidental loss.

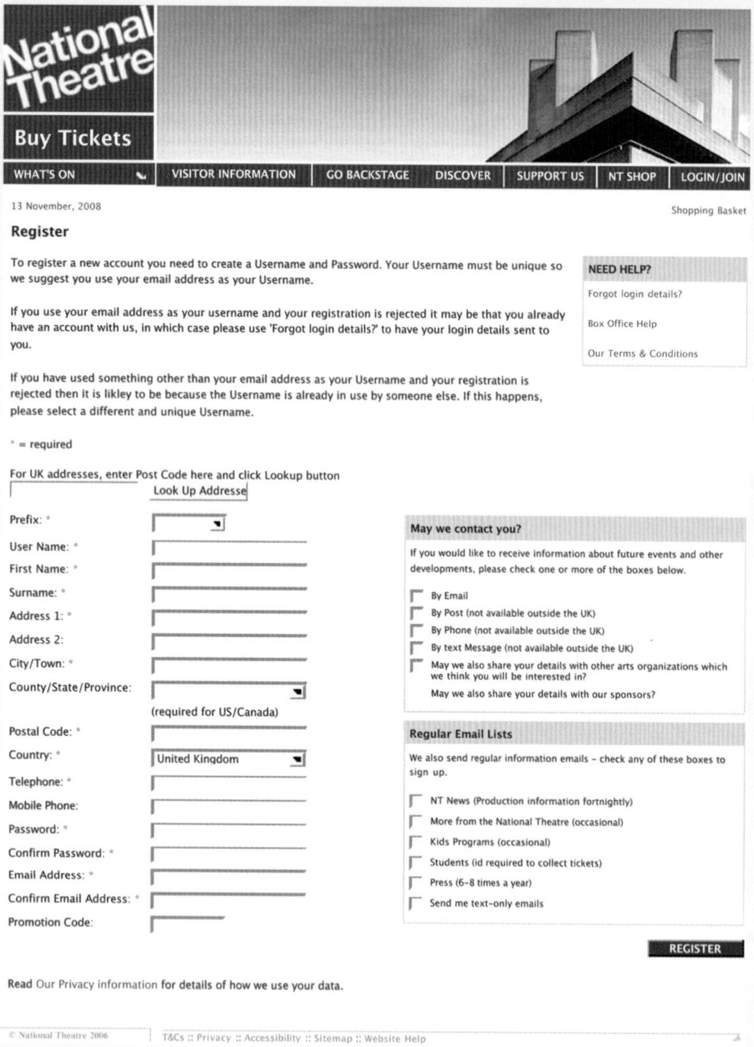
National Theatre

Buy Tickets

WHAT'S ON | VISITOR INFORMATION | GO BACKSTAGE | DISCOVER | SUPPORT US | NT SHOP | LOGIN/JOIN

13 November, 2008

Shopping Basket

Register

To register a new account you need to create a Username and Password. Your Username must be unique so we suggest you use your email address as your Username.

If you use your email address as your username and your registration is rejected it may be that you already have an account with us, in which case please use 'Forgot login details?' to have your login details sent to you.

If you have used something other than your email address as your Username and your registration is rejected then it is likley to be because the Username is already in use by someone else. If this happens, please select a different and unique Username.

NEED HELP?
Forgot login details?
Box Office Help
Our Terms & Conditions

* = required

For UK addresses, enter Post Code here and click Lookup button

Look Up Addresses

Prefix: *
User Name: *
First Name: *
Surname: *
Address 1: *
Address 2:
City/Town: *
County/State/Province: (required for US/Canada)
Postal Code: *
Country: * United Kingdom
Telephone: *
Mobile Phone:
Password: *
Confirm Password: *
Email Address: *
Confirm Email Address: *
Promotion Code:

May we contact you?

If you would like to receive information about future events and other developments, please check one or more of the boxes below.

- By Email
- By Post (not available outside the UK)
- By Phone (not available outside the UK)
- By text Message (not available outside the UK)
- May we also share your details with other arts organizations which we think you will be interested in?

May we also share your details with our sponsors?

Regular Email Lists

We also send regular information emails – check any of these boxes to sign up.

- NT News (Production information fortnightly)
- More from the National Theatre (occasional)
- Kids Programs (occasional)
- Students (id required to collect tickets)
- Press (6–8 times a year)
- Send me text-only emails

REGISTER

Read Our Privacy information for details of how we use your data.

© National Theatre 2006 | T&Cs :: Privacy :: Accessibility :: Sitemap :: Website Help

Figure 1 Online registration form for the National Theatre

If you fill in the form in Figure 1 to register with the National Theatre website, your details can be passed on if you tick the last box in the 'May we contact you?' panel.

Principle 8 means that personal data cannot be transferred to countries outside the European Union unless the country provides an adequate level of protection.

Here's one way to remember the eight principles:

P registered **purposes** (2)
E not transferred outside the **EU** (8)
R **relevant** (3)
S **secure** (7)
O you can inspect your **own** records (6)
N **not kept** for longer than is necessary (5)
A **accurate** (4)
L **lawfully** processed (1).

Exemptions from the Data Protection Act 1988

The following exemptions exist from complying with the principles of the Act:

- if the information is used to safeguard national security
- if the information is used for the prevention and detection of crime
- if the information is used for the collection of taxes
- if personal data relates to someone's own family or household affairs, it does not need to be registered.

What is the role of the Information Commissioner?

The **Information Commissioner** has the responsibility of ensuring that the data protection legislation is enforced.

The Commissioner keeps a public register of data controllers. Each register entry must include the name and address of the data controller as well as a description of the processing of personal data carried out under the control of the data controller. An individual can consult the register to find out what processing of personal data is being carried out by a particular data controller.

The Data Protection Act 1998 requires every data controller who is processing personal data to notify the Commissioner unless one of the exemptions listed in the Act applies. A complete copy of the public register is kept at the Information Commissioner's Office and is updated weekly.

Other duties of the Commissioner include giving advice on data protection issues, promoting good information handling and encouraging data controllers to develop suitable codes of practice. He also acts as an ombudsman.

> The Information Commissioner was previously called the Data Protection Registrar under the 1984 Act.

Case Study 4 – The DPA in the news

Marks and Spencer admit breaking DPA for 15 years

In 1999, Marks and Spencer had to change its procedures after learning it had been breaking the Data Protection Act for almost 15 years.

The company had been disclosing charge-card account details to supplementary cardholders – people who were authorised to charge goods to another person's account.

Lloyds TSB accused of breaking the DPA

In 2004 a customer alleged that Lloyds TSB had broken the Data Protection Act by transferring work to India. The bank was accused of sending its customers' personal financial data outside the European Union without their written consent.

Organ-group president fined

In 1996 Trevor Daniels, the president of the Association of Organ Enthusiasts, was fined £50 for keeping the membership list on his home computer without being registered.

Solicitor fined for failing to register

A solicitor, Ralph Donner, was prosecuted by the Information Commissioner's Office in 2005 for failing to register under the Data Protection Act 1998. He was fined £3150 and ordered to pay £3500 towards prosecution costs. Mr Donner had been contacted more than five times by the Information Commissioner over a period of two years without registering.

Complaint against mobile-phone company

In 2007 a complaint was made to the Information Commissioner about the way in which a mobile-phone operator processed personal information. Apparently new members of staff were allowed to share user names and passwords when accessing the company IT system.

Utility companies break DPA

In 1997 the Information Commissioner reprimanded two utility companies for breaking the Data Protection Act. The companies stored names and addresses for sending bills to customers. They then used these details to send out direct-mail advertisements to their customers.

1 Which data protection principle was Lloyds TSB accused of breaking?
2 Which data protection principle did Marks and Spencer break?
3 What did Mr Daniels do wrong?
4 What should Mr Donner have done?
5 Which data protection principle did the mobile-phone company break?
6 Which data protection principle did the utility companies break?
7 Use the Internet to search for details of other breaches of the Data Protection Act. Use sites such as http://www.guardian.co.uk/ or http://www.independent.co.uk

▶ Copyright, Designs and Patents Act 1988

Copyright laws have long protected the intellectual rights of authors, composers, artists and others, so that books, music and works of art cannot be copied without their permission and/or payment of a fee. Copyright applies to all work, whatever format it is produced in – material made available on the World Wide Web is covered by copyright. It is an offence to download music or video files without the permission of the copyright holder.

Copyright laws now also apply to computer software. The Copyright, Designs and Patents Act 1988 has made copying software illegal and aims to protect software producers by deterring copying, ensuring that they do not lose money.

The Act makes it illegal to do any of the following without permission:

▶ copy (or pirate) software
▶ sell or distribute copies of software
▶ adapt software
▶ transmit software.

A person who 'buys' software does not buy the program, only the right to use it under the terms of the **licence**. It is illegal to copy or use software without having obtained the appropriate licence. Criminal penalties include unlimited fines, two years' imprisonment or both.

A software copying and licensing agreement is a legal contract between the software producer and the user that sets out how the piece of software may be used.

It is very important for organisations to ensure that, in the workplace, all their employees are working within the law. If an employee is found using unlicensed software on the organisation's computer then the organisation can be held responsible and prosecuted. As a result the organisation could be fined. This would apply both if the software was related to work, perhaps an unlicensed copy of a desktop publishing package, or if it was for recreational purposes, such as a game.

Software piracy

Piracy is the name given to the unauthorised copying of software. It applies whether the copying is carried out on a large scale, where copies are sold for financial gain, or by an individual user for personal use. A user is allowed to make copies of software for backup only.

Software piracy is a very large problem. Many people do not seem to realise that whenever they take a copy of software from a friend to use on their own computer they are breaking the law.

Computer crime and malpractice

▶ What is computer crime?

Computer **crime** is any illegal act that has been committed using a computer as the principal tool. As the role of computers in society has increased, opportunities for crime have been created that never existed before.

Computer crime can take the form of:

▶ the theft of money – for example, transferring payments to the wrong account
▶ the theft of information – for example, from files or databases
▶ the theft of goods – for example, diverting them to the wrong destination.

Committing a crime breaks the law as passed by Parliament. Crimes are punished through the courts. Punishments are likely to take the form of a fine or, in severe cases, prison.

Examples of computer crime include gaining unauthorised access to an ICT system, illegally copying a piece of software from a computer in the workplace and taking it home, or applying for a loan via the Internet using a false identity.

▶ What is malpractice?

Malpractice is defined as negligent or improper professional behaviour. It is an act of breaking professional rules set by an employer or professional body that results, intentionally or unintentionally, in harm to their organisation or clients. An employee who carelessly leaves their workstation logged on, or divulges their password to others, could be enabling unauthorised access to data. This could be considered to be malpractice.

Excessive personal use of a computer at work by an employee could be considered to be malpractice. With so many workers having a computer with Internet access on their desks, there is a growing concern about Internet misuse at work. This could be through:

▶ wasting time surfing the net
▶ e-shopping
▶ sending and receiving personal e-mails
▶ accessing inappropriate sites such as those displaying pornographic images
▶ visiting chat rooms.

See Activity 3, page 142 for some examples.

Punishment for malpractice is likely to be a warning, downgrading, dismissal or expulsion from the professional body depending on the severity of the malpractice.

Case Study 5 – 28 arrested in global web fraud sting

In 2004, police officers working for the UK's National Hi-Tech Crime Unit (NHTCU) joined forces with investigators from the US Secret Service to crack an international criminal gang allegedly dealing in identity theft, computer fraud, credit-card fraud and conspiracy.

Twenty-eight suspects from seven countries, including a 19-year-old British man from Camberley, Surrey, were arrested. They were alleged to be members of a global Internet-based organised criminal network who used three websites to commit various offences, such as fraud involving counterfeit credit cards and false identification information,

driver's licences, passports and birth certificates. The gang used the websites to provide information helpful for would-be fraudsters as well as selling the 'tools of the trade'.

'We believe that the suspects have trafficked at least 1.7 million stolen credit-card numbers, leading to losses by financial institutions running into the millions,' said one of the police officers heading the investigation.

1 What is meant by identity theft?
2 Research other cases of Internet-based crime.

Case Study 6 – Bank fraud

A woman who opened a bank account using false information, saying that she expected to receive her divorce settlement shortly, carried out a more elaborate fraud. She later returned to the bank and surreptitiously removed all the paying-in slips (used by customers to pay money into their accounts) and replaced them with paying-in slips that she had had specially printed.

These fake paying-in slips were exactly the same as the genuine ones except that they had her account number printed at the bottom in MICR characters – just like the paying-in slips at the back of a personal chequebook.

When reading paying-in slips, the computer

looks for the MICR numbers. If there are none, the operator has to type in the bank account number given. If there are MICR numbers, the information is automatically read and not checked.

Money paid in with the fake paying-in slips was paid directly into the woman's account. Customers did not notice any errors until they checked their bank statements. By this time the woman had withdrawn over $150 000 in cash from her 'divorce settlement', disappeared and was never seen again.

1 Was the woman's act an internal or external threat?
2 Was the act a crime or malpractice?

▶ Viruses, worms and Trojan horses

A **virus** is a program that is written with the sole purpose of infecting computer systems. Most viruses cause damage to files that are stored on the computer's hard disk. A virus on the hard disk of an infected computer can reproduce itself onto a floppy disk. When the floppy disk is used on a second computer, the virus copies itself onto this computer's hard disk.

This spreading of the virus is hidden and automatic, and the user is usually unaware of its presence until something goes wrong. Thousands of viruses exist, with their damage varying from the trivial to the disastrous. Some viruses have little effect. Others delete all your data. Many viruses are distributed by e-mail. You may get an e-mail that says something like:

> Hi! I am looking for new friends.
> My name is Jane, I am from Miami, FL.
> See my homepage with my weblog and latest webcam photos!
> See you!

If you open an attached file or click on a hyperlink, you will probably contract the virus. This sort of virus is very prevalent, as Case Study 7 reveals.

Activity 5

1 Find out about the latest virus threats at
   http://us.mcafee.com/virusInfo/default.asp
2 Copy and complete the following table:

Name of virus	What it does

Case Study 7 – Christmas-card virus hits one in ten e-mails

In December 2004, a virus masquerading as a Christmas greeting infected computers world wide.

Only a few days after the Zafi-D worm (W32/Zafi-D) was discovered, it was already the culprit in about 75 per cent of all virus reports, according to IT security experts. It may have infected as many as one in ten e-mails.

Zafi-D spread inside e-mails giving what appeared to be a jokey Christmas greeting. It is thought to have originated from Hungary but the e-mails used several different languages, including English, French, Spanish and Hungarian.

▶ Give **three** pieces of advice about how to avoid such viruses.

A **worm** is a type of stand-alone executable program that exploits the facilities of the host computer to copy itself. It then carries out an action such as using up all the computer's memory and processing capability, forcing the system to close down.

Yet another destructive program type is the **Trojan horse**. This passes itself off as an innocent program. One example of a Trojan horse claims to remove a virus from your computer but, if downloaded, will actually introduce a virus.

Summary

▶ Regular use of ICT equipment over a long period of time may lead to **health problems**, particularly:

a RSI (Repetitive Strain Injury), often stiffness and swelling in the wrists

b eye strain

c stress

d back problems

e ELF radiation.

These problems can be reduced by taking sensible precautions: not using equipment for too long; introducing adjustable chairs and screens; using wrist supports and screen filters.

▶ A **code of practice** is a behaviour code for ICT users describing their responsibilities, rules for maintaining security and the penalties for misuse.

▶ The **Computer Misuse Act 1990** makes the following illegal:

a accessing computer material without permission – for example, hacking

b unauthorised access to a computer to commit another crime

c editing computer data without permission – for example, spreading a virus.

▶ The **Data Protection Act 1998** concerns the storage of personal data. **Data controllers** must:

a register with the Information Commissioner

b follow the eight data protection principles.

The principles say that personal data must be kept secure, be accurate, up to date and be used only for the registered purpose.

Data subjects have various rights under the Act, including the right to inspect data about themselves, have any errors corrected and claim compensation for any distress.

▶ The **Copyright, Designs and Patents Act 1988** makes copying software illegal. It aims to protect software producers, by deterring copying, ensuring that they do not lose money.

The Act makes it illegal to do any of the following without permission:

a copy (or pirate) software

b sell or distribute copies of software

c adapt software

d transmit software.

It requires all users of software to have a valid **licence**.

Computer owners must be aware of the terms of the licence agreement which comes with software.

▶ Computer **crime** is any crime that has been committed using a computer as the principal tool.

▶ **Malpractice** is behaviour that is legal but goes against a professional code of practice.

Chapter 10 Questions

1 Explain, using an example for each, what is covered by:

a the Data Protection Act 1998 (3)

b the Computer Misuse Act (3)

c copyright and licensing agreements. (3)

2 In 1990 an Act was introduced to allow the prosecution of people who accessed computer systems without authorisation.

a Name the Act. (1)

b State, and give an example of, each of the **three** sections of the Act. (6)

c Few companies ever prosecute people under this Act. Explain why this is so. (2)

3 If software is not designed properly, it can cause stress in a user. For example, if a data entry screen is cluttered with multicoloured and unnecessary images the user can become confused and disoriented.

Describe **three other** features in the design of a software package that could cause stress in a user. (6)

4 An ICT professional within a company has been asked to produce health and safety guidelines for employees working with ICT. The guidelines will be stored on the company's intranet so that all employees can access them at all times.

State **four** guidelines that you would include and explain the reason for each. (8)

5 Mr Hadawi is setting up a new office for his car hire business. He needs to equip the office with a computer that will be used all day by an employee. Mr Hadawi wishes to ensure the health and safety of his employee.

Describe **two** features that Mr Hadawi should consider when buying and installing **each** of the following:

a the screen

b the chair

c the keyboard

d the desk and surroundings. (8)

6 The Data Protection Act 1998 is designed to regulate the processing of personal data.

a State what is meant by *personal data*. (1)

b State with whom a company should register if they store personal data. (1)

c Explain the rights of a data subject who thinks that the data stored is incorrect. (2)

7 Using a suitable, relevant example describe one health issue raised by the increased use of ICT systems in the home. (2)

8 Downtown College uses an ICT system to store details on staff and students and to manage its finances.

a Discuss in detail the legal requirements of storing personal data on this ICT system. (4)

b Discuss the responsibilities of the staff and students in relation to maintaining the security of the ICT system. (3) WJEC June 07

9 A school has installed a new local area network (LAN) to help with its school administration.

a Describe how the school staff could use the LAN to help with administration. (4)

b Discuss **two** health and safety issues which the school should consider when designing the LAN. (2)

c Explain how the school can prevent:

   i accidental loss of data (3)

   ii deliberate destruction of data. (3)

d Discuss the measures, **other than** keeping data secure, that the school must take to comply with the Data Protection Act 1998. (4) WJEC Jan 07

10 Banks must protect their online banking systems from both deliberate crimes and accidental destruction of data.

a Describe, using examples relating to online banking, **two** different crimes identified by the Computer Misuse Act. (4)

b Describe suitable strategies a bank could use to prevent accidental loss of or damage to data. (3) WJEC June 06

11 In response to modern businesses' concerns about the use of computers for criminal purposes, the government has introduced legislation such as the Computer Misuse Act 1990, the Data Protection Act 1998 and the Copyright, Designs and Patents Act 1988.

With reference to suitable examples, suggest how this legislation has tried to address these concerns. (5) WJEC June 05

Activity 3 | Answers

Unacceptable practice	Reason
Using password that is easy to guess	A simple password presents a security risk
Reading personal e-mail	Using work time, for which he is being paid, for personal matters
Downloading photos	Putting unnecessary load on network resources
Opening SPAM e-mail from unknown source	Likely to be in breach of security policy: potential of a virus
Using database password originally assigned to him by administrator	Not changing the password regularly could present a security risk
Sticking password on screen	Passwords should be kept secret
Failing to log off	Leaves computer vulnerable to use by others who may gain unauthorised access to data
Installing game on hard drive	Likely to be in breach of security policy. Unauthorised software installed without licence
Playing computer game	Wasting work time
Telling colleague his password	Passwords should be kept secret
Downloading music	Putting unnecessary load on network resources. Likely to be in breach of copyright
Downloading and storing pornographic images	Inappropriate behaviour

Chapter 11

Database Systems 4.1.11

A **database** is a collection of data items and links between them, structured in a way that allows it to be accessed by a number of different applications programs.

Flat files

Traditionally computer systems stored data in files like this one:

Forename	Surname	Exam	Teacher	Result
Dai	Thomas	French	Miss Knight	E
Dai	Thomas	Art	Mr Hill	C
Gareth	Davies	Physics	Ms Edwards	A
Gareth	Davies	French	Miss Knight	B
Fay	Hunt	French	Miss Knight	B
Fay	Hunt	Art	Mr Hall	C
Fay	Hunt	English	Ms Cornwell	B
Fay	Hunt	History	Mr Galloway	D
Jamie	Smith	Art	Mr Hill	E

This **flat file** stores examination results in a school. It consists of a number of records.

Each record in the file stores the details of a separate exam result and contains five fields: forename, surname, exam, teacher and result. In a real system there would be many more fields such as other forenames, date of birth, class group and unique candidate number.

A flat-file system like this would work but it is not efficient for the following reasons:

▶ Data is **duplicated**. We can see that Fay Hunt has been entered for four exams. Each time a new exam result is received, her full name is included. Typing in repeated data wastes time. It can also waste space on the disk as the file is bigger than necessary. If the file is larger, it will take longer to load and save.

▶ Data can be **inconsistent**. Three students have results for the Art exam. In one the Art teacher is Mr Hall. In the other two it is Mr Hill. We don't know if this is the same teacher. If so, how do we know which name is correct? If the same data is entered several times, mistakes like this are more likely to occur.

Each field has a **data type**. The record structure and the data type for each field are decided when the database is designed.

There are a number of data types to choose from. They include:

▶ **Integer** – a whole number. In the example, NumberInStock would be of type integer.
▶ **Currency** – a number representing money in pounds and pence (in the UK). In the example, Price would be of type currency.
▶ **String** – made up of characters that can be letters, digits or special characters such as **&** or ***** or **?** in any combination. Description, Colour and ProductId would be of type string.
▶ **Date** – holds a current date. DateOfLastDelivery would be of type date.
▶ **Boolean** – this data type allows just two values which represent two alternatives such as 'true' or 'false', 'yes' or 'no'. EndOfLine would be of type Boolean.

The record structure could be shown like this:

	Field name	Data type
1	ProductId	String
2	Description	String
3	Colour	String
4	NumberInStock	Integer
5	Price	Currency
6	DateOfLastDelivery	Date
7	EndOfLine	Boolean

Chapter 1, page 4 explains more about coding data.

Fields can be **coded** to reduce storage space and speed up data entry. In the example, Colour is coded as **RE** for red, **BR** for brown and **BL** for black.

Chapter 3, pages 21–22 discusses validation checks in detail.

A database allows **validation checks** to be assigned to fields. For example, there may be a range check on NumberInStock which will check that the number entered is between 0 and 20, say.

Each record will have a field that uniquely identifies it. This field is known as a **key field**. In the example, ProductId is the key field as no two products have the same ProductId.

Summary

▶ The term **flat file** refers to a single file that is like a two-dimensional table.
▶ The use of flat-file systems can produce **data duplication** where the same data item is stored in two or more different files.
▶ Unnecessary data duplication is known as **data redundancy**.
▶ Redundancy often leads to **data inconsistency** where the same item of data is stored differently in different places.

▶ Advantages of a **database** over a set of flat files include:
  a no data redundancy
  b no data inconsistency
  c a centralised pool of data that can be used for many applications
  d data being independent of the applications
  e the possibility of different users being allocated different access rights to different parts of the database.

▶ Disadvantages of a relational database over a set of flat files include:
  a the system is more complex to set up
  b greater security and confidentiality issues arise if the data is used for a range of applications
  c users need to be trained to use the system.

▶ A database is made up of **records**. The record structure specifies the **fields** that will be in each record.

▶ Every field has a **data type**. Data types include:
  a integer
  b currency
  c string
  d date
  e Boolean.

▶ Fields can contain **coded** data and can be assigned **validation** checks.

Chapter 11 Questions

1 Give **four** advantages of using a database rather than a flat-file information storage and retrieval system. **(4)**

2 A sports club stores data about its members on a database. Part of this database is shown below.

Membership number	Gender	Date of birth	Disabled	Name
678	M	12/05/90	✓	S Johnston
986	F	13/12/82		R Begum
243	M	16/09/78		P Davies
734	F	01/04/80	✓	L Phillips
175	M	10/07/79		D Kowolski
764	F	16/11/75		A Jones

a Give **one** field that has coded data and explain **one** advantage of coding data. **(2)**

b The field **Disabled** is a Boolean data type. Describe what you understand by the term *Boolean data type* and describe **one** disadvantage of using this data type for this field. **(2)**

c Data validation techniques were used in creating this database. Explain what is meant by *data validation* and describe in detail **one** example of a type of data validation which could have been used **with this database**. **(3)**

3 a A school uses a database to store students' details. Some of the fields and data types used in this database are shown in the table below.

   i Give the most suitable data types for the **Surname** and **FreeSchoolMeals_Y/N** fields. (1)

   ii Give **two other** fields which would be suitable for this database. (1)

	Field name	Data type
1	StudentNumber	integer
2	FirstName	string
3	Surname	
4	Address1	string
5	Address2	string
6	Postcode	string
7	TelNo	string
8	DateofBirth	date
9	FreeSchoolMeals_Y/N	

b The school's database might contain some errors.

   i Describe how **two different** types of error could occur. (2)

   ii Describe how **each** of the errors you have identified above could be prevented or found. (2) WJEC Jan 2005

4 A health centre is considering replacing its single (flat) filing system, used for storing details of staff, patients and treatments, with a relational database system.

   a State **two** advantages and **one** disadvantage of relational databases over single filing systems. (3)

   b Give **one** example of a Boolean field that could appear in the health centre's database. (1)

   c Verification and validation are methods used to reduce errors in databases.

      i Define the term *verification* and state **one** method that could be used with the health centre's database. (2)

      ii A date field is used in this database. Name a validation method suitable for a date field and describe how it can prevent errors. (2) WJEC June 2005

Unit 1B

Spreadsheets and Business Modelling

> The examples and activities in this unit will help you to produce your own spreadsheets. They do not in themselves provide a complete solution for this work.

In this unit we shall look at examples of how spreadsheets are used in business for performing automatic financial calculations and making predictions. There is also a section on simulation modelling.

Spreadsheets are useful because they offer automatic recalculation if some of the data, such as rate of pay, changes. Calculations are quick and accurate.

Spreadsheets can be used to draw graphs in order to present information in an easy-to-read format. They can perform 'what ifs' so that you can see the effects of changing data such as prices. This is used to help a business make decisions about its actions.

Among the documents we shall look at are:

- order forms
- cash-flow forecasts
- break-even charts
- invoices
- balance sheets.

The spreadsheets will be presented in Microsoft Excel but they would also work in OpenOffice.org Calc or other spreadsheet software.

The spreadsheets developed in this unit are examples of how spreadsheet software can be used for business modelling. They are designed to prepare students for carrying out an assessment task.

This assessment task should involve using the techniques shown in this unit. Students must develop their own spreadsheets and should not simply duplicate spreadsheets from this book.

Order forms

Large organisations such as banks, businesses, councils and hospitals often buy a lot of the same items: for example, A4 paper and printer cartridges.

These organisations negotiate contracts with a supplier, which means that the items can be bought at a considerable discount because they are bought in bulk.

Whenever staff buy these items on behalf of the organisation, they must use this supplier. Staff are provided with a price list, such as the example shown (in part) in Figure 1 on the following page.

Figure 1

	A	B	C	D
1	Product ID	Item	Price	Supplier
2	110414	Compatible black HP DeskJet 540 ink cartridge	£9.99	Cartridges 4U
3	110415	Compatible colour HP DeskJet 540 ink cartridge	£12.99	Cartridges 4U
4	118671	HP Colour LaserJet 4600 toner cartridge	£64.99	Cartridges 4U
5	119186	Epson AcuLaser 2600N toner cartridge yellow	£116.99	Cartridges 4U
6	119187	Epson AcuLaser 2600N toner cartridge magenta	£116.99	Cartridges 4U
7	119188	Epson AcuLaser 2600N toner cartridge cyan	£116.99	Cartridges 4U
8	119189	Epson AcuLaser 2600N toner cartridge black	£56.99	Cartridges 4U
9	119200	Epson AcuLaser C1100 toner cartridge yellow	£90.99	Cartridges 4U
10	119201	Epson AcuLaser C1100 toner cartridge magenta	£90.99	Cartridges 4U
11	119202	Epson AcuLaser C1100 toner cartridge cyan	£90.99	Cartridges 4U
12	119203	Epson AcuLaser C1100 toner cartridge black	£51.99	Cartridges 4U

Purchases are made with a standard order form. The **order form** will contain:

▶ the name and address of the organisation
▶ the date
▶ the details of the items to be purchased
▶ the price of these items
▶ the quantity required
▶ the total cost
▶ the name and address of the supplier.

An order form involves one or more columns of figures, looking up data in the price list, carrying out various calculations and the need for accuracy is high. Order forms are thus a very suitable application for spreadsheets.

Staff can also use a spreadsheet for price modelling:

▶ What would it cost if I ordered three yellow cartridges?
▶ What would it cost if I bought one of each cartridge for the AcuLaser?

In the example in Figure 2, the order form has been set up on sheet 2.

Figure 2

	A	B	C	D	E
1			**Lakin and Twigg**		
2			Market Street, Llangollen, LL99 8YU		
3			(01798) 202020		
4			www.lakinandtwigg.co.uk		
5					
6	31/03/2008				
7					
8	Product ID	Quantity	Item	Price	Total price
9	119187	4	Epson AcuLaser 2600N toner cartridge magenta	£116.99	£ 467.96
10	119201	2	Epson AcuLaser C1100 toner cartridge magenta	£90.99	£ 181.98
11	110414	12	Compatible black HP DeskJet 540 ink cartridge	£9.99	£ 119.88
12					
13					
14					
15					
16					
17					
18					
19					£ 769.82

WJEC Information & Communication Technology for AS

The table of prices is on sheet 1. The VLOOKUP function is used so that when the product ID of an item is entered the name of the item and its price are automatically inserted.

The total cost of the order is calculated in cell E19.

Giving a name such as **Product_ID** to cells A2 to A12 in sheet 1 means that the product ID can be chosen from a drop-down list (see Figure 3).

This means that the data can be validated. Normally the product ID will be selected using the mouse, but if the product ID is typed in and does not appear in the table on sheet 1, it will be rejected (see Figure 4).

Figure 5 shows the formulas.

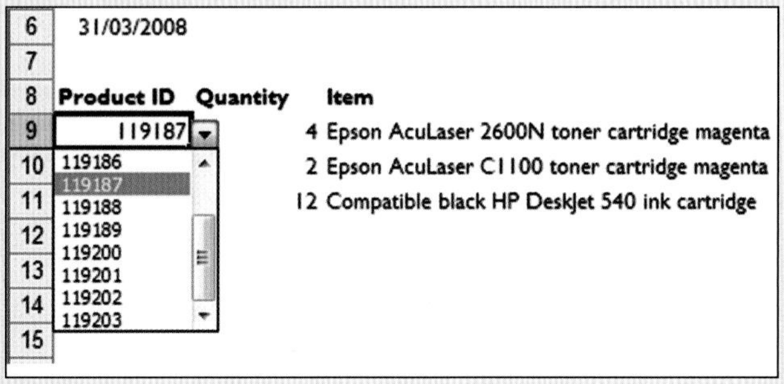

Figure 3

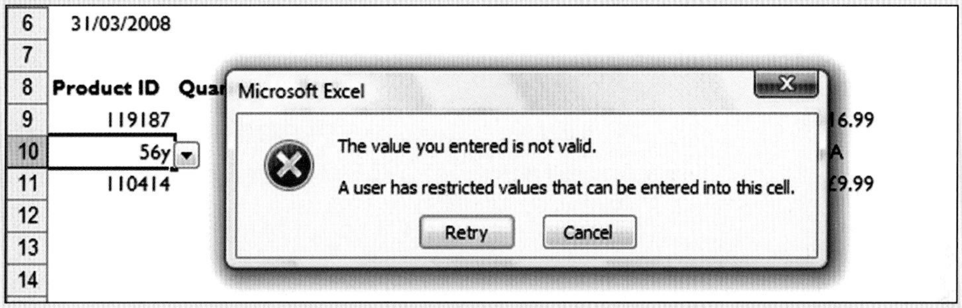

6	31/03/2008		
7			
8	**Product ID**	**Quantity**	**Item**
9	119187 ▾		4 Epson AcuLaser 2600N toner cartridge magenta
10	119186		2 Epson AcuLaser C1100 toner cartridge magenta
11	119187 / 119188		12 Compatible black HP DeskJet 540 ink cartridge
12	119189		
13	119200 / 119201		
14	119202 / 119203		
15			

Figure 4

Microsoft Excel

The value you entered is not valid.

A user has restricted values that can be entered into this cell.

Retry   Cancel

	A	B	C	D	E
1			**Lakin and Twigg**		
2			Market Street, Llangollen, LL99 8YU		
3			(01798) 202020		
4			www.lakinandtwigg.co.uk		
5					
6	=TODAY()				
7					
8	**Product ID**	**Quantity**	**Item**	**Price**	**Total price**
9	119187	4	=VLOOKUP(A9,pricelist,2)	=VLOOKUP(A9,pricelist,3)	=B9*D9
10	119201	2	=VLOOKUP(A10,pricelist,2)	=VLOOKUP(A10,pricelist,3)	=B10*D10
11	110414	12	=VLOOKUP(A11,pricelist,2)	=VLOOKUP(A11,pricelist,3)	=B11*D11
12					
13					
14					
15					
16					
17					
18					
19					=SUM(E9:E11)

Sheet1 \ **Sheet2** / Sheet3 /

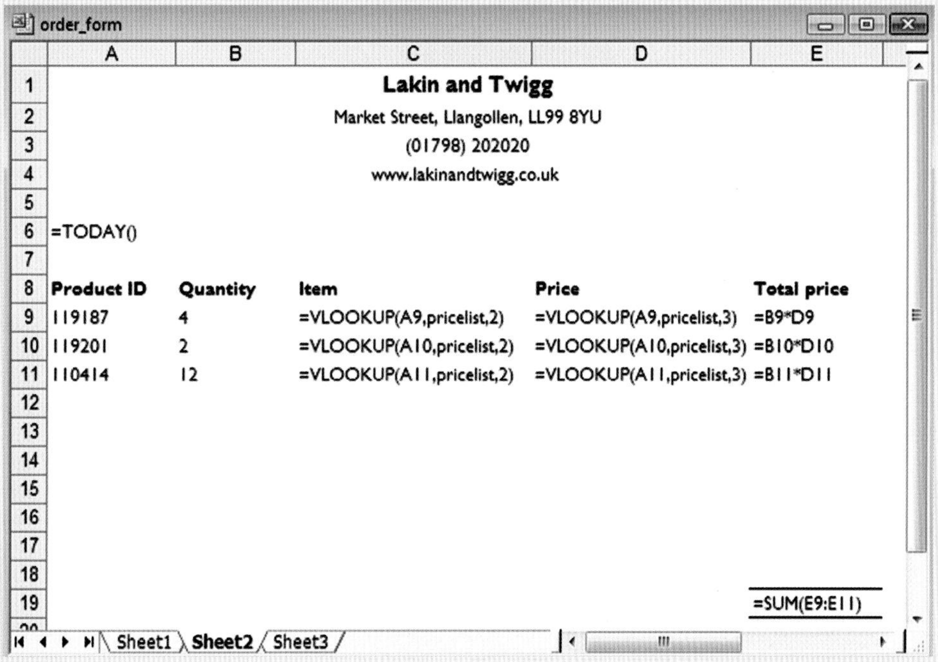

Figure 5

▶ Problems with this spreadsheet

At present this spreadsheet can only deal with orders involving three items. If I want more items, I will need to copy the formulas into cells C12, D12 and E12. However, if the formulas are entered and no product ID chosen, I will get an error message **#N/A** (as in Figure 6).

Figure 6

How can I set up the formulas so that if the cell in column A is blank, I don't get the dreaded **#N/A**?

This is called **error trapping**.

In cell C9, instead of **=VLOOKUP(A9,pricelist,2)** I should enter:
=IF(A9="","",VLOOKUP(A9,pricelist,2))

This sets the cell C9 to be blank if cell A9 is blank.

Of course then I would have to change the formulas in cells D9 and E9 and copy them down to all the rows, as in Figure 7.

Figure 7

Activity 1

Evans and Davies Ltd have a contract with a local supplier for stationery. Amongst the items that can be purchased are the following:

Product ID	Item	Price
21	50 pencils	£1.99
22	25 ballpoint pens (black)	£2.99
23	25 ballpoint pens (blue)	£2.99
24	25 ballpoint pens (red)	£2.99
25	Sellotape (large)	£0.60
26	Sellotape (small)	£0.45
27	One ream (500 sheets) A4 copier paper (white)	£3.49
28	One ream (500 sheets) A4 copier paper (yellow)	£6.99
29	One ream (500 sheets) A4 copier paper (blue)	£6.99
30	One ream (500 sheets) A4 copier paper (pink)	£6.99

Use spreadsheet software to produce an order form for Evans and Davies Ltd. You should include:

▶ a table of prices
▶ use of VLOOKUP to look up prices
▶ use of formulas to calculate total costs
▶ validation to prevent entry of wrong data
▶ error trapping.

Cash-flow forecasts

It is important for businesses to plan their finances. They need to predict income and expenditure to make sure that the business has enough money to trade.

A **cash-flow forecast** looks at a company's predicted income and outgoings over a set time, usually every month over the next year.

As cash-flow forecasts have traditionally involved presenting figures in rows and columns and doing calculations with these figures, cash-flow forecasts are a very good example of using spreadsheet software for business modelling. Figure 8 on the following page shows an example of a cash-flow forecast for a new garage and service station owned by Graham Doggett.

	A	B	C	D	E	F	G	H	I	J	K	L	M	N
1	Cash flow forecast template													
2		Jan	Feb	Mar	Apr	May	Jun	Jul	Aug	Sep	Oct	Nov	Dec	Total
3	Cash flow into the business													
4	Investment capital	£300,000												£300,000
5	Sales - petrol	£24,000	£24,000	£24,000	£24,000	£24,000	£24,000	£24,000	£24,000	£24,000	£24,000	£24,000	£24,000	£288,000
6	Sales - car servicing	£5,000	£5,000	£5,000	£5,000	£8,000	£10,000	£10,000	£10,000	£8,000	£5,000	£5,000	£5,000	£81,000
7	Sales - food	£2,000	£2,000	£2,000	£2,000	£2,000	£2,000	£2,000	£2,000	£2,000	£2,000	£2,000	£2,000	£24,000
8	Sales other	£1,000	£1,000	£1,000	£1,000	£1,000	£1,500	£1,500	£1,500	£1,000	£1,000	£1,000	£1,000	£13,500
9	TOTAL CASH FLOW IN	£332,000	£32,000	£32,000	£32,000	£35,000	£37,500	£37,500	£37,500	£35,000	£32,000	£32,000	£32,000	£706,500
10														
11	Cash flow out of the business													
12	Capital expenditure													
13	Break-down vehicle lease	£2,000	£2,000	£2,000	£2,000	£2,000	£2,000	£2,000	£2,000	£2,000	£2,000	£2,000	£2,000	£24,000
14	Equipment lease	£3,500	£3,500	£3,500	£3,500	£3,500	£3,500	£3,500	£3,500	£3,500	£3,500	£3,500	£3,500	£42,000
15	Capital expenditure Total	£5,500	£5,500	£5,500	£5,500	£5,500	£5,500	£5,500	£5,500	£5,500	£5,500	£5,500	£5,500	£66,000
16														
17	Operating expenditure													
18	Wages and salaries	£9,000	£9,000	£9,000	£9,000	£9,000	£9,000	£9,000	£9,000	£9,000	£9,000	£9,000	£9,000	£108,000
19	National insurance/pensions (18%)	£1,620	£1,620	£1,620	£1,620	£1,620	£1,620	£1,620	£1,620	£1,620	£1,620	£1,620	£1,620	£19,440
20	Rent	£4,000	£4,000	£4,000	£4,000	£4,000	£4,000	£4,000	£4,000	£4,000	£4,000	£4,000	£4,000	£48,000
21	Rates	£325	£325	£325	£325	£325	£325	£325	£325	£325	£325	£325	£325	£3,900
22	Insurance	£314	£314	£314	£314	£314	£314	£314	£314	£314	£314	£314	£314	£3,768
23	Utilities and phone	£225	£225	£225	£225	£225	£225	£225	£225	£225	£225	£225	£225	£2,700
24	Accounting, payroll & audit charges	£50	£50	£50	£50	£50	£50	£50	£50	£50	£50	£50	£50	£600
25	Stationery, postage, office expenses	£100	£100	£100	£100	£100	£100	£100	£100	£100	£100	£100	£100	£1,200
26	Stock purchase	£22,870	£22,870	£22,870	£22,870	£23,870	£23,870	£23,870	£23,870	£22,870	£22,870	£22,870	£22,870	£278,440
27	Operating expenditure Total	£38,504	£38,504	£38,504	£38,504	£39,504	£39,504	£39,504	£39,504	£38,504	£38,504	£38,504	£38,504	£466,048
28														
29	Total expenses	£44,004	£44,004	£44,004	£44,004	£45,004	£45,004	£45,004	£45,004	£44,004	£44,004	£44,004	£44,004	£532,048
30														
31	Monthly Net Cash Flow	£287,996	-£12,004	-£12,004	-£12,004	-£10,004	-£7,504	-£7,504	-£7,504	-£9,004	-£12,004	-£12,004	-£12,004	
32	Monthly Bank Balance	£287,996	£275,992	£263,988	£251,984	£241,980	£234,476	£226,972	£219,468	£210,464	£198,460	£186,456	£174,452	
33														

Cash flow forecast

Figure 8

Formulas are used in:

- column N to add the figures for each month to give a yearly total
- row 9 to calculate total cash flow in
- row 15 to calculate total capital expenditure
- row 27 to calculate total operating expenditure
- row 29 to calculate total outgoings
- row 31 to calculate monthly cash flow
- row 32 to calculate monthly bank balance
- row 19 to calculate 18% of wages and salaries.

The formulas for these calculations can be protected using **Tools > Protect > Protect Sheet** so that it is possible to change the figures but not the formulas or the column/row headings.

According to this cash-flow forecast, the monthly cash flow is negative – the garage is making a loss. Graham can try to turn this loss into a profit by:

- increasing income
- reducing expenditure.

Activity 2

1 Load the spreadsheet. (To get the file for it, use the download link above.)
2 Adjust the spreadsheet by reducing some of the costs: for example, by cutting salaries to £8000 per month.
3 Increase the income figures but remember that if sales go up, so does the cost of purchasing stock.
4 Can you make the spreadsheet predict a profit?

WJEC Information & Communication Technology for AS

Activity 3

Karen Morris owns riding stables.

Income: She has invested £75000 of her own money and charges £350 a month per horse for stabling. She has enough room for 18 horses but expects only 12 to start with. She also has 4 horses of her own and expects to get about £2000 a month from giving riding lessons.

Expenditure: Karen has leased a Land Rover and horsebox for £1300 a month. Petrol will be around £150 a month. She will employ two part-time grooms for £450 each per month. This means that there will be no pension or National Insurance costs. Rent for the stables is £1400 per month. Rates are £328 per month and insurance is £90 per month.

She estimates accountancy costs will be £50 per month. Other costs include:

► utilities – £105 a month
► office expenses – £115 a month
► advertising in the local newspaper – £300 per month
► miscellaneous – £30 per month.

It costs roughly £100 per month per horse for feed, hay, shoes, vet's fees, etc.

1 Produce and fill in a cash-flow forecast for the stables for the next year. Use Figure 9 below to help you.
2 Does Karen make a profit with 12 horses?
3 How many horses does she need to make a profit?
4 What is her profit if the stables are full?
5 Can you record a macro to clear out all the data at the year end ready for the next year?

	A	B	C	D	E	F	G	H	I	J	K	L	M	N
	Cash flow forecast stables													
1	Cash flow forecast template													
2		Jan	Feb	Mar	Apr	May	Jun	Jul	Aug	Sep	Oct	Nov	Dec	Total
3	Cash flow into the business													
4	Investment capital													£0
5	Stabling													£0
6	Riding lessons													£0
7	TOTAL CASH FLOW IN	£0	£0	£0	£0	£0	£0	£0	£0	£0	£0	£0	£0	£0
8														
9	Cash flow out of the business													
10	Capital expenditure													
11	Car and horse box lease													£0
12	Capital expenditure Total	£0	£0	£0	£0	£0	£0	£0	£0	£0	£0	£0	£0	£0
13														
14	Operating expenditure													
15	Wages													£0
16	Rent													£0
17	Rates													£0
18	Insurance													£0
19	Utilities and phone													£0
20	Accountancy													£0
21	Office expenses													£0
22	Advertising													£0
23	Feed, hay, etc													£0
24	Miscellaneous purchases													£0
25	Operating expenditure Total	£0	£0	£0	£0	£0	£0	£0	£0	£0	£0	£0	£0	£0
26														
27	Total expenses	£0	£0	£0	£0	£0	£0	£0	£0	£0	£0	£0	£0	£0
28														
29	Monthly Net Cash Flow	£0	£0	£0	£0	£0	£0	£0	£0	£0	£0	£0	£0	
30	Monthly Bank Balance	£0	£0	£0	£0	£0	£0	£0	£0	£0	£0	£0	£0	
31														
32														
33														

Cash flow forecast

Figure 9

Break-even charts

A **break-even chart** is a graph that plots total costs and total revenue to find the break-even point. (Revenue means income – money coming in.) The **break-even point** is the point at which costs and revenue are equal. At this point, the organisation has made neither a profit nor a loss.

How to produce a break-even chart

Suppose a business is making baseball caps. The caps cost £1 to make and the business makes 5000 caps. They sell the caps to shops for £2.50 each.

We are going to draw a break-even chart to find the break-even point. First we need to create a spreadsheet:

1. Load Excel.
2. Type the labels **Cost price** into cell A1, **Selling price** into cell A2 and **Number made** into cell A3 and format them to bold.
3. Click on cell B1. Click on **Insert** > **Name** > **Define** and call this cell **costprice**.
4. Type the number **1** into this cell and format it to currency. It will appear as **£1.00**.
5. Click on cell B2. Click on **Insert** > **Name** > **Define** and call this cell **sellingprice**.
6. Type the number **2.5** into this cell and format it to currency. It will appear as **£2.50**.
7. Click on cell B3. Click on **Insert** > **Name** > **Define** and call this cell **numbermade**.
8. Type the number **5000** into this cell.
9. In cell A5 type the label **Sales** and format it to bold.
10. In cell B5 type the label **Costs** and format it to bold.
11. In cell C5 type the label **Revenue** and format it to bold.
12. Type **0** in cell A6 and **250** in cell A7.
13. Highlight cells A6 and A7 and use the fill handle to copy down to cell A26. (This column should now go from 0 to 5000.)
14. In cell B6 type **=numbermade*costprice**
15. Highlight cells B6 to B26 and click on **Edit > Fill >Down**.
16. In cell C6 type **=A6*sellingprice**
17. Highlight cells C6 to C26 and click on **Edit > Fill >Down**.

The spreadsheet should look like Figure 10.

break even

	A	B	C	D
1	Cost price	£ 1.00		
2	Selling price	£ 2.50		
3	Number made	5000		
4				
5	Sales	Costs	Revenue	
6	0	£ 5,000.00	£ -	
7	250	£ 5,000.00	£ 625.00	
8	500	£ 5,000.00	£ 1,250.00	
9	750	£ 5,000.00	£ 1,875.00	
10	1000	£ 5,000.00	£ 2,500.00	
11	1250	£ 5,000.00	£ 3,125.00	
12	1500	£ 5,000.00	£ 3,750.00	
13	1750	£ 5,000.00	£ 4,375.00	
14	2000	£ 5,000.00	£ 5,000.00	
15	2250	£ 5,000.00	£ 5,625.00	
16	2500	£ 5,000.00	£ 6,250.00	
17	2750	£ 5,000.00	£ 6,875.00	
18	3000	£ 5,000.00	£ 7,500.00	
19	3250	£ 5,000.00	£ 8,125.00	
20	3500	£ 5,000.00	£ 8,750.00	
21	3750	£ 5,000.00	£ 9,375.00	
22	4000	£ 5,000.00	£ 10,000.00	
23	4250	£ 5,000.00	£ 10,625.00	
24	4500	£ 5,000.00	£ 11,250.00	
25	4750	£ 5,000.00	£ 11,875.00	
26	5000	£ 5,000.00	£ 12,500.00	

Sheet1 / Sheet2 / Sheet3

Figure 10

We are now going to create the break-even chart:

18 Highlight cells A5 to C26.
19 Click on the **Chart Wizard** icon.
20 Choose **Line Graph**. Click on **Next**.

At the moment the graph is wrong. We need the sales to be the horizontal (x) axis.

21 Click on the **Series** tab.
22 Select **Sales** in the **Series** list and choose **Remove**.
23 In the Category (x) axis labels enter **=Sheet1!A6:A26** as in Figure 11.
24 Click on **Next**.
25 Add the title **Break-even chart**.
26 Make the x-axis label **Sales**.

The break-even chart should look like Figure 12.

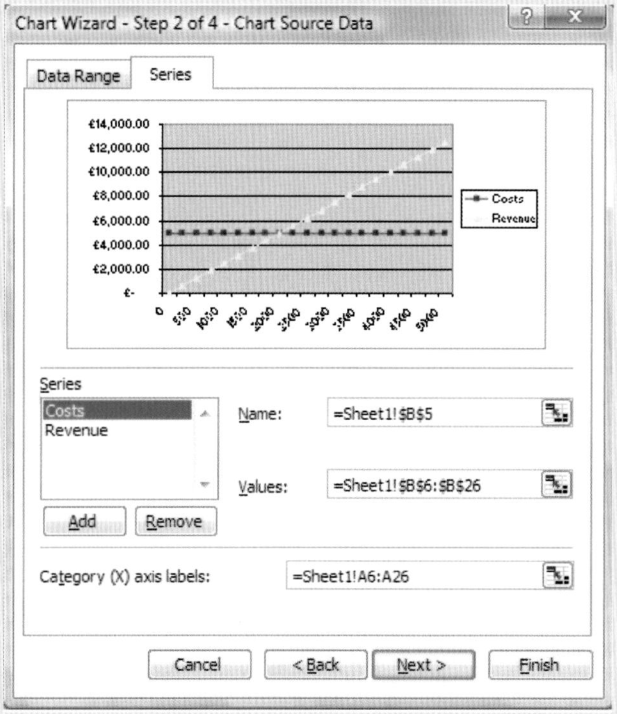

Figure 11

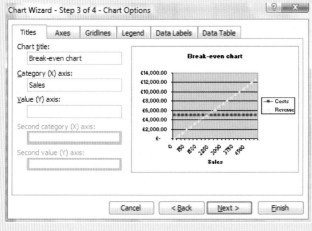

Figure 12

27 Click on **Next**.
28 Click on **Finish**.

The break-even chart should look like Figure 13.

The break-even point is where the yellow line crosses the purple line – that is, 2000 sales. Anything more than that is profit. Anything less is a loss.

	A	B	C
1	Cost price	£ 1.00	
2	Selling price	£ 2.50	
3	Number made	5000	
4			
5	Sales	Costs	Revenue
6	0	£ 5,000.00	£ -
7	250	£ 5,000.00	£ 625.00
8	500	£ 5,000.00	£ 1,250.00
9	750	£ 5,000.00	£ 1,875.00
10	1000	£ 5,000.00	£ 2,500.00
11	1250	£ 5,000.00	£ 3,125.00
12	1500	£ 5,000.00	£ 3,750.00
13	1750	£ 5,000.00	£ 4,375.00
14	2000	£ 5,000.00	£ 5,000.00
15	2250	£ 5,000.00	£ 5,625.00
16	2500	£ 5,000.00	£ 6,250.00
17	2750	£ 5,000.00	£ 6,875.00
18	3000	£ 5,000.00	£ 7,500.00
19	3250	£ 5,000.00	£ 8,125.00
20	3500	£ 5,000.00	£ 8,750.00
21	3750	£ 5,000.00	£ 9,375.00
22	4000	£ 5,000.00	£ 10,000.00
23	4250	£ 5,000.00	£ 10,625.00
24	4500	£ 5,000.00	£ 11,250.00
25	4750	£ 5,000.00	£ 11,875.00
26	5000	£ 5,000.00	£ 12,500.00

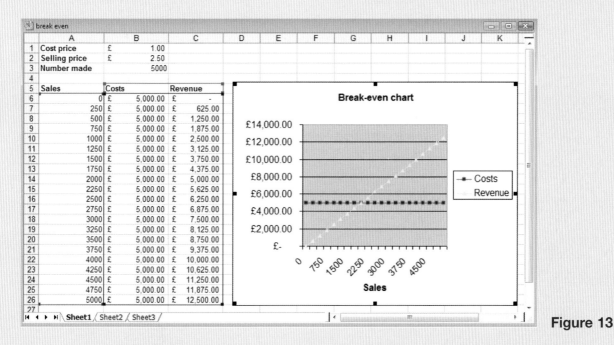

Figure 13

▶ Customising your graph

You can do the following:

▶ Change the numbers in cells B1, B2 and B3. The graph will adjust automatically.

▶ Adjust the colours of the lines in the chart. To do this, simply double click on the line and choose the colour and style you want.

▶ Remove the grey background. To do this, choose **None** in the Marker list.

Figure 14 shows a customised version of the break-even chart.

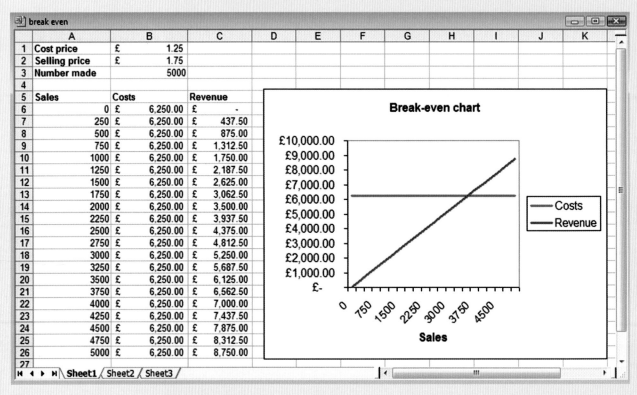

Figure 14

Activity 4

Clive is a baker. It costs 80p to make a wholemeal loaf, which he sells for £1.25. He makes a batch of 3000 loaves.

Create the break-even chart.

WJEC Information & Communication Technology for AS

Invoices

An **invoice** is a bill. Spreadsheet software can be used for invoices in the same way as for order forms (see pages 165–169). The spreadsheet can also include VAT, delivery and service charges if appropriate.

A stock file for Cartridges 4U is shown in Figure 15. Invoices are printed with a standard layout containing:

▶ the name and address of Cartridges 4U
▶ the date
▶ an invoice number
▶ the details of the items purchased
▶ the unit price of these items
▶ the quantity required
▶ the total cost
▶ VAT, delivery and service charges.

invoice

	A	B	C
1	Product ID	Item	Price
2	110414	Compatible black HP DeskJet 540 ink cartridge	£9.99
3	110415	Compatible colour HP DeskJet 540 ink cartridge	£12.99
4	118671	HP Colour LaserJet 4600 toner cartridge	£64.99
5	119186	Epson AcuLaser 2600N toner cartridge yellow	£116.99
6	119187	Epson AcuLaser 2600N toner cartridge magenta	£116.99
7	119188	Epson AcuLaser 2600N toner cartridge cyan	£116.99
8	119189	Epson AcuLaser 2600N toner cartridge black	£56.99
9	119200	Epson AcuLaser C1100 toner cartridge yellow	£90.99
10	119201	Epson AcuLaser C1100 toner cartridge magenta	£90.99
11	119202	Epson AcuLaser C1100 toner cartridge cyan	£90.99
12	119203	Epson AcuLaser C1100 toner cartridge black	£51.99
13			

Sheet1 / Sheet2 / Sheet3

Figure 15

As with an order form, there are several columns of figures, data has to be looked up in a price list and various calculations carried out. The need for accuracy is high so invoices are again a very suitable application for spreadsheets.

The spreadsheet in Figure 16 uses VLOOKUP and formulas to work out the total cost of the order, which is calculated in cell E24.

invoice

	A	B	C	D	E	F
1			**Cartridges 4U**			
2			High Street, Llangollen, LL99 8YZ			
3			(01798) 203456			
4			www.cartridges4u.co.uk			
5						
6	07/07/2008					
7	Invoice no: 4512					
8						
9	**Product ID**	**Quantity**	**Item**	**Price**	**Total price**	
10	119187	4	Epson AcuLaser 2600N toner cartridge magenta	£116.99	£ 467.96	
11	119201	2	Epson AcuLaser C1100 toner cartridge magenta	£90.99	£ 181.98	
12	110414	12	Compatible black HP DeskJet 540 ink cartridge	£9.99	£ 119.88	
13						
14						
15						
16						
17						
18					£ 769.82	
19				Delivery	£ 5.50	
20				Sub total	£ 775.32	
21						
22				VAT @ 17.5%	£ 135.68	
23						
24				Total owed	£ 911.00	
25						

Sheet1 \ **Sheet2** / Sheet3

Figure 16

Figure 17 shows the formulas. Drop-down lists for validation and error trapping can be used as on an order form.

	A	B	C	D	E	F
1			**Cartridges 4U**			
2			High Street, Llangollen, LL99 8YZ			
3			(01798) 203456			
4			www.cartridges4u.co.uk			
5						
6	=TODAY()					
7	Invoice no:	4512				
8						
9	Product ID	Quantity	Item		Price	Total price
10	119187	4	=IF(A10="","",VLOOKUP(A10,pricelist,2))	=IF(A10="","",VLOOKUP(A10,pricelist,3))	=IF(A10="","",B10*D10)	
11	119201	2	=IF(A11="","",VLOOKUP(A11,pricelist,2))	=IF(A11="","",VLOOKUP(A11,pricelist,3))	=IF(A11="","",B11*D11)	
12	110414	12	=IF(A12="","",VLOOKUP(A12,pricelist,2))	=IF(A12="","",VLOOKUP(A12,pricelist,3))	=IF(A12="","",B12*D12)	
13			=IF(A13="","",VLOOKUP(A13,pricelist,2))	=IF(A13="","",VLOOKUP(A13,pricelist,3))	=IF(A13="","",B13*D13)	
14			=IF(A14="","",VLOOKUP(A14,pricelist,2))	=IF(A14="","",VLOOKUP(A14,pricelist,3))	=IF(A14="","",B14*D14)	
15			=IF(A15="","",VLOOKUP(A15,pricelist,2))	=IF(A15="","",VLOOKUP(A15,pricelist,3))	=IF(A15="","",B15*D15)	
16			=IF(A16="","",VLOOKUP(A16,pricelist,2))	=IF(A16="","",VLOOKUP(A16,pricelist,3))	=IF(A16="","",B16*D16)	
17			=IF(A17="","",VLOOKUP(A17,pricelist,2))	=IF(A17="","",VLOOKUP(A17,pricelist,3))	=IF(A17="","",B17*D17)	
18					=SUM(E10:E17)	
19				Delivery	5.5	
20				Sub total	=SUM(E18:E19)	
21						
22				VAT @ 17.5%	=17.5%*E20	
23						
24				Total owed	=SUM(E20:E22)	
25						

I◄ ◄ ► ►I \ Sheet1 \ **Sheet2** / Sheet3 /

Figure 17

Activity 5

E. Williams Ltd is a local stationery supplier. These are some of the items that can be purchased:

Product ID	Item	Price
21	50 pencils	£1.99
22	25 ballpoint pens (black)	£2.99
23	25 ballpoint pens (blue)	£2.99
24	25 ballpoint pens (red)	£2.99
25	Sellotape (large)	£0.60
26	Sellotape (small)	£0.45
27	One ream (500 sheets) A4 copier paper (white)	£3.49
28	One ream (500 sheets) A4 copier paper (yellow)	£6.99
29	One ream (500 sheets) A4 copier paper (blue)	£6.99
30	One ream (500 sheets) A4 copier paper (pink)	£6.99

Use spreadsheet software to produce an invoice template for E. Williams Ltd. You should include:
- ▶ a table of prices
- ▶ use of VLOOKUP to look up prices
- ▶ use of formulas to calculate total costs
- ▶ validation to prevent entry of wrong data
- ▶ error trapping.

Balance sheets

A **balance sheet** is a statement of the assets and liabilities of an organisation. An **asset** is anything that is owned by a business, such as land, buildings and equipment. Any amounts of money owed by a business are its **liabilities**.

The Companies Act states that a balance sheet must be included in a limited company's accounts.

Balance sheets set out figures in a table and calculations have to be performed on these figures, so they are very suitable applications for spreadsheets. However you should be aware that balance sheets like the one shown in Figure 18 use only very simple formulas and do not include many of the features needed at this level.

	A	B	C	D
1	**Griffiths and Morgan plc**			
2	Balance Sheet (in £ millions)	**31 July 2009**	**31 July 2008**	
3				
4	**Fixed Assets**	10,522	9,034	
5				
6	Current Assets	1,994	1,782	
7	Short-term creditors	-5,189	-3,676	
8				
9	**Net Current Liabilites**	-3,195	-1,894	
10				
11	Total Assets less Current Liabilities	7,327	7,140	
12				
13	Long-term creditors	-1,809	-1,595	
14	Provisions	-45	-34	
15				
16	**Total Net Assets**	5,473	5,511	
17				
18	**Total Capital Employed**	5,473	5,511	
19				
20				

Figure 18 Balance sheet in normal view

Figure 19 on the following page shows the same balance sheet in formula view. Notice how Excel stores dates. The date 31st July 2009 is stored as 40025. This is because dates are stored as the number of days since 1 January 1900.

	A	B	C	
1	**Griffiths and Morgan plc**			
2	Balance Sheet (in £ millions)	40025	39660	
3				
4	**Fixed Assets**	10522	9034	
5				
6	Current Assets	1994	1782	
7	Short-term creditors	-5189	-3676	
8				
9	**Net Current Liabilites**	=SUM(B6:B7)	=SUM(C6:C7)	
10				
11	Total Assets less Current Liabilities	=B4+B9	=C4+C9	
12				
13	Long-term creditors	-1809	-1595	
14	Provisions	-45	-34	
15				
16	**Total Net Assets**	=SUM(B11:B14)	=SUM(C11:C14)	
17				
18	**Total Capital Employed**	=B16	=C16	
19				
20				

Figure 19 Balance sheet in formula view

What you have to do

▶ The examination

You have to produce a spreadsheet solution for section B of the ICT1 examination.

Your solution must be sufficiently complex to need the features listed in the section *Design and implementation of your spreadsheet* on pages 179–180.

▶ You must produce your spreadsheet in your ICT lessons with a teacher present.
▶ You **cannot** create your spreadsheet at home or outside lessons.
▶ You must print the finished spreadsheet in both normal and formula view and take the printouts into the exam.
▶ You cannot print any annotation on your spreadsheet.

There will be two sections in the exam. Section A will consist of traditional exam questions based on *Unit 1A: Chapters 1–11* in this book. The marks for this section will be 75% of the total for the whole exam.

Section B will consist of questions about spreadsheets. You can use your spreadsheet to help answer the questions. The remaining 25% of the marks for the exam will be for this section.

At the end of the exam, you will hand in the printouts of your spreadsheet with your answers to the other questions.

In the exam you will be expected to spend roughly one third of the time on section B.

► What do I need to show?

Your printouts should include evidence of the following:

- ► worksheets showing labels, data, formulas
- ► multiple sheets and the use of 3D referencing between them
- ► use of LOOKUP or VLOOKUP or HLOOKUP
- ► drop-down boxes
- ► spinners
- ► true/false or tick boxes or option boxes
- ► start-up user interface
- ► data entry forms
- ► validation techniques and error messages produced
- ► use of sorting
- ► searching for specific criteria
- ► buttons to run macros
- ► use of appropriate graphs such as bar or column graphs, line graphs, pie charts, scatter graphs, pictographs.

You will need to make sure that you print:

- ► all worksheets
- ► different versions of the same worksheet with different data if appropriate
- ► copies in formula view with columns wide enough so that all the formulas are visible.

For the examination you should be prepared to answer questions about the spreadsheet and identify techniques used.

► User requirements

You should be prepared to give answers to these questions:

- ► What is the purpose of the spreadsheet? What will it be used to do?
- ► What are the outputs? What does the user interface look like? How many worksheets are there? What data do they each store?
- ► What processes are used? This could include calculations, searching, sorting, validation, macros.
- ► What is the printed output?

► Design and implementation of your spreadsheet

You should be prepared to:

- ► Identify and explain the purpose of labels and data.
- ► Identify evidence of at least **two** of these functions:
  a SUM   d MIN
  b COUNT   e AVERAGE
  c MAX   f RAND.

▶ Identify evidence of at least **two** of these functions:
   a Single IF   c Date =TODAY()
   b Multiple (Nested) IF   d ROUND.

▶ Identify evidence of multiple sheets and 3D links.

▶ Identify evidence of simplification of data entry such as:
   a drop-down boxes
   b choosing from a list
   c spinners
   d true/false or tick boxes or option boxes
   e LOOKUP or VLOOKUP or HLOOKUP.

▶ Identify evidence of ease of use and professionalism:
   a start-up user interface
   b data entry forms
   c use of control buttons to initiate macros – for example, navigation/print/data transfer.

▶ Identify evidence of error trapping – for example, validation techniques and error messages produced **not** spinners or lists.

▶ Identify evidence of processing used:
   a sorting techniques
   b searching for specific criteria, including single and multiple criteria.

▶ Identify appropriate use of graphs such as:
   a bar or column graphs   d scatter graphs
   b line graphs   e pictographs.
   c pie charts

Your answers must relate to the spreadsheet that you have created and must be supported by clear evidence.

▶ Evaluation

You will also need to be able to reflect on the creation of your spreadsheet:

▶ Are there ways in which your spreadsheet could be improved?
▶ Are there ways in which it could be developed further?

Simulation modelling

Simulation modelling means using a computer and mathematical formulas to imitate a real phenomenon. Simulations have become common in science and economics. They look at **what if** scenarios: what will happen if this happens?

It is possible to use sophisticated computer programs to simulate:
▶ weather conditions such as the effects of heavy rainfall
▶ tidal flows
▶ chemical reactions
▶ atomic reactions
▶ traffic flows such as the effect of building new roads or installing traffic lights

▶ geological surveys
▶ the effects of a car crash
▶ financial models.

Thanks to the development of powerful computers, models can be used to forecast the weather, locate the whereabouts of oil and other minerals, analyse, predict and perform.

▶ Why use simulation modelling?

▶ It enables predictions to be made in areas which may be dangerous to humans, such as prospecting for oil under water.
▶ It is usually much cheaper: for example, using a computer to simulate the effects of a car crash would be cheaper than crash testing real cars.
▶ Some situations cannot be performed for testing purposes in real life, such as the effects of heavy rainfall or of increasing the price of goods by 10%.
▶ A simulation can often be operated more quickly than the real system, so the effects over a long period of time can be studied easily.
▶ Conversely, if the actual system operates very quickly, the simulation can slow it down to study results more easily.

▶ Problems with simulation modelling

▶ It is only a model and not the real thing. Predictions may not be accurate. They are only as accurate as the formulas on which they are based.
▶ Powerful and expensive computer hardware is required.
▶ It can be expensive to create the model. For example, aerodynamic wind tunnels, used to model the performance of cars and aeroplanes, are very costly.
▶ Some things cannot be predicted accurately and so are hard to simulate – for example, earthquakes.

▶ Parallel and distributed processing

Simulation modelling can allow millions and millions of calculations to be performed. A weather forecast needs huge computation power as it has to process real-time data from satellite observations, balloons, ships and weather stations.

It will often take a very long time to perform these calculations. Sometimes more than one central processing unit (CPU) is used to execute the program. This is called **parallel processing** and the program runs faster.

Distributed processing may also be used. This is when a program is split up so that some processing is done locally – for example, input and initial processing of data from a weather station – rather than all processing being done by one central computer.

Case Study 1 – Virtual crash tests save Rover £2 500 000 on cost of introducing a new car

There are two ways of testing the safety of new cars:

1 use a physical prototype (a real car) and crash it
2 use digital prototypes (computer models) and simulate crashes.

Rover have improved car safety and at the same time cut costs and testing times by using digital prototypes.

The cost of a building a physical prototype car can be as much as £250 000. It can take over four months to build and the crash test lasts only a tenth of a second.

Using digital prototypes means Rover can test the safety of vehicles at an early stage in the design process. Changes can be made to designs at this stage without incurring high costs. This reduces the cost and time of the total design process because it reduces the number of physical prototypes that need to be made.

The new system has already helped Rover to reduce the length and cost of the design process. The new hardware, software and modelling facilities enabled analysts to predict safety performance with greater accuracy. It has allowed Rover to remove one phase of physical-prototype crash simulation. This could use up to ten cars which, at £250 000 per prototype, means a saving of £2.5 million.

Case Study 2 – Weather forecasting

Computer-assisted weather forecasting at the Met Office

Computer models are used by the Meteorological Office (Met Office) to produce weather forecasts. These forecasts have become far more accurate since the introduction of computer models.

These models are derived from the laws of physics and involve analysing a large number of measurements such as pressure, temperature, humidity and wind. Readings come from all around the world from sources including radar, satellites and balloons in the upper atmosphere. The models provide a set of equations to solve in order to predict the future weather.

The models produce a global forecast twice a day based on readings taken at midnight and midday. This forecast requires 160 million equations to be solved. The supercomputer at the Met Office takes only about an hour to produce a six-day global forecast.

Case Study 3 – Financial modelling

Credit-card companies such as Capital One offer interest-free balance transfers.

This means that a customer of another credit-card company with a balance of, say, £1000 can switch to Capital One and not have to pay any interest for perhaps as long as 12 months.

Obviously having not to pay interest is attractive to customers. Conversely, the lack of interest is costly to Capital One. But they hope to recoup this cost in the long run.

How do Capital One decide what to offer to attract new customers? They use financial modelling. Using a sophisticated computer model which includes interest rates, average balance transfers, credit-card spend, income, average length of time before the cardholder switches again, etc., they can predict whether they can profit from new customers.

Activity 6

Read Case Studies 1–3. For each of the three areas below, describe the benefits of simulation modelling:

1 financial forecasting
2 simulating car crashes
3 weather forecasting.

Unit

2

Introduction

⬤ What you have to do in this unit

The examples and activities in this unit will help you to produce your own documents and presentations. They do not in themselves provide a complete solution for this work.

In this unit you have to use ICT hardware and software applications to solve a problem involving three separate tasks:

1 the production of a document such as a leaflet or magazine
2 the production of a document containing automated routines, such as a mail-merged letter
3 the production of a presentation to show to an audience, such as a web pages or a slide show.

The three tasks should be for the same organisation. For example, you could produce a magazine, automated documents and a website for the same business.

At the start of the first task, you should describe the organisation and consider its ethos/house style. You will need to study documents used in the organisation such as:

Terms in **blue bold** are defined in the DTP Glossary on page 256.

▶ letters to all customers (promotional material/junk mail)
▶ flyers
▶ brochures, leaflets or catalogues

▶ compliments slips
▶ posters
▶ web pages
▶ slide shows.

From these you can identify the house style. What colours do they use? What **fonts**? What text size are headings, standard text, etc. Your documents will need to conform to this style.

⬤ What you must hand in

You will have to hand in work for each of the three tasks but you will also need to hand in work covering **all three** tasks. You will need to include:

▶ Background to the organisation. What is the organisation? What does it do? Where is it? How big is it? (See example on page 185.)
▶ Documents used in the organisation (either scanned or in their original form)
▶ The ethos of the organisation. Are they go ahead? Modern? Stuck in the past? Forward thinking? Exciting? Dull but reliable? How is the ethos reflected in the document(s)?
▶ An evaluation (see page 185)

▶ Data compression techniques, including methods used to compress and store your files and a justification of the chosen methods (see example below). You will probably wish to refer to different methods of storing still images, sounds and video images if these are included in your documents or presentation.

Example – Background information

Chris Jackson is a friend of my father's. He owns a business called CMJ Digital that installs satellite dishes and TV aerials in the area around Sheldon. The business employs just four people including Chris.

With the switch to digital TV, a lot of people need a dish or a new aerial. Chris is keen to get work from these people.

At present he advertises by posting flyers through people's letterboxes near where he lives. Chris has asked me to redesign the flyer to make it more eye-catching and to include the Freesat logo.

CMJ Digital is a modern business fitting the latest technology in satellite dishes and TV aerials. They have a top-quality modern image. They pride themselves on the quality of their work, their reliability and providing a top-class service.

As the quality of their work is so important, I will need to emphasise this and the fact that all the staff are qualified.

▶ Evaluation

This should comprise a well-organised and clear evaluation of all three tasks, including:
▶ whether or not you have met your original aims
▶ strengths and weaknesses of your documents
▶ evidence on which you have based these comments
▶ possible future modifications of your documents

and demonstrating:
▶ specialist vocabulary
▶ legible text
▶ accurate spelling, punctuation and grammar
▶ clarity of meaning.

See the DTP Glossary, page 256, for some specialist terms you may need to use.

A running commentary on what you did to create the documents is **not** necessary.

Example – Documentation of compression and storage techniques

There were 6 HTML files created, called:

cmjfreeview.htm	cmjprices.htm	cmjsatellite.htm
cmjhome.htm	cmjradio.htm	cmjswitch.htm

There were 15 image files, called:

dc1.jpg	dr2.jpg	freesat.gif	home2.jpg	sky.jpg
dc2.jpg	free1.jpg	freeview.gif	prices1.jpg	stv1.jpg
dr1.jpg	free2.jpg	home1.jpg	prices2.jpg	stv2.jpg

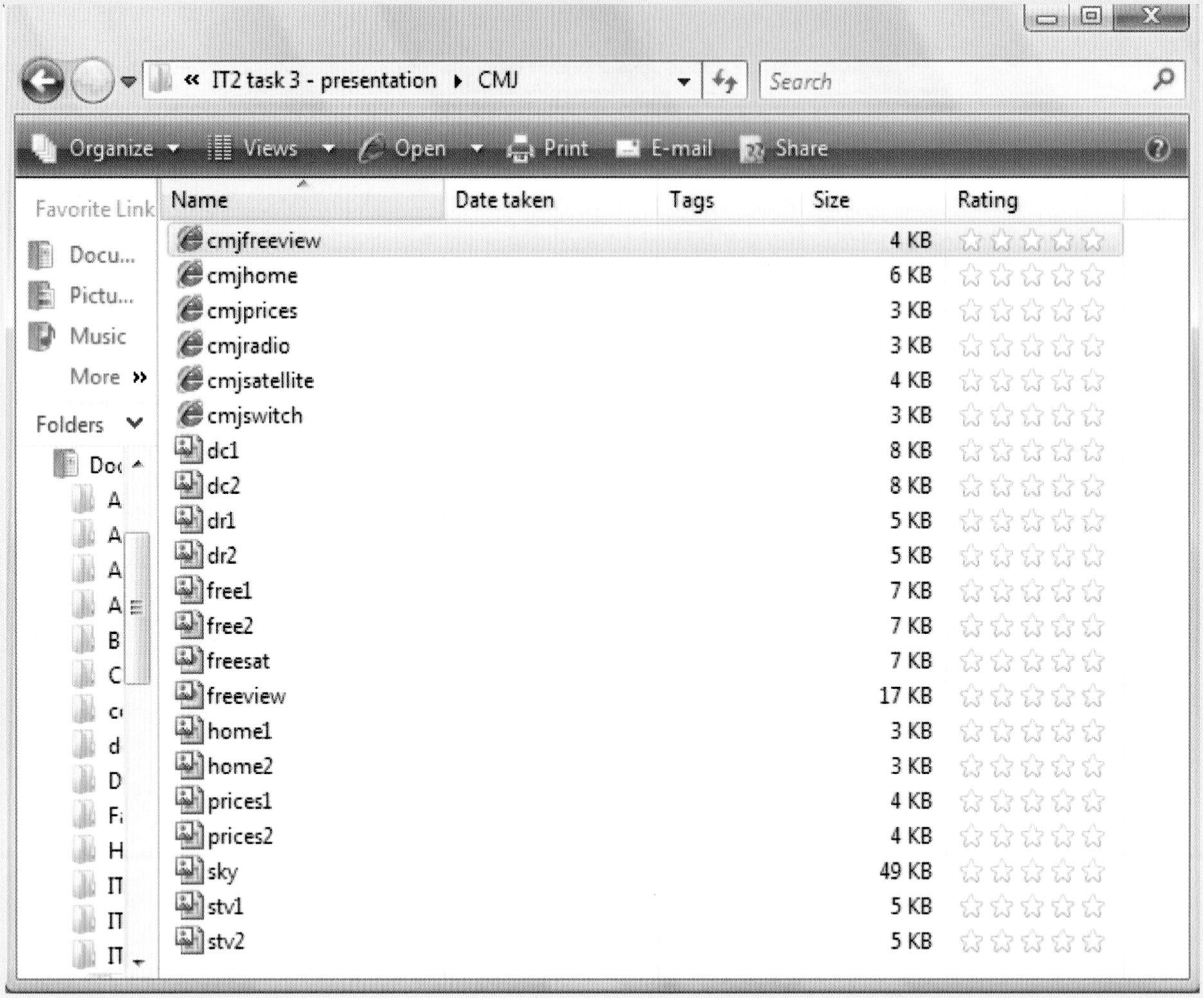

Figure 1

The images are all stored in either gif or jpg format. These formats use compression techniques to reduce the size of each image and are much, much smaller than bitmap images.

As these files have been compressed, they are very small, as you can see from the above screenshot (Figure 1). These files are so small that they would load very quickly and the web pages would load in just a few seconds.

This means that customers visiting the website do not have to wait.

These files have been stored on the computer's internal hard disk in a folder called CMJ so that it can easily be found and opened. As can be seen from the screenshot, the size of the files in this folder is only 160 KB.

This folder would easily fit on a hard disk, memory stick or even a floppy disk so further compression is not necessary.

If the file sizes were much larger I could compress them by right clicking on the file name, choosing **Send To > Compressed (zipped) Folder**. This would mean they would take up less disk space and would not take as long to e-mail if I wished to send them to a colleague.

Project ideas

Here are some possible ideas on which to base your project.

You could produce for an organisation:

▶ a brochure saying what services they offer or a programme for an event or a promotional calendar
▶ a mail-merge letter to potential customers about a new service that they are offering
▶ a website advertising their services or a presentation to show to potential customers.

Some organisations that might want these items are:

▶ a local recording studio wishing to expand their business
▶ a local car hire company
▶ a caravan site
▶ a new pizza takeaway
▶ a gardening service
▶ a school/college putting on a performance
▶ a leisure centre
▶ a music company.

Whatever you choose for your project, it must be sufficiently detailed to be able to demonstrate the skills listed in the *What you have to do in this task* section for each task.

1 Desktop Publishing (DTP)

What you have to do in this task

For this task you have to use an appropriate software application to produce a document such as a leaflet or magazine. The document should be at least two sides of A4 and contain at least 150 words.

You will need to produce evidence of using:

- different font styles
- different font sizes
- bold and underline
- align centre, align right or fully **justify**
- AutoShapes
- **bullet** points
- WordArt
- shading effects
- **headers** and **footers**
- at least **two** forms of electronic combination of graphical images – for example, scanned images, graphics from the Internet, **clip-art** from disk, digital-camera images, graphs from a spreadsheet, graphics from a paint or CAD package
- tables.

> Terms in **blue bold** are defined in the DTP Glossary, page 256.

To get higher marks you will need to produce evidence of using some of the following features:

- customising tables – for example, cell merging or splitting or text orientation
- different paragraph formats
- different line spacing
- superscripts and subscripts
- page or frame borders
- setting and using your own tabs
- setting and using your own indents
- watermarks
- **pagination**
- layering
- creating your own styles.

Choosing your task

This is often the hardest part of a project.

A poor choice of task might mean that you can't get all the marks available because some features listed on page 188 are not needed.

An exciting choice will motivate you. You will enjoy it and welcome the challenge of getting good marks.

It is a good idea to have a real project such as:

▶ redesigning an existing document to make it better
▶ producing a new document for somebody else.

It is much easier to describe the purpose of the document if it is a real document for a real business and not something that you have made up.

If the document is smaller than A4 size, such as a CD box insert, you can produce it in a larger size that will be reduced when it is printed.

Whatever you choose, it must be sufficiently detailed to be able to use many of the features listed on page 188.

Designing your document

Your design should show:

▶ page size
▶ page orientation
▶ outline layout of the page
▶ position of headings, titles, etc., stating the font, colour and size to be used
▶ position of text frames, stating the font, colour and size to be used
▶ format of frames, giving details such as background colour and border
▶ position of images
▶ **margins**
▶ **paragraph styles**
▶ tables where appropriate
▶ tab settings or indents.

Before you start designing your document, study at least two different existing DTP documents produced by your chosen organisation to find out the house style.

Next, produce some rough layout designs. It is best to sketch these using pencil and paper. Draw them to scale – if possible, the exact size.

▶ Issues to consider

Page size

What size will the paper be? Will it be **portrait** or **landscape**? Try to stick to standard sizes such as A4 or A5. Try a few design mock-ups so that you find the best size. Show your designs to other people to get their opinions.

Name

What is the name of the document? Try to think of something catchy. A newsletter called *The South Pemberton Social Services Newsletter* may do exactly what it says on the tin, but is the name snappy? Can you imagine anyone saying, 'Did you see that article in *The South Pemberton Social Services Newsletter*?'

Call your document something snappy like *Explore, The Gist, The Picture, The Level, The Pipeline* or *Bulletin*. The name should be one or two words and in large type to attract the reader. Use a subtitle to explain more about the content.

Nameplate position

The **nameplate** is where you put the name of the publication. Does it have to be at the top? Maybe it could be rotated through 90 degrees and put along the side. Could it be at the bottom?

Paper

There are several different thicknesses of paper available. Would card be better for a flyer? Generally, the thicker the paper, the more it costs, but the less likely it is to get screwed up. If the paper is too thin, ink may show through on the other side.

Paper colour

You don't have to print onto white paper. Would it be better to print onto yellow? Or maybe pink or pale blue? Experiment with how different colours look. Pale colours are best for clarity. But whatever you choose it must fit in with the house style.

House style

Has the organisation for which you are producing the document got its own style? Does it have a logo? What font is used? Is there a standard colour for text?

Fonts

Which font or fonts will be used? This should be determined by the house style but if there isn't a house style, you should create one. It is best if all pages and all documents use the same style. This means they should use the same fonts, colours and sizes throughout.

Serif fonts such as Times New Roman are often regarded as old-fashioned and fuddy-duddy. **Sans serif** fonts such as Arial or Calibri are seen as more modern and clearer.

Font sizes

Which font sizes are best? Study professional documents to see what font sizes they have used. Text is often as small as 10 **point** or even 8 point.

Flyers where you need to grab someone's attention in a short time will have larger text.

Of course, font, font colour and font size can be varied a little. Reverse colour, which is white text on a dark background, works well for subheadings. But use variations sparingly. It is generally OK to use two different fonts on a page but any more than that is over the top.

Colour

The colour of ink should complement the colour of paper. Black ink on white paper is the most readable combination. Whichever colours you choose, you need good contrast so you should use a dark colour for text.

Pull quotes

Pull quotes are short interesting quotes taken from an article and repeated in a larger font. They attract attention and also help break up a long article.

Balance

If you include two pictures on a page, you will need to ensure that there is a good balance. This means that one image should be on the right-hand side of the page and one on the left. But don't put them next to each other (unless they belong together). One image bottom left and one middle right would give good balance. Figures 1 and 2 show two designs with a similar layout but which one is better balanced?

Figure 1   Figure 2

Note that:

▶ Use of shading can make an article stand out.
▶ Lines separating pull quotes from the text make them stand out.
▶ The face in Figure 1 is looking into the rest of the page, whereas the face in Figure 2 is looking away from the page. Which is better?

Upper or lower case?

Should headings be entirely in **upper case** (capital letters)? **Lower-case** letters are easier to read and they are smaller, so they take up less space. Upper-case text is more eye-catching.

▶ Creating the page design

Once you have made these decisions you will be ready to put together some drawings of what your document might look like. Try images in different positions. Experiment with the position of the nameplate. Produce a few different designs and get some opinions from others.

Look at similar documents to see how the text is laid out. What font size do they use? Where are the images?

If you are producing an A4 document consider using columns. Text can be hard to read if a column goes across a whole page. Have at least two columns for A4 portrait and at least three columns for A4 landscape.

Other features that you might want to think about are:

▶ shaded background to a text box
▶ lines/borders around a text box, an image or even the whole page
▶ watermarks
▶ **text wrap** around an image
▶ text printing on top of an image, but only if it is clear.

Your designs should be annotated so that it is clear which features you intend to use, including:

▶ page size
▶ page orientation
▶ margins, with sizes
▶ styles
▶ fonts

▶ font sizes
▶ paragraph styles
▶ **imported** graphics
▶ tables
▶ settings for tabs or indents.

Figure 3 shows an example of a flyer redesigned by a student. Chris, the owner of CMJ Digital, advertises by posting flyers through people's letterboxes near where he lives. He asked the student to redesign the flyer shown in Figure 3 to make it more eye-catching and include the Freesat logo. The original flyer is A5 size and double sided.

The design in Figure 3 is very cluttered. This is partly because the margins around the edge are too big. It uses four different fonts, one of

See page 185 for more background information on CMJ Digital.

Figure 3 **Front page of a flyer used by CMJ Digital**

which is hard to read. There are no images and there is no colour. The new design needed to be less cluttered and to use some of the advanced features of the software such as:

▶ borders ▶ layering

▶ tables ▶ line spacing.

▶ watermarks

The new design is shown in Figure 4 on the following page. The student also produced a design for the reverse of the flyer and again labelled features to be used.

Superscripts and subscripts

Superscripts are small characters set above the normal letters or figures. They are often used for ordinal numbers such as 1st, 2nd and 3rd.

1 To format text to superscript, highlight the text concerned (e.g. **st** in 1st).

2 Click on **Format > Font** and tick the **Superscript** box as in Figure 6.

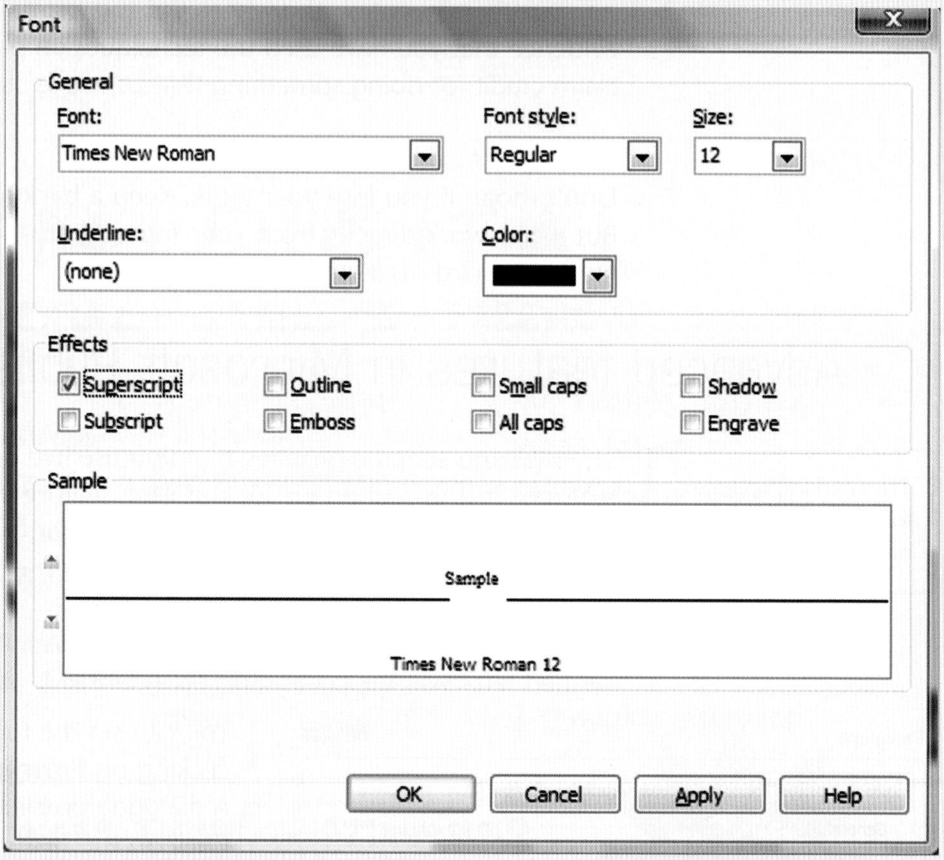

Figure 6

Subscripts are similar but the characters are set below the normal letters as in CO_2. They are used for chemical formulas and, sometimes, in numbering for footnotes.

3 To format text to subscript, highlight the text concerned, click on **Format > Font** and tick the **Subscript** box.

Customising tables

1 To insert a table, click on **Table > Insert > Table**.

You will see a dialogue box (as in Figure 7) which you can use to customise your table. You can select the number of rows and columns here, as well as choosing from a variety of layouts.

2 You could, for example, set up a table of three rows and four columns with no formatting. To start with, it would look like Figure 8.

3 To format a column to background colour yellow, highlight the cells in the column, click on the **Fill Colour** icon and choose yellow. You could format columns 1 and 3 to yellow and 2 and 4 to pale green as in Figure 9.

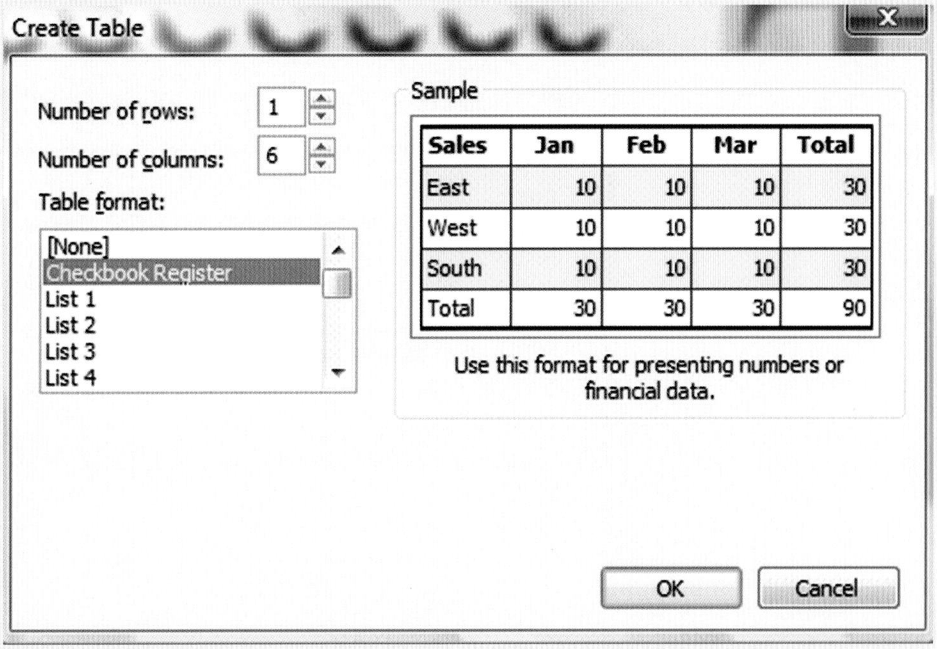

Figure 7

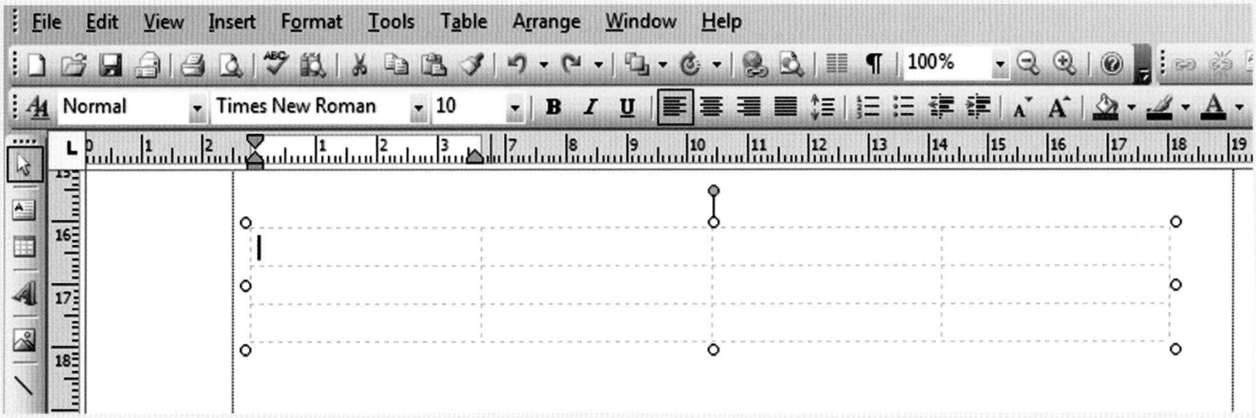

Figure 8

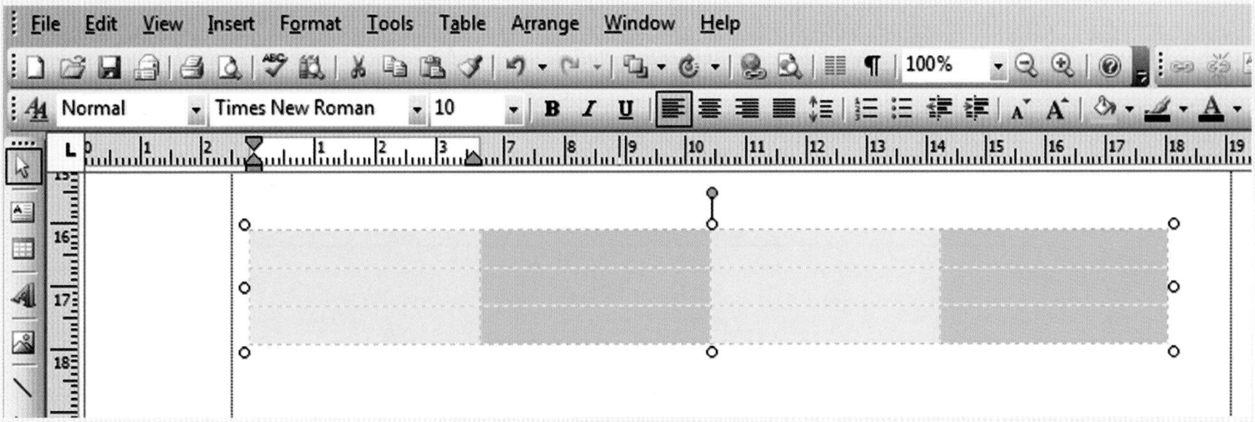

Figure 9

4 To give the table borders between the cells, highlight the whole table and click on **Format > Table**.

5 Click on the **Colors and Lines** tab if not already selected.

6 Click on the **All Borders** icon in the Presets (see Figure 10 on the following page) then choose the required line colour.

All Borders icon

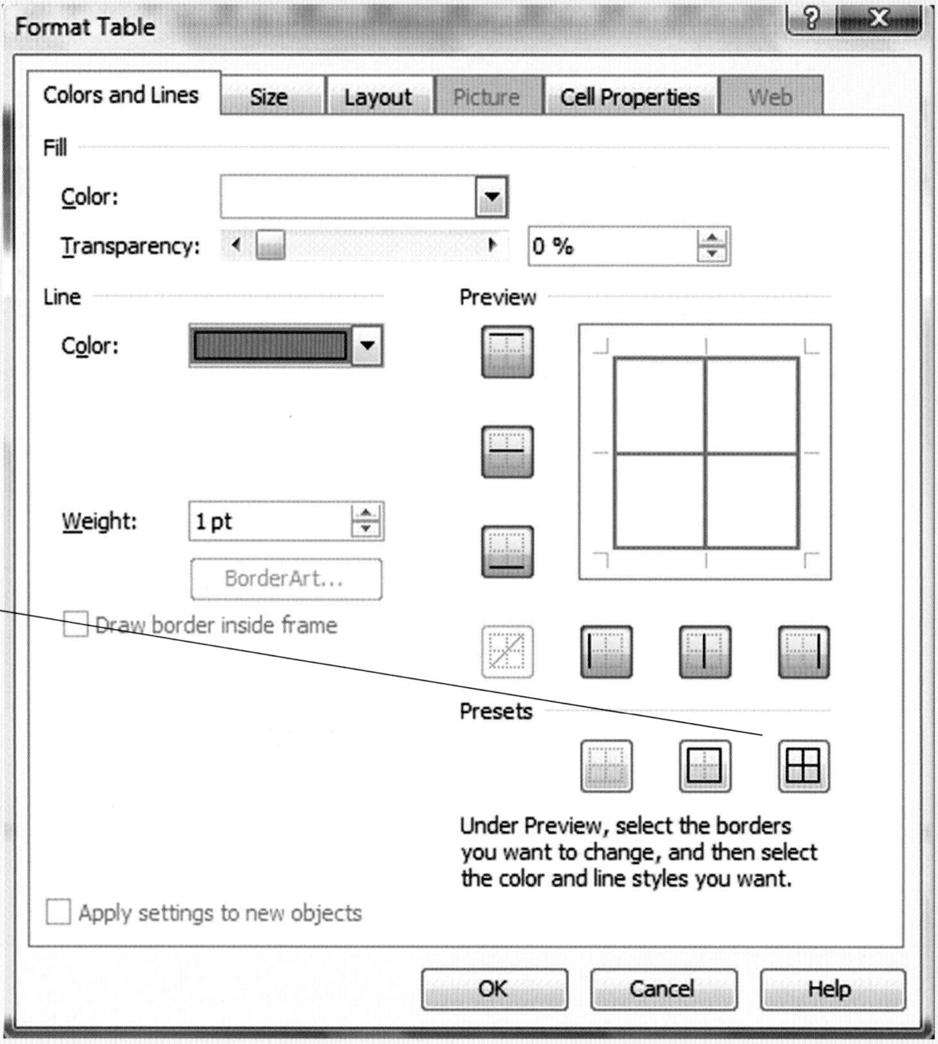

Figure 10

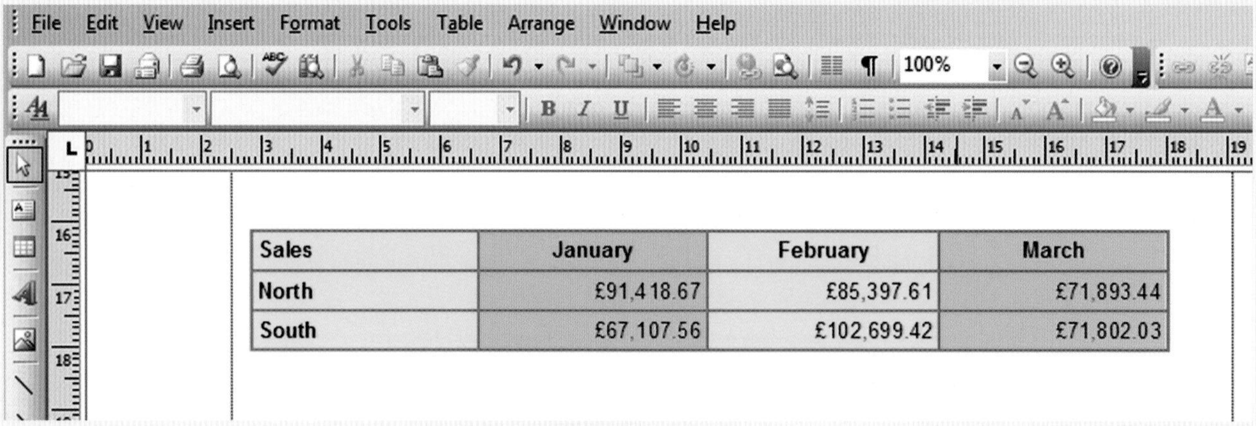

Figure 11

7 Click on **OK**.

8 Format the fonts in the table in the usual way. Tables often have the row and column headings in bold as in Figure 11.

Page or frame borders

You can put borders around **objects** such as text boxes and images to make them stand out. You can also put a border round a whole page.

WJEC Information & Communication Technology for AS

Figure 12

Adding a border to an object such as a text box

1 Select the text box and click on **Format > Text box**.
2 Choose a colour using the **Line Color** drop-down list.
3 Adjust the thickness of the border by adjusting **Weight** then click on **OK**.

Using images for the border of a text box

1 Select the text box as before and click on **Format > Text box**.
2 Click on **BorderArt**. A number of different images are available.
3 Select the one you want then click on **OK** twice.

Adding a page border

1 Select the page where you want to add the border.
2 On the Objects toolbar, click on the **Rectangle** icon shown in Figure 12.
3 Drag out a rectangle that covers nearly the whole page.
4 Select the rectangle then click on **Format > AutoShape**.
5 Click on the **Colors and Lines** tab.
6 Choose the colour and line style options you want for your border.
7 Click on **OK**.

Using images for a page border

1 Select the rectangle as before then click on **Format > AutoShape**.
2 Click on **BorderArt**. A number of different images are available.
3 Select the one you want then click on **OK** twice. You will get a border like the one in Figure 13.

Figure 13

Setting and using tabs

If you want text to appear directly underneath other text, you will need to use tabs as in Figure 14. Microsoft Publisher has a preset tab stop every centimetre.

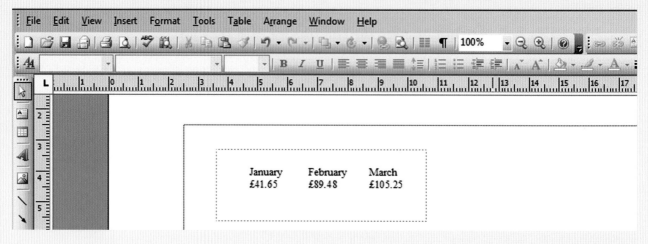

Figure 14

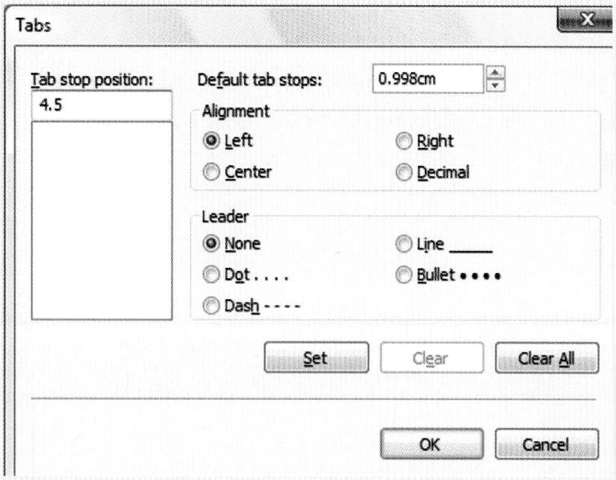

You can also set your own tabs as follows:

1 Click in the paragraph that you want to align with tabs.
2 Click on **Format > Tabs**.
3 In the **Tab Stop Position** box, type the measurement for the tab stop – for example, 4.5, as in Figure 15.
4 Click on **Set**.
5 Repeat steps 3 and 4 for each tab stop you want to set.
6 Click on **OK**.

Figure 15

Setting and using indents

An indent is a blank space between a margin and the beginning of a line. Sometimes the first line of a paragraph is indented.

▶ Flush left means that none of the lines in a paragraph are indented.
▶ A first-line indent means that the first line of a paragraph is indented but not the other lines.
▶ A hanging paragraph is the opposite: the first line is not indented but the other lines are.

You can set indents by clicking on **Format > Paragraph**.

In Figure 16 the options chosen mean that the first line only will be indented by a centimetre.

The paragraph will look like Figure 17. Note that this paragraph has been set up with **greeking**.

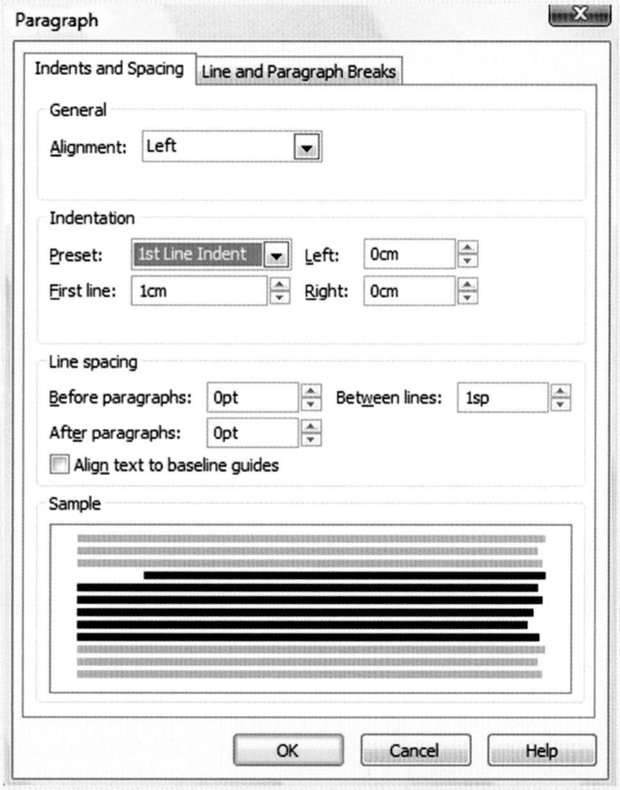

Figure 16

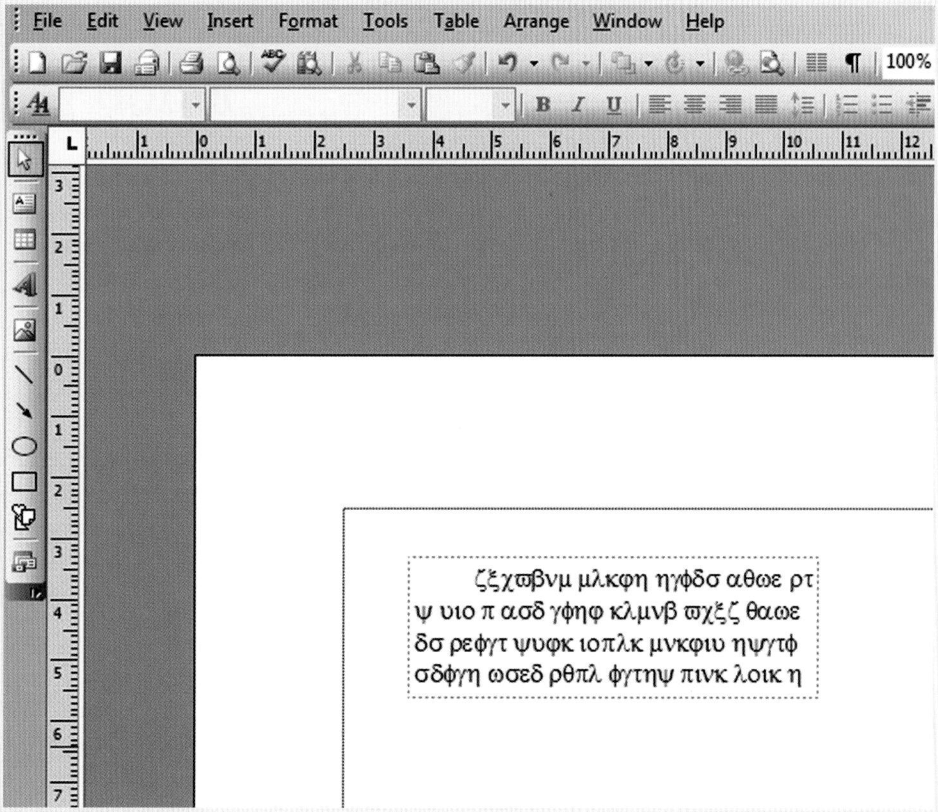

Figure 17

Watermarks

A watermark is an image reproduced in a colour such as light grey that appears under the text in a document. The text can still be read easily as the watermark is very pale.

To add a watermark to a page:

1 Press CTRL + M to enter master view.
2 Click on **Insert > Picture > From File**.
3 Find the required picture and click on **Insert**.
4 Right click on the picture and click on **Format Picture**.
5 Click on the **Picture** tab.
6 Click on **Washout** in the **Color** drop-down list, and then click on **Recolor**.
7 Choose a colour for your watermark. Click on **Apply** then click on **OK**.
8 Click on **OK**. The image is now a single-colour washed-out version of the original image.
9 Press CTRL + M to leave master view or click on **Close Master View**.

The page will look like Figure 18. (This page has also been set up with greeking.)

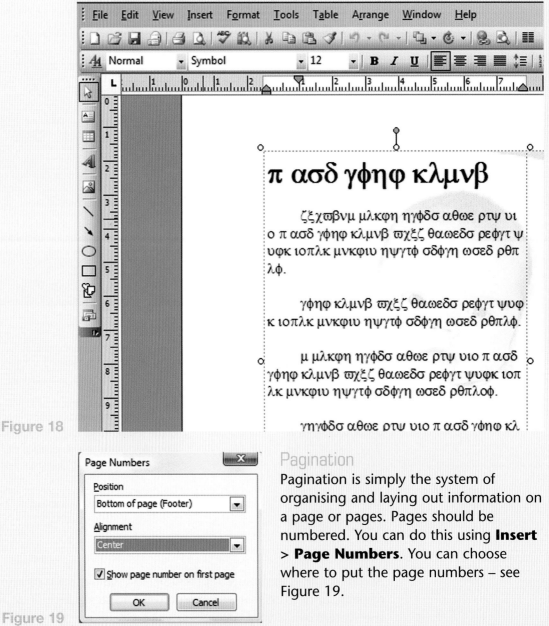

Figure 18

Figure 19

Pagination

Pagination is simply the system of organising and laying out information on a page or pages. Pages should be numbered. You can do this using **Insert > Page Numbers**. You can choose where to put the page numbers – see Figure 19.

Layering (forward and behind)

Sometimes you may want to place one object (say some text) on top of another object, such as an image. You can do this using layers. To put one object behind another, select the first object and click on **Arrange > Order > Send Backward**.

You can also bring an object forward, send it to the back (behind all objects) or bring it to the front (in front of all objects).

Creating your own styles

You can easily set your own styles in Microsoft Publisher. For example:

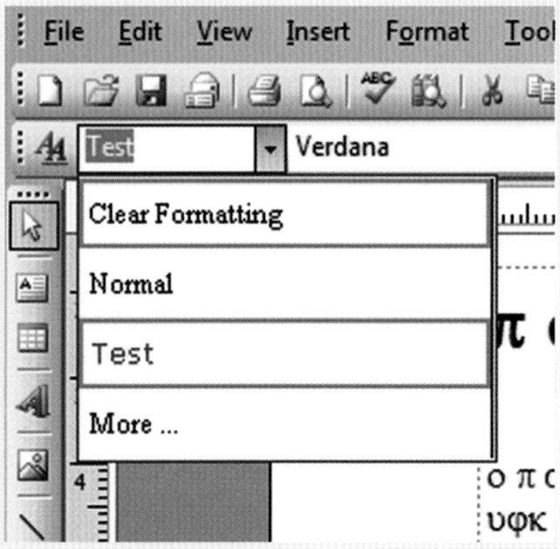

Figure 20

1 Click on **Format > Styles and Formatting** (or **Format Styles** in Publisher 2007).
2 Click on **Create new style**.
3 In the dialogue box enter the new style name **Test**.
4 Click on **Font** to set the font to **Verdana**, size **10**, colour **red**.
5 Click on **OK**.
6 Click on **Create new style**.
7 Click on **Paragraph**.
8 Set the indentation to **Flush Left** and the line spacing after paragraphs to **10** point.
9 Click on **OK** twice.
10 Set the style by selecting a paragraph then selecting **Test** from the style drop-down list as in Figure 20.

Fifteen useful Microsoft Publisher tips and tricks

Here are some more features that you might want to use when creating your document.

Nudging objects

For fine-positioning of an object, use the nudge option. Select the object then use the ALT + ARROW keys to move your object just one pixel.

Or use **Arrange > Nudge > Up** (or **Down**, **Left** or **Right**) to move the object.

Inserting a new page

To insert a new page after the one that is currently displayed, press CTRL + SHIFT + N.

Selecting two or more objects

To select two objects such as two text boxes, first select one of the objects. Then hold down the SHIFT key and select the second object. Now you can move or resize both objects at the same time.

Grouping objects

You can group several objects so that they become one object. To do this, select all the objects that you want to group as one and click on **Arrange > Group** or press CTRL + SHIFT + G.

To reverse this, select the grouped objects and click on **Arrange > Ungroup** or, as before, press CTRL + SHIFT + G.

Using the design checker to check for errors

This is a quick and easy way to check for errors in your document. Click on **Tools > Design Checker**. This will tell you about errors such as text in the overflow area or space below the margins at the top of the page.

Using fancy letters to begin a paragraph

Highlight the letter that you wish to make fancy. Click on **Format > Drop Cap**. Choose the format that you want and click on **OK**.

Removing hyphenation

Very annoyingly, Publisher hyphenates text automatically. With narrow columns, this can lead to lots of hyphens. To turn off the hyphenation, select the text box concerned. Click on **Tools > Language > Hyphenation**. Make sure **Automatically hyphenate this story** is turned off, as in Figure 21.

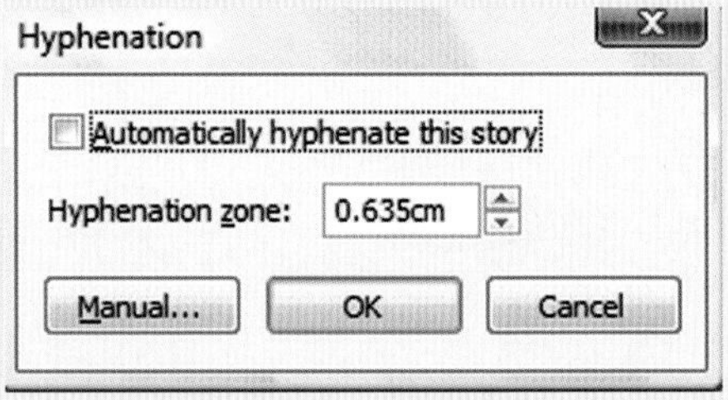

Figure 21

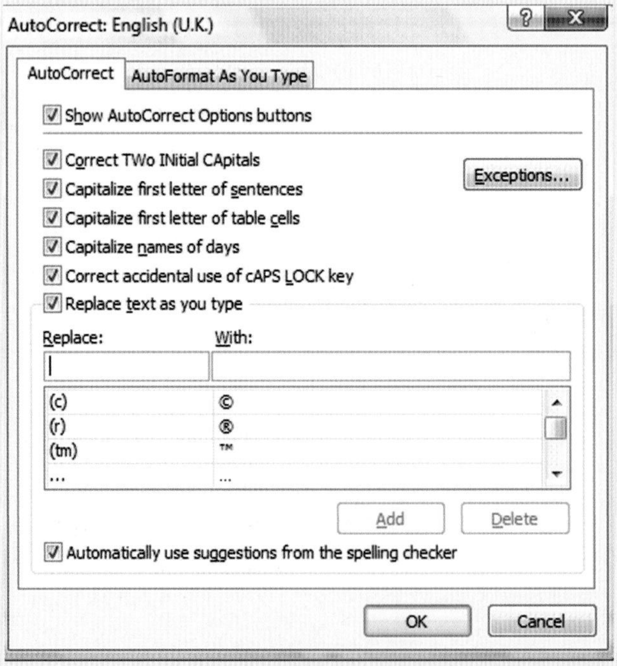

Figure 22

AutoCorrect

The AutoCorrect feature in Microsoft Publisher can correct mistakes without you even knowing. AutoCorrect will automatically correct common spelling mistakes. If you type in 'recieve', it will automatically be corrected to 'receive'.

Click on **Tools > AutoCorrect Options** and make sure that all the boxes are ticked, as in Figure 22.

Text wrap

Text wrap is where text goes round a picture. In the example in Figure 23, we can get the text to go around the image of the car.

WJEC Information & Communication Technology for AS

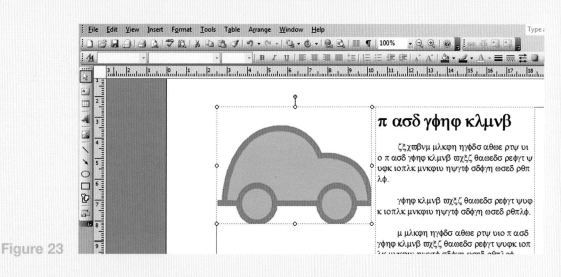

Figure 23

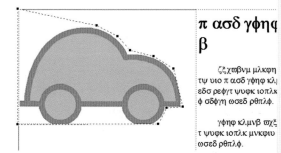

1 Select the car image.
2 Click on **Arrange > Text Wrapping > Edit Wrap Points**.
3 Bend the red dashed line around the front of the car as shown in Figure 24.
4 Move the text box over the car. The text should wrap around the image as shown in Figure 25.

Linking text boxes

Suppose you have a story in a text box on page 1 of your document. The story does not fit in its text box so you want to continue it on page 2. To make sure that, whatever the font or the size of the text boxes, the story still continues on page 2, you need to link two text boxes together.

1 Create a blank text box on page 2.
2 Select the text box on page 1.
3 Click on the **Create Text Box Link** icon shown in Figure 26.
4 The pointer changes to a jug. Switch to page 2 and click on the text box you want to connect to.

Columns

You can put text into columns as follows:

1 Highlight the text box you wish to put into columns.
2 Click on **Format > Text Box**.

Figure 24

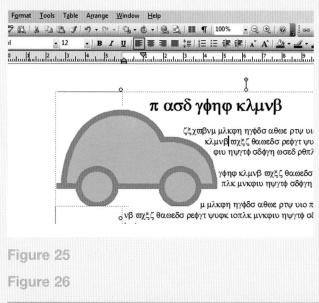

Figure 25

Figure 26

3 Click on the **Text Box** tab.
4 Click on **Columns**. Set the number of columns then click on **OK** twice.

If you format a story to, say, two columns, the whole story will be in two columns, including any headline within the text box. You will need to put the headline in a different text box, formatted to just one column.

Margins

You can change the page margins by clicking on **Arrange > Layout Guides** and setting the margin guides, as in Figure 27.

AutoShapes

AutoShapes are fancy shapes such as arrows, speech bubbles and stars.

1 Add an AutoShape by clicking on the **AutoShapes** icon in the Objects menu – see Figure 28.
2 Choose the required shape then drag a rectangle onto the screen to create the shape.
3 To format the colour of the shape, right click on the shape and choose **Format AutoShape**.

Figure 27

Figure 28

Spacing objects equally

If you have a number of objects such as text boxes that you wish to space out equally:

1 Select all the objects (as in *Selecting two or more objects*, page 203).
2 Click on **Arrange > Align** or **Distribute > Distribute Vertically**.

Keyboard shortcuts

Here are some time-saving keyboard shortcuts for some of the most commonly used options:

CTRL + =	superscript
CTRL + SHIFT + =	subscript
CTRL + B	bold text
CTRL + I	italic
CTRL + U	underline
CTRL + SHIFT + K	small caps
CTRL + SHIFT + <	decreases the font size by a half point
CTRL + SHIFT + >	increases the font size by a half point
CTRL + SHIFT + G	group/ungroup
CTRL + SPACEBAR	removes all style formats from the highlighted text
ALT + F6	bring to the front
ALT + SHIFT + F6	send to the back.

WJEC Information & Communication Technology for AS

What you must hand in

You must hand in the final printout of your document. But you must also hand in evidence that you have covered every part of the marking scheme (see page 209).

You will need to include the following:

1 The background and user requirements

Example

Chris Jackson is a friend of my father's. He owns a business called CMJ Digital that installs satellite dishes and TV aerials. With the switch to digital, a lot of people need a dish or a new aerial.

Chris is keen to get work from these people. At present he advertises by posting flyers through people's letterboxes near where he lives.

Chris has asked me to redesign the flyer to make it more eye-catching and include the Freesat logo.

2 How similar information is processed and communicated by the organisation at present

Example

At present CMJ Digital produce a large number of these flyers, which are individually delivered through the letterboxes of local homes. This will continue with the new design.

3 The purpose of document(s) you are creating

Example

The purpose of the flyer is to inform residents of the services offered by CMJ Digital. The design must be eye-catching. The resident will pick up the flyer by their front door and within five seconds deposit it in the recycling bin. I have just five seconds in which to attract their attention.

4 The intended audience

Example

The audience is any local residents.

5 Detailed designs of the document(s)

Example

See Figure 4, page 194.

6 Printouts of all your completed documents. These printouts should be annotated to point out use of features in the marking scheme, as in Figure 29. For example, if you have used bullet points or WordArt, annotate your printout to say so. Include 'before and after' screenshot evidence of features such as layering, use of subscripts or superscripts and customising tables. If you have used watermarks and styles, include screenshot evidence of creating them.

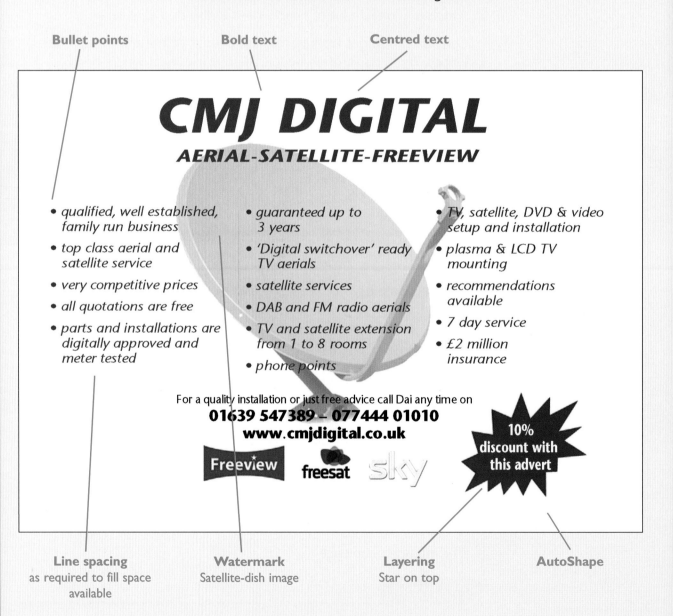

Bullet points

Bold text

Centred text

CMJ DIGITAL
AERIAL-SATELLITE-FREEVIEW

- *qualified, well established, family run business*
- *top class aerial and satellite service*
- *very competitive prices*
- *all quotations are free*
- *parts and installations are digitally approved and meter tested*

- *guaranteed up to 3 years*
- *'Digital switchover' ready TV aerials*
- *satellite services*
- *DAB and FM radio aerials*
- *TV and satellite extension from 1 to 8 rooms*
- *phone points*

- *TV, satellite, DVD & video setup and installation*
- *plasma & LCD TV mounting*
- *recommendations available*
- *7 day service*
- *£2 million insurance*

For a quality installation or just free advice call Dai any time on
01639 547389 – 077444 01010
www.cmjdigital.co.uk

Freeview   freesat   sky

10% discount with this advert

Line spacing
as required to fill space available

Watermark
Satellite-dish image

Layering
Star on top

AutoShape

Figure 29 Annotated printout of new flyer for CMJ Digital

Marking scheme – Task 1

Components	Criteria	Marks
Design of document	Purpose of document/intended user	2
	Detailed design of document	4
Use of basic features	Different font styles and sizes	1
	Bold, centre and underline	1
	AutoShapes	1
	Right or full justification	1
	Bullet points	1
	WordArt	1
	Shading effects	1
	Headers and footers	1
	At least **two** forms of electronic combination of graphical images – for example, scanned images, graphics from the Internet, clip-art from disk, digital-camera images, graphs from a spreadsheet, graphics from a paint or CAD package	2
	Tables	1
Use of advanced features	*Each of the following may be awarded 1 mark – up to a maximum of 5 marks for this section.*	
	Different paragraph formats	1
	Different line spacing	1
	Superscripts and subscripts	1
	Customised tables	1
	Page or frame borders	1
	Setting and using own tabs	1
	Setting and using own indents	1
	Watermarks	1
	Pagination	1
	Layering (forward and behind)	1
	Own style sheets	1
		Max 5

Automated Documents

What you have to do in this task

For this task you have to use a word-processing package to produce documents containing automated routines such as mail-merged letters including macros.

You will need to produce evidence of:

▶ importing data from an external file
▶ designing and using a professional format and layout for data
▶ testing that automated routines work.

To get higher marks you will need to produce evidence of using some of the following features:

▶ individual macros or modules created using internal programming capabilities of the software package
▶ individually designed templates (other than the normal template or standard templates provided by wizards in the software package).

Mail merge

In this chapter you will learn how to create a mail-merged letter using Microsoft Word.

A **mail-merged letter** includes data imported from a database, such as a name and address, to give the impression that the letter has been individually written just for you.

For example, if Mrs Harris has bought a Ford Mondeo and Mr Jones has bought a Ford Focus, part of the seller's database will look like this:

Mrs Harris	Ford Mondeo
Mr Jones	Ford Focus

A mail-merged letter can be set up so that Mrs Harris receives this letter:

Dear Mrs Harris
Thank you for purchasing a new Ford Mondeo ...

while Mr Jones receives this letter:

Dear Mr Jones
Thank you for purchasing a new Ford Focus ...

▶ Importing data

You can import the data for your letter from a variety of software applications. For example:

▶ a table in Microsoft Word
▶ a worksheet in Microsoft Excel
▶ a table in Microsoft Access.

In the examples in this chapter, we shall use a worksheet in Microsoft Excel but you could use Word or Access if you prefer.

You do not need the latest version of the software for this work. You can produce mail-merged letters in all versions of Microsoft Word but the commands and icons in Word 2007 are slightly different from those in Word XP or 2003.

Your screen may differ slightly from the screenshots shown here depending on the version of Windows you are using and the screen resolution.

Download link
The file for the spreadsheet **customer file.xls**, which appears in Figure 1 and is used later in this task, can be downloaded from www.hodderplus.co.uk/wjec-ict-as

	A	B	C	D	E	F	G	H	I	J	K
1	Account no	Title	Forename	Surname	Address1	Address2	Postcode	Instalment	January	February	March
2	8560001	Mr	Philip	Rogers	49 Arthurs Court	Neath	SA10 0GS	£580.87	Y	Y	Y
3	8560002	Miss	Nicky	Ellis	42 Manchester Close	Swansea	SA3 2DK	£163.46	Y	Y	Y
4	8560003	Mr	ApOwen	Morgan	28 Blackpool Drive	Neath	SA10 8KF	£248.15	Y	Y	Y
5	8560004	Ms	Carla	Price	17 Green Street	Swansea	SA4 0DK	£381.60	Y	N	N
6	8560005	Mr	Matthew	Evans	31 Church Street	Neath	SA10 0FS	£59.85	Y	Y	Y
7	8560006	Miss	Vicky	Jones	23 Greenacres Drive	Swansea	SA4 0KS	£320.86	Y	Y	Y
8	8560007	Miss	Gwladys	Wicks	67 Main Street	Swansea	SA4 9QW	£65.25	Y	Y	Y
9	8560008	Ms	Lucy	Davis	21 Tipping Road	Neath	SA10 0PP	£38.31	Y	N	N
10	8560009	Mr	Keith	Wardle	101 Spencer Close	Neath	SA10 0LS	£250.3	Y	Y	Y
11	8560010	Mrs	Lucy	Pugh	19 Heol Trefor	Swansea	SA9 9PK	£232.88	Y	Y	Y
12	8560011	Miss	Megan	Evans	10 Greenacres Drive	Swansea	SA4 0KS	£190.47	Y	Y	Y
13	8560012	Mr	Iwan	Davies	74 Heol Gerrig	Swansea	SA4 0BS	£27.29	Y	Y	Y
14	8560013	Mrs	Rachel	Edwards	37 Arennig Road	Swansea	SA4 0GS	£372.44	Y	Y	Y
15	8560014	Mrs	Gemma	Green	23 Orchard Road	Swansea	SA4 8GF	£119.21	N	N	N
16	8560015	Miss	Samantha	Harding	12 Arennig Road	Swansea	SA4 0GS	£460.7	Y	Y	Y
17	8560016	Mrs	Katy	Walters	34 Green Street	Neath	SA10 0DK	£280.17	Y	Y	Y
18	8560017	Mr	Dylan	Williams	42 Heol Trefor	Swansea	SA9 9PK	£180.31	Y	Y	Y
19	8560018	Miss	Carys	Williams	12 Riverside Close	Neath	SA10 0GS	£240.11	Y	Y	Y
20	8560019	Mrs	Catrin	Roberts	23 Heol Trefor	Swansea	SA9 9PK	£297.81	Y	Y	Y
21	8560020	Mr	Gwyn	Griffiths	75 Heol Gerrig	Swansea	SA4 0BS	£106.60	Y	Y	N
22	8560021	Mrs	Katy	Jones	23 Blackpool Drive	Swansea	SA4 8KF	£351.33	Y	Y	Y

Customers / Sheet2 / Sheet3 /

Figure 1

Figure 1 shows part of a customer file in Excel. The worksheet contains the names and addresses of customers who have borrowed money from PDQ Finance to buy a car. It also contains the instalment that they must pay every month in order to pay off the loan and indicates whether or not they have paid the instalment due in January, February, etc.

We are going to:

▶ compose **conditional** mail-merged letters which will be sent to only some of the people in a database, such as:

  a customers who have not paid their instalment for a certain month

  b customers who are in arrears (for example, no payment in February, March or April)

▶ automate tasks with macros.

We must also ensure that the letters look professional.

Creating a letter

▶ Professional-looking design

The exam specification says that you must use a professional format and layout for your letter. It is a good idea to look at professional letterheads. Look at your school's/college's headed paper:

▶ What information is on the headed paper?

▶ Where is it? Left aligned? Right aligned? Centred?

▶ Is there any information at the bottom of the page?

There are also several templates for letters in Microsoft Word. You can choose one of these:

1 Click on **File > New > General Templates** (**General Templates** is in the menu on the right of the screen).

2 Click on the **Letters & Faxes** tab then select **Professional Letter** and click on **OK**.

We shall start creating the letter from scratch, but if you look at the various templates available for professional letters, you will find that most of them follow these rules:

▶ The company address, phone number, fax number and e-mail address appear first, at the top of the letter (usually left aligned or centred).

▶ The date comes next, left aligned.

▶ The name and address of the recipient (the person who you are writing to) comes next, left aligned.

▶ Then comes the **salutation** (for example, 'Dear Mrs Roberts'), left aligned.

▶ Then comes the title of the letter – what is it about. This may be centred or left aligned and may be in bold.

▶ Then comes the text of the letter, left aligned with a line space after each paragraph. Paragraphs are not indented.

▶ The letter finishes with 'Yours sincerely', left aligned, followed by a 5-line gap in which to sign the letter.

▶ The name of the writer of the letter and their job title, left aligned, come after the 5-line gap.

▶ Designing your letter

1 Describe, in detail, the purpose of the document. What will it be used for? What data will be merged into your document?

2 Draw some rough sketches of what you think the page should look like. They don't have to be exact but they should be neat – use a ruler. You can do your design on computer if you wish but it is probably easier to draw it A4 size on plain paper using a pencil.

Your design should show:

a page size
b page orientation
c margins
d an outline layout of the page
e position of address, date, etc.
f fonts, colours and sizes to be used
g position of fields
h position of images such as a logo
i paragraph styles
j tab settings or indents.

3 Decide on the fields you will need to create in your database, such as (see Figure 1):

a Account no
b Title
c Forename
d Surname
e Address1
f Address2
g Postcode.

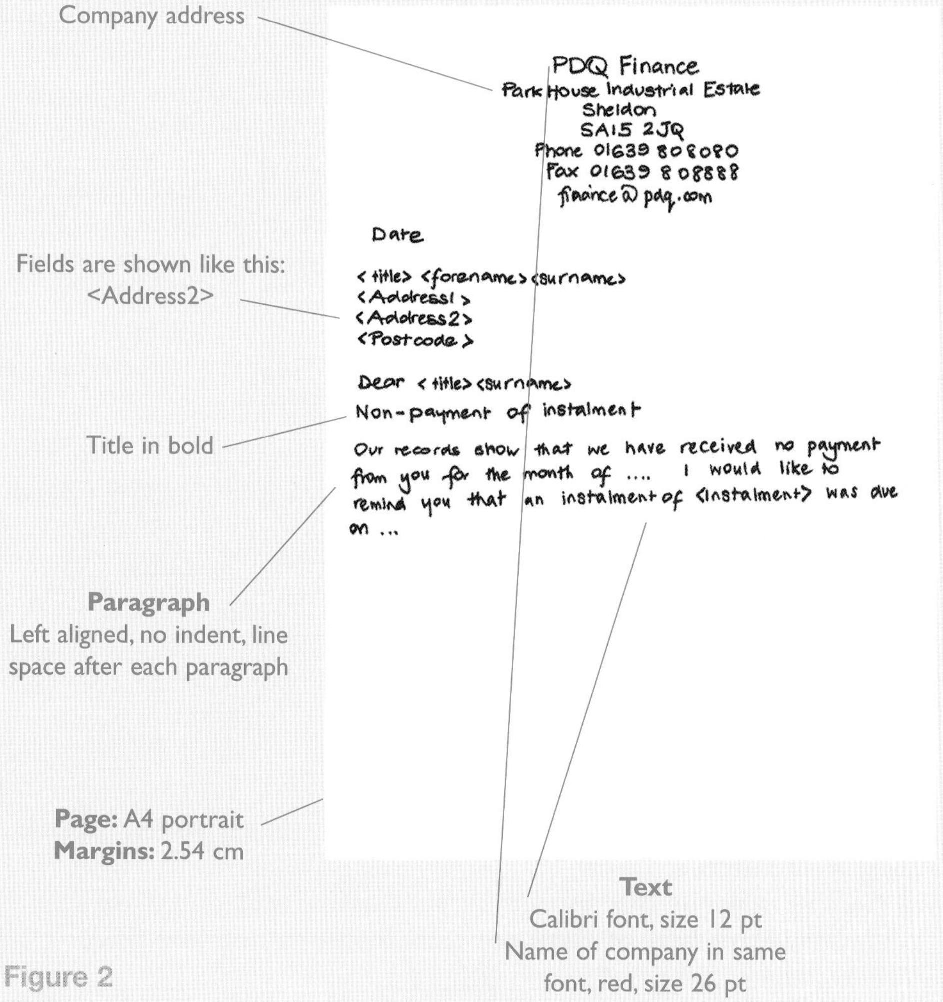

This is not always as easy as it seems, particularly deciding on how to store customers' names. It is generally better to store names in three fields: title, forename and surname. This means that it is possible to put a customer's full name above their address but to have a salutation such as 'Dear Mrs Roberts'.

4 Remember to follow the rules about professional layout in your design.

5 Take your time. You may not get it right first go.

Figure 2 shows a design for a letter to PDQ Finance.

Company address

Fields are shown like this:
<Address2>

Title in bold

Paragraph
Left aligned, no indent, line space after each paragraph

Page: A4 portrait
Margins: 2.54 cm

PDQ Finance
Park House Industrial Estate
Sheldon
SA15 2JQ
Phone 01639 808080
Fax 01639 808888
finance@pdq.com

Date

< title> <forename> <surname>
<Address1>
<Address2>
<Postcode>

Dear < title> <surname>
Non-payment of instalment

Our records show that we have received no payment from you for the month of .... I would like to remind you that an instalment of <instalment> was due on ...

Text
Calibri font, size 12 pt
Name of company in same font, red, size 26 pt

Figure 2

Creating the document

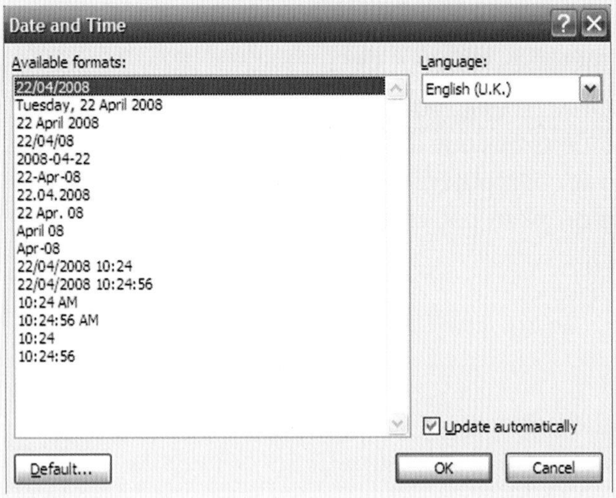

Figure 3

When you are happy with your design, you can begin to create your document:

1 Open a new blank document and enter the company name, address and other details at the top of the page as in your design.
2 Give your file a name and save it – for example, as **PDQ Finance.doc**.
3 Enter the date by clicking on **Insert > Date & Time**. Choose the format of the date that you require then tick the **Update automatically** box as shown in Figure 3. Then click on **OK**.

Creating the database

You will need a database of names and addresses to merge with the letter. You can either use a database that you have created yourself or, to save time, you can download the file used here called **customer file.xls** which is shown in Figure 1. The address to use for downloading the file is www.hodderplus.co.uk/wjec-ict-as. If you set up your own file, you will need to use the same fields as in **customer file.xls**.

You are now in a position to set up the mail merge so that the recipients' names and addresses, etc., can be imported into your letter.

The next two sections show how to do this in Word 2007 and Word XP or 2003 using a letter saved as **PDQ Finance.doc** (based on a design like that shown in Figure 2) and the database **customer file.xls**.

Setting up the mail merge in Word 2007

1 Open the letter and click on **Mailings > Start Mail Merge > Step by Step Mail Merge Wizard**.
2 The **Mail Merge Task Pane** will appear on the right of the screen as shown in Figure 4. Choose **Letters** (if not already selected) then click on **Next: Starting document**.
3 Choose **Use the current document**.
4 Click on **Next: Select recipients**.
5 Choose **Use an existing list**.
6 Click on **Next: Write your letter**.
7 A dialogue box opens as in Figure 5. Find the file **customer file.xls**. Click on **Open**.
8 Another dialogue box appears. Select **Customers$** and make sure that the **First row of data contains column headers** box is ticked as in Figure 6. Click on **OK**.

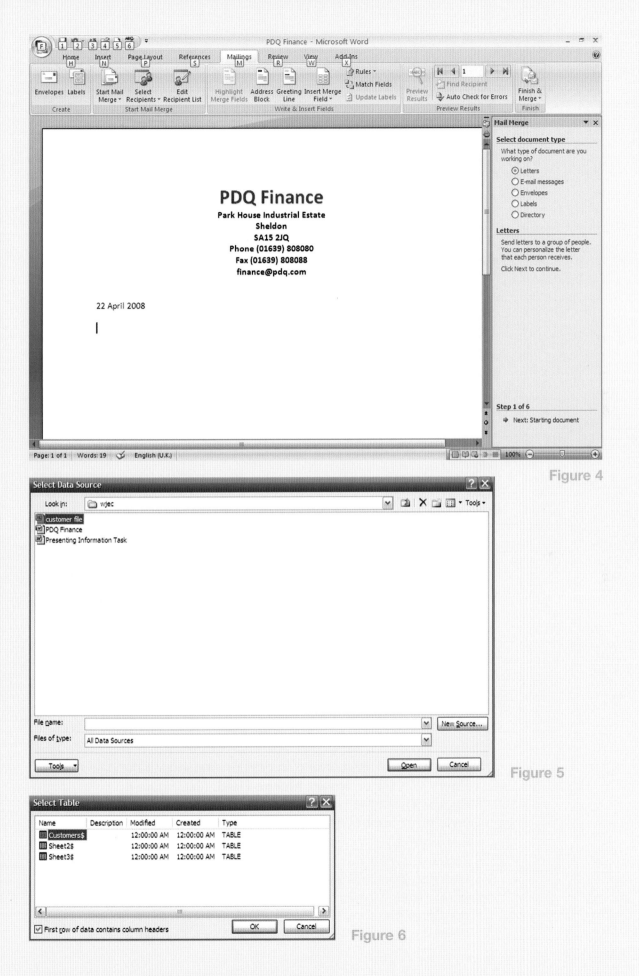

Figure 4

Figure 5

Figure 6

9 A third dialogue box appears as in Figure 7. Simply choose **OK**.

We are now ready to put in the mail-merge fields.

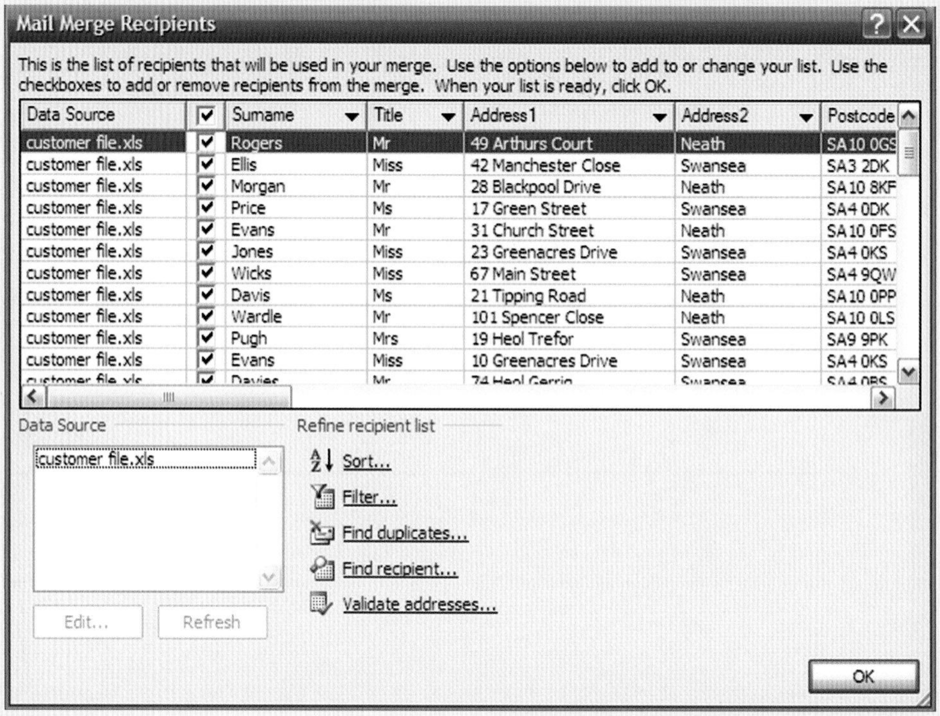

Mail Merge Recipients

This is the list of recipients that will be used in your merge. Use the options below to add to or change your list. Use the checkboxes to add or remove recipients from the merge. When your list is ready, click OK.

Data Source	✔	Surname ▼	Title ▼	Address1 ▼	Address2 ▼	Postcode ▲
customer file.xls	✔	Rogers	Mr	49 Arthurs Court	Neath	SA10 0GS
customer file.xls	✔	Ellis	Miss	42 Manchester Close	Swansea	SA3 2DK
customer file.xls	✔	Morgan	Mr	28 Blackpool Drive	Neath	SA10 8KF
customer file.xls	✔	Price	Ms	17 Green Street	Swansea	SA4 0DK
customer file.xls	✔	Evans	Mr	31 Church Street	Neath	SA10 0FS
customer file.xls	✔	Jones	Miss	23 Greenacres Drive	Swansea	SA4 0KS
customer file.xls	✔	Wicks	Miss	67 Main Street	Swansea	SA4 9QW
customer file.xls	✔	Davis	Ms	21 Tipping Road	Neath	SA10 0PP
customer file.xls	✔	Wardle	Mr	101 Spencer Close	Neath	SA10 0LS
customer file.xls	✔	Pugh	Mrs	19 Heol Trefor	Swansea	SA9 9PK
customer file.xls	✔	Evans	Miss	10 Greenacres Drive	Swansea	SA4 0KS
customer file.xls	✔	Davies	Mr	74 Heol Gerrig	Swansea	SA4 0BS

Data Source

customer file.xls

Refine recipient list

A↓ Sort...
Filter...
Find duplicates...
Find recipient...
Validate addresses...

Edit...   Refresh

OK

Figure 7

Figure 8

Insert Merge Field

Insert:
○ Address Fields   ◉ Database Fields

Fields:
Account no
Title
Forename
Surname
Address1
Address2
Postcode
Instalment
January
February
March
April
May
June
July

Match Fields...   Insert   Cancel

PDQ Finance - Microsoft Word

Mailings   Review   View   Add-Ins

Highlight   Address   Greeting   Insert Merge
Merge Fields   Block   Line   Field ▼

Rules ▼
Match Fields
Update Labels

Write & Insert Fields

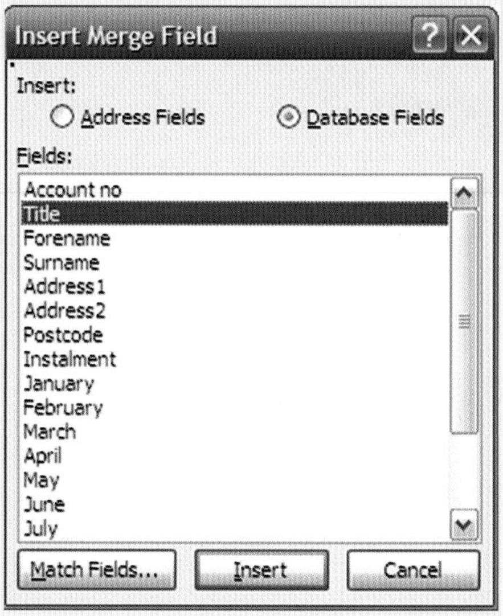

Figure 9

10 Make sure that the cursor is in position underneath the date (as in Figure 4). Click on **Insert Merge Field**. (See Figure 8.)
11 Choose **Title** as in Figure 9 then click on **Insert**. Click on **Close**.
12 Press the space bar (to insert a space between the title and the forename).
13 Repeat steps 10 and 11 for the **Forename**.
14 Press the space bar again.
15 Repeat steps 10 and 11 for the **Surname**. The letter will now look like Figure 10.
16 Continue adding fields until the letter looks like Figure 11.

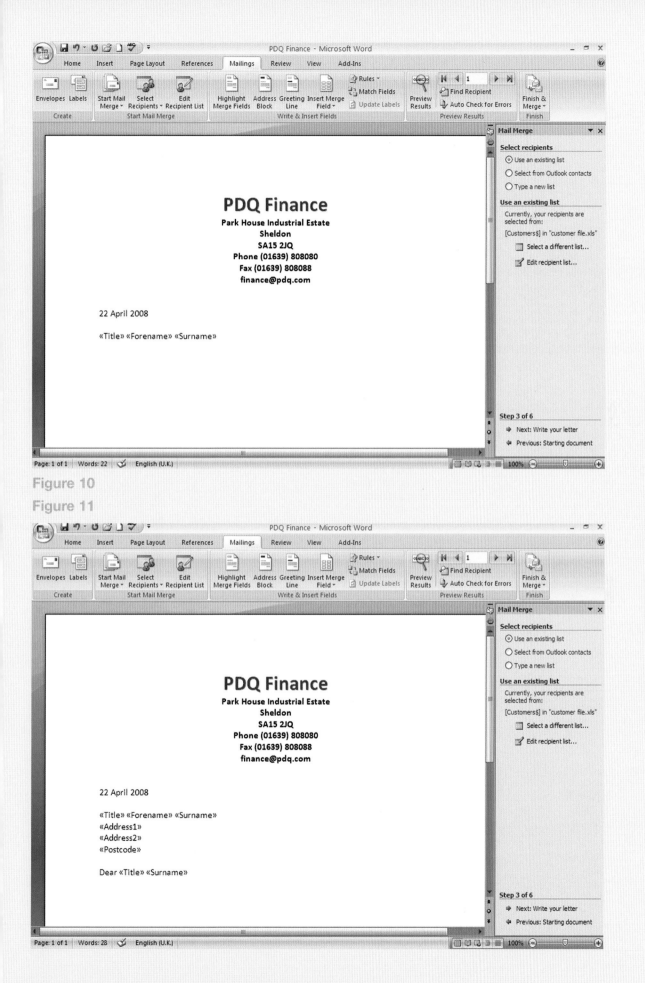

Figure 10

Figure 11

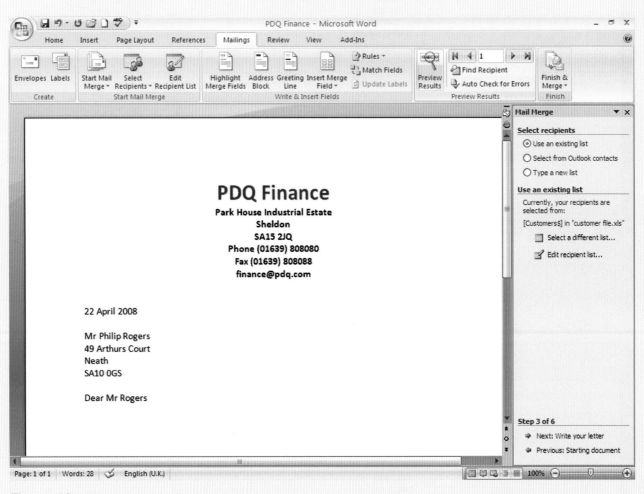

Figure 12

17 Click on the **Preview Results** icon (see Figure 12) to see what the first letter will look like. It should look like Figure 13.

Figure 13

By clicking on the **Next record** arrow (see Figure 14), you can scroll through all the records.

18 Continue writing the letter so that it looks like Figure 15.

At present the letter will go to all customers whether they have paid in April or not. We need to filter the customer file so that the letter only goes to the non-payers.

Next record

Figure 14

19 Click on the **Edit Recipient List** icon (see Figure 16). The dialogue box shown in Figure 7 will reappear.

20 Click on **Filter** as in Figure 17 and enter the data shown in Figure 18. Click on **OK**.

WJEC Information & Communication Technology for AS

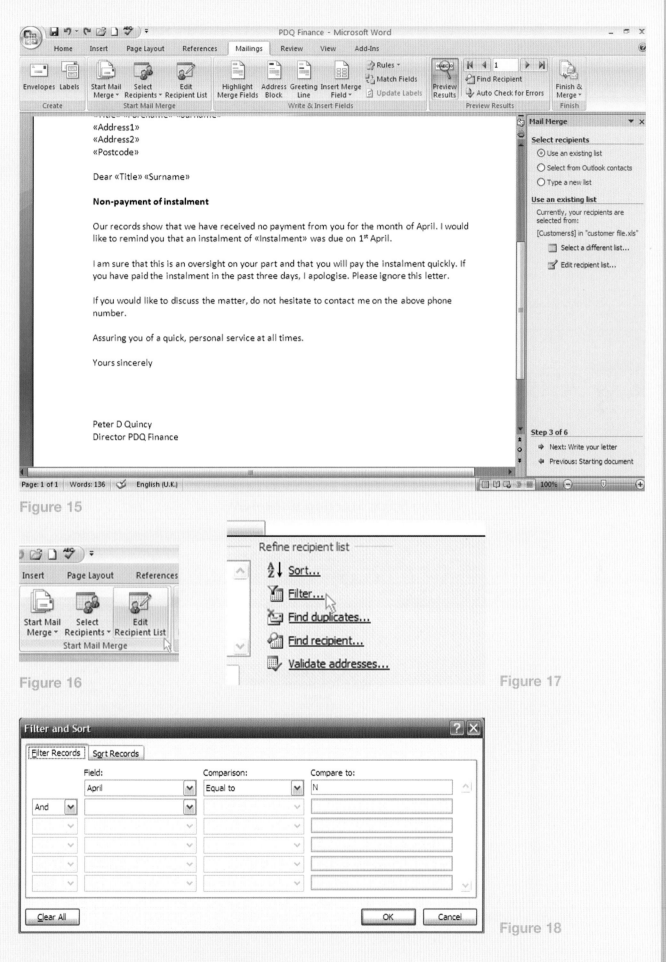

Figure 15

Figure 16

Figure 17

Figure 18

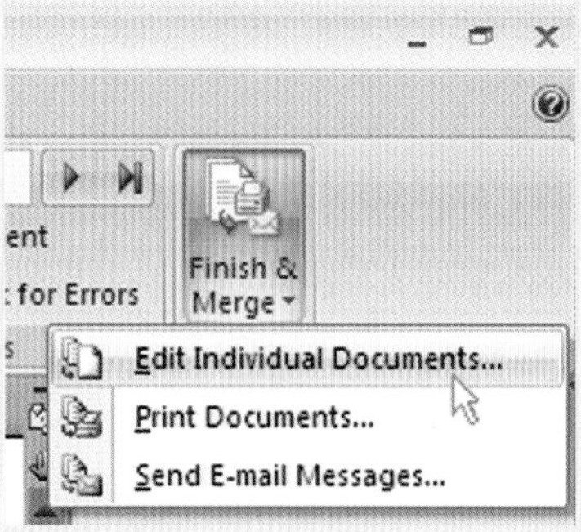

21 Clicking on the **Next Record** icon would show that in this example there are only seven records – corresponding to the seven customers who have not paid the April instalment.

22 Click on the **Finish & Merge** icon then **Edit Individual Documents** as in Figure 19.

Figure 19

23 A new document called **Letters1** loads. In this example, there should be seven different letters in this document.

24 Select **All** as in Figure 20. Click on **OK**.

25 Save **Letters1** – for example, as **April nonpayers.doc**. You can print this document if required.

Figure 20

Setting up the mail merge in Word XP or 2003

1 Open the letter and click on **Tools > Letters and Mailings > Mail Merge Wizard**.

2 The **Mail Merge Task Pane** will appear on the right of the screen as shown in Figure 21. Choose **Letters** (if not already selected) then click on **Next: Starting document**.

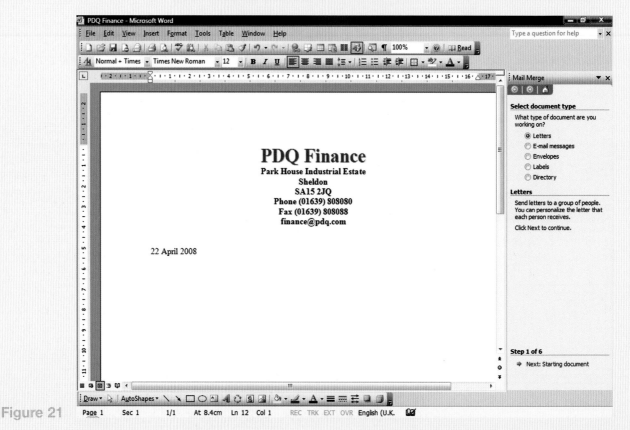

Figure 21

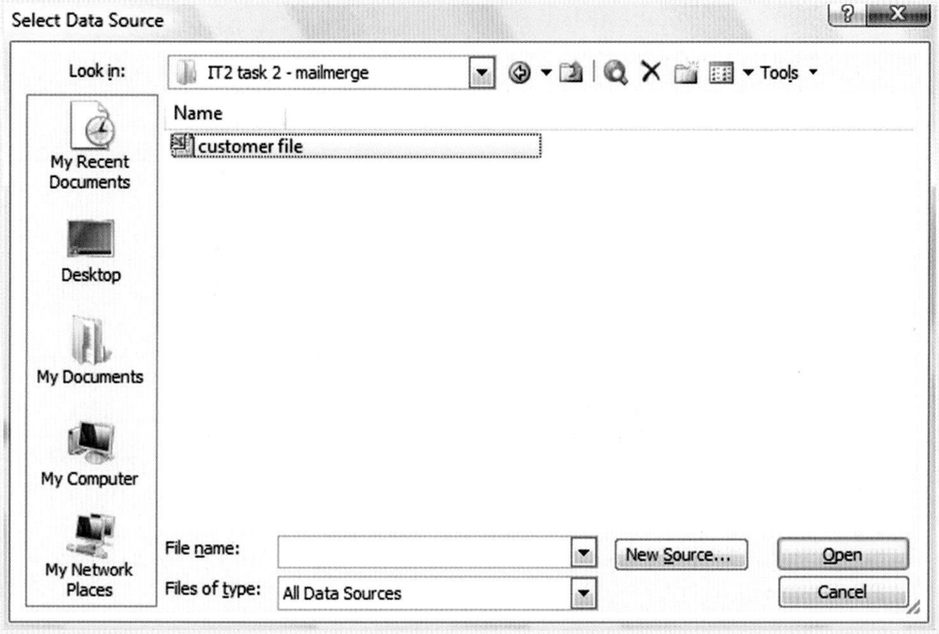

Select Data Source

Look in: IT2 task 2 - mailmerge

Name

customer file

My Recent Documents

Desktop

My Documents

My Computer

My Network Places

File name:

Files of type: All Data Sources

New Source...

Open

Cancel

Figure 22

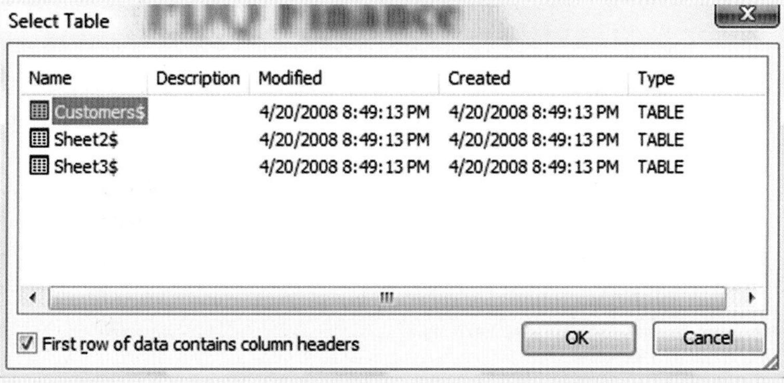

Select Table

Name	Description	Modified	Created	Type
Customers$		4/20/2008 8:49:13 PM	4/20/2008 8:49:13 PM	TABLE
Sheet2$		4/20/2008 8:49:13 PM	4/20/2008 8:49:13 PM	TABLE
Sheet3$		4/20/2008 8:49:13 PM	4/20/2008 8:49:13 PM	TABLE

☑ First row of data contains column headers

OK   Cancel

Figure 23

3 Choose **Use the current document**.
4 Click on **Next: Select recipients**.
5 Choose **Use an existing list**.
6 Click on **Next: Write your letter**.
7 A dialogue box opens as in Figure 22. Find the file **customer file.xls** Click on **Open**.
8 Another dialogue box appears. Select **Customers$** and make sure that the **First row of data contains column headers** box is ticked as in Figure 23. Click on **OK**.
9 A third dialogue box appears as in Figure 24. Simply choose **OK**.

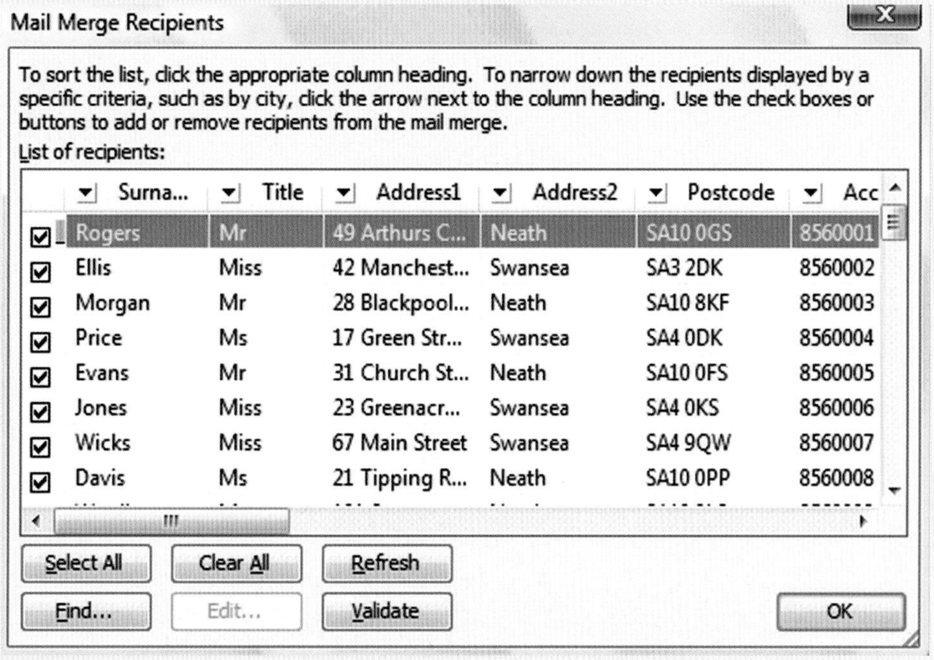

Mail Merge Recipients

To sort the list, click the appropriate column heading. To narrow down the recipients displayed by a specific criteria, such as by city, click the arrow next to the column heading. Use the check boxes or buttons to add or remove recipients from the mail merge.

List of recipients:

	Surna...	Title	Address1	Address2	Postcode	Acc
☑	Rogers	Mr	49 Arthurs C...	Neath	SA10 0GS	8560001
☑	Ellis	Miss	42 Manchest...	Swansea	SA3 2DK	8560002
☑	Morgan	Mr	28 Blackpool...	Neath	SA10 8KF	8560003
☑	Price	Ms	17 Green Str...	Swansea	SA4 0DK	8560004
☑	Evans	Mr	31 Church St...	Neath	SA10 0FS	8560005
☑	Jones	Miss	23 Greenacr...	Swansea	SA4 0KS	8560006
☑	Wicks	Miss	67 Main Street	Swansea	SA4 9QW	8560007
☑	Davis	Ms	21 Tipping R...	Neath	SA10 0PP	8560008

Select All   Clear All   Refresh

Find...   Edit...   Validate   OK

Figure 24

We are now ready to put in the mail-merge fields.

10 Make sure that the cursor is in position underneath the date. If the mail-merge toolbar is not visible, click on **View > Toolbars > Mail Merge**.

11 Click on the **Insert Merge Fields** icon (see Figure 25).

12 Choose **Title** as in Figure 26 then click on **Insert**. Click on **Close**.

13 Press the space bar (to insert a space between the title and the forename).

14 Repeat steps 11 and 12 for the **Forename**.

15 Press the space bar again.

16 Repeat steps 11 and 12 for the **Surname**. The letter will now look like Figure 27.

17 Continue adding fields until the letter looks like Figure 28.

18 Click on the **View Merged Data** icon (see Figure 29) to see what the first letter will look like. It should look like Figure 30.

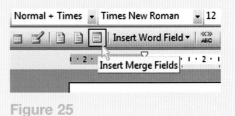

Figure 25

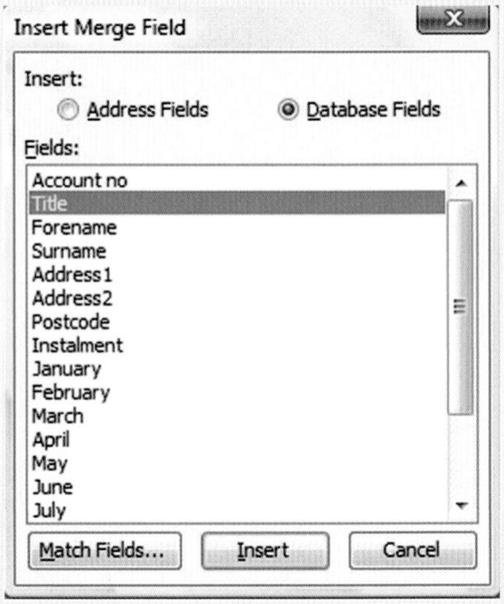

Figure 26

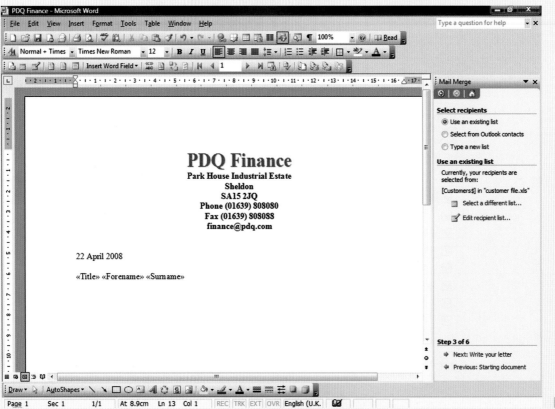

Figure 27

WJEC Information & Communication Technology for AS

Figure 28

UNIT 2 Presenting Information

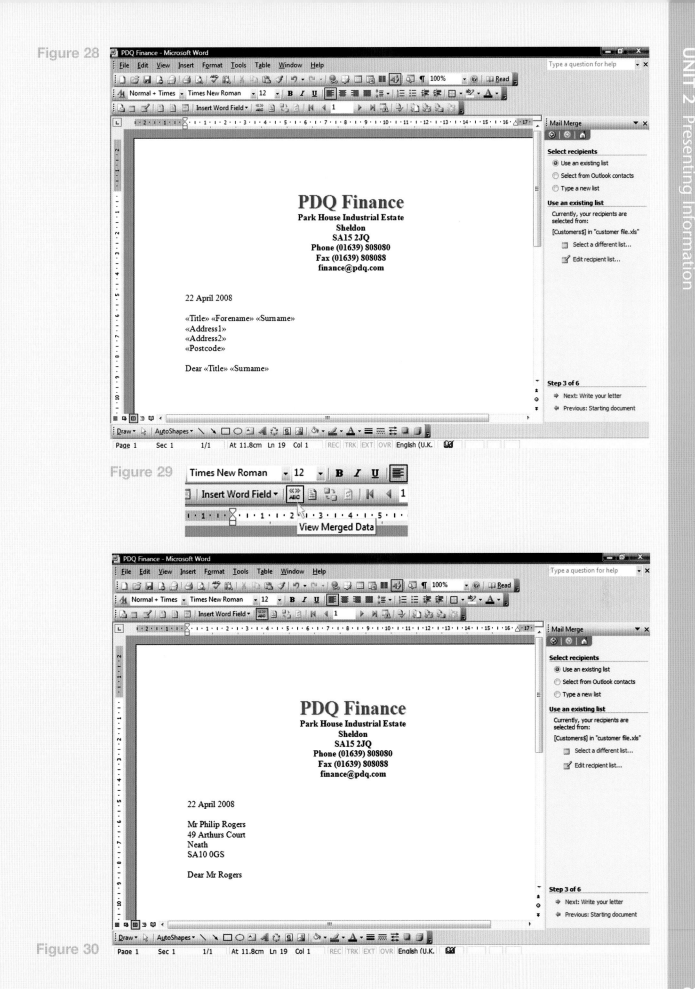

Figure 29

View Merged Data

Figure 30

By clicking on the **Next record** arrow (Figure 31), you can scroll through all the records.

19 Continue writing the letter so that it looks like Figure 32.

Figure 31

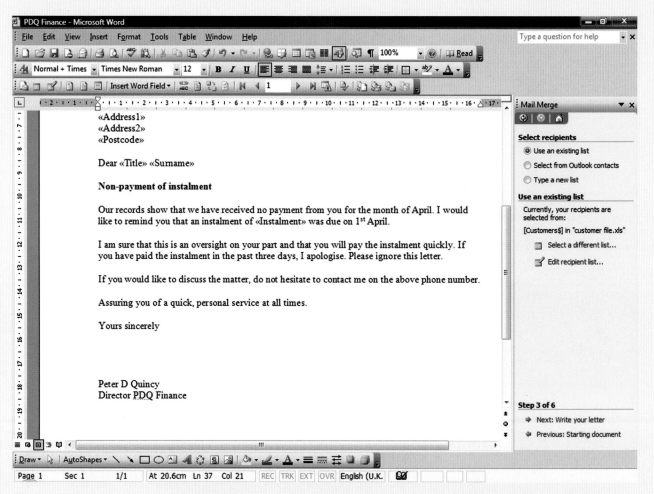

Figure 32

At present the letter will go to all customers whether they have paid in April or not. We need to filter the customer file so that the letter only goes to the non-payers.

20 Click on the **Mail Merge Recipients** icon (see Figure 33). The dialogue box shown in Figure 24 will reappear.

21 Scroll to the right until you see the April column heading. Click on the arrow to the left of **April** and choose **N** from the drop-down list as in Figure 34.

22 Click on **OK**.

23 Click on the **View Merged Data** icon. Clicking on the **Next Record** icon would show that in this example there are only seven records – corresponding to the seven customers who have not paid the April instalment.

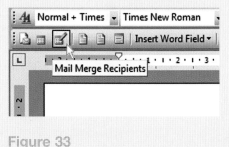

Figure 33

WJEC Information & Communication Technology for AS

24 Click on the **Merge to New Document** icon (see Figure 35). The dialogue box shown in Figure 36 appears. Click on **OK**.

25 A new document called **Letters1** loads. In this example, it should contain seven different letters. Save this document – for example, as **April nonpayers.doc**. You can print it if required.

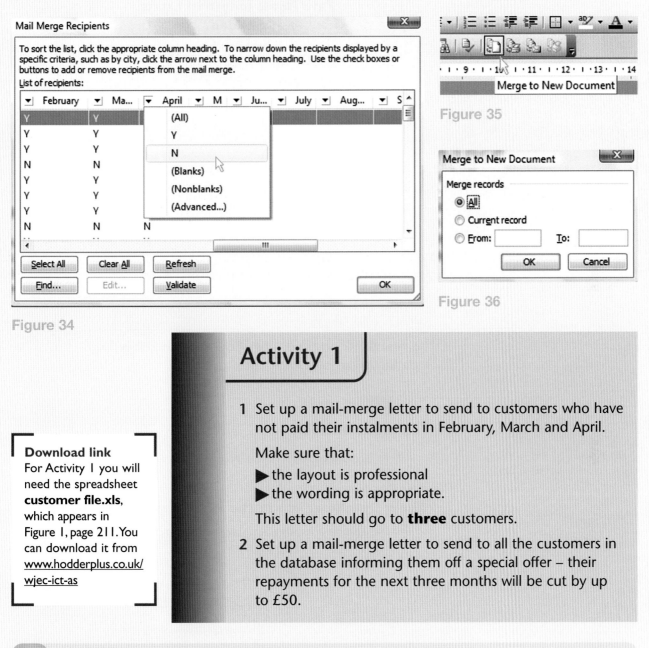

Figure 34

Figure 35

Figure 36

Activity 1

Download link
For Activity 1 you will need the spreadsheet **customer file.xls**, which appears in Figure 1, page 211. You can download it from www.hodderplus.co.uk/wjec-ict-as

1 Set up a mail-merge letter to send to customers who have not paid their instalments in February, March and April.

Make sure that:
▶ the layout is professional
▶ the wording is appropriate.

This letter should go to **three** customers.

2 Set up a mail-merge letter to send to all the customers in the database informing them off a special offer – their repayments for the next three months will be cut by up to £50.

Automating actions with macros and customising toolbars

▶ What is a macro?

A macro is a way of simplifying use of the computer. It replaces a commonly used long sequence of commands with one command (called a **macro**).

For example, PDQ Finance always put their address and other details at the top of a letter as follows:

PDQ Finance
Park House Industrial Estate
Sheldon
SA15 2JQ
Phone (01639) 808080
Fax (01639) 808088
finance@pdq.com

This is followed by the date.

We can set up a macro to enter this data at the click of a button. This will save a lot of time spent typing it all out.

▶ What is meant by customising the toolbars?

You can customise the **toolbars** in any way you like. You can add, edit or remove icons. You can add a button to run a macro.

▶ Recording a macro in Word 2007

1 Start a new blank document by clicking on the **New** icon.
2 Click on the Microsoft Office button:

3 Click on **Word Options**:

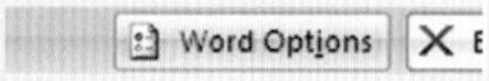

    [Word Options] ✕ E

4 Click on **Popular** (if not already selected).
5 Tick **Show Developer tab in the Ribbon** as in Figure 37.

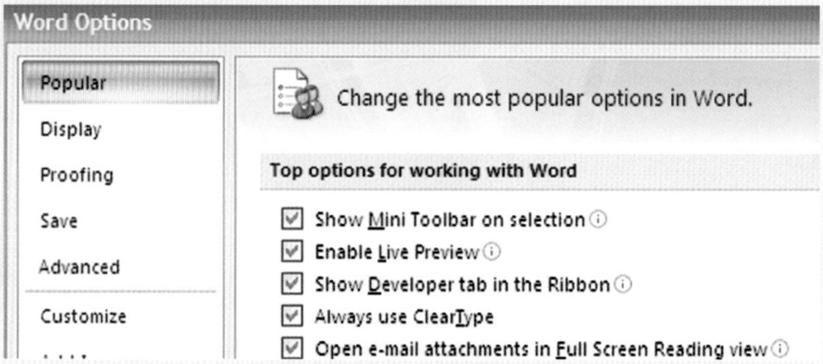

Word Options

Popular		Change the most popular options in Word.
Display		
Proofing		**Top options for working with Word**
Save		☑ Show Mini Toolbar on selection ⓘ
Advanced		☑ Enable Live Preview ⓘ
Customize		☑ Show Developer tab in the Ribbon ⓘ
		☑ Always use ClearType
. . . .		☑ Open e-mail attachments in Full Screen Reading view ⓘ

Figure 37

6 Click on the **Developer** tab.
7 Click on the **Record Macro** tab. Alternatively, click on the **Record Macro** icon at the bottom of the screen (see Figure 38).

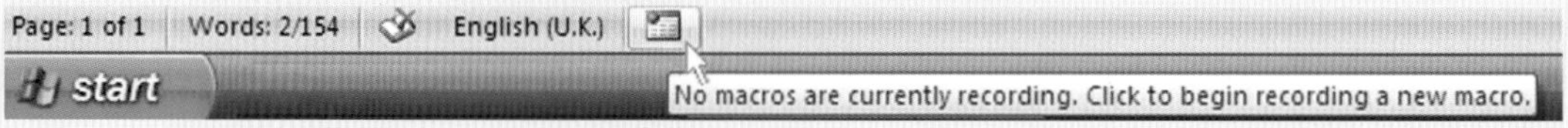

Page: 1 of 1 | Words: 2/154 | 🕮 | English (U.K.) | 📖

🏁 **start**   No macros are currently recording. Click to begin recording a new macro.

Figure 38

226

Record Macro

Macro name:
Address

Assign macro to

Button   Keyboard

Store macro in:
All Documents (Normal.dotm)

Description:

OK   Cancel

Figure 39

8 The Record Macro dialogue box appears. Set the macro name to **Address** as in Figure 39.

9 Click on **OK**.

The macro is now recording every keystroke that you make. Note that in the toolbar there are now two new commands: **Stop Recording** and **Pause Recording** (see Figure 40).

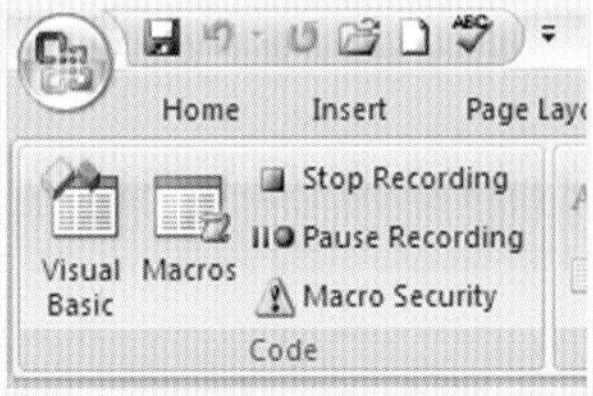

Home   Insert   Page Layo

Stop Recording
Pause Recording
Macro Security

Visual   Macros
Basic

Code

Figure 40

10 Click on the **Home** tab then the **Align Center** icon. Set the font to **Calibri**, size **26**, colour **red**. Type in **PDQ Finance**.

11 Press ENTER. Set the font size to **12**, colour **black**.

12 Type in **Park House Industrial Estate**. Press ENTER.

13 Type in **Sheldon**. Press ENTER.

14 Type in **SA15 2JQ**. Press ENTER.

15 Type in **Phone (01639) 808080**. Press ENTER.

16 Type in **Fax (01639) 808088**. Press ENTER.

17 Type in **finance@pdq.com**. Press ENTER twice.

18 Click on the **Align Left** icon. Click the **Insert** tab and choose **Date & Time.** Choose the version of the date that you want then click on **OK**.

19 Press ENTER twice then click on the **Developer** tab and choose **Stop Recording**.

▶ Recording a macro in Word XP or 2003

1 Start a new blank document by clicking on the **New** icon.

2 Click on **Tools > Macro > Record New Macro**.

3 The Record Macro dialogue box appears. Set the macro name to **Address** as in Figure 41.

4 Click on **OK.**

Record Macro

Macro name:
Address

Assign macro to

Toolbars   Keyboard

Store macro in:
All Documents (Normal.dot)

Description:
Macro recorded 24/4/2008

OK   Cancel

Figure 41

The macro is now recording every keystroke that you make.

The Stop Recording toolbar

will now be visible. It has just two icons: **Stop Recording** and **Pause Recording**.

Note that in the status bar at the bottom of the screen **REC** is now in black instead of grey to show that you are recording (see Figure 42). You will also see that the cursor has turned into an arrow and a miniature cassette tape.

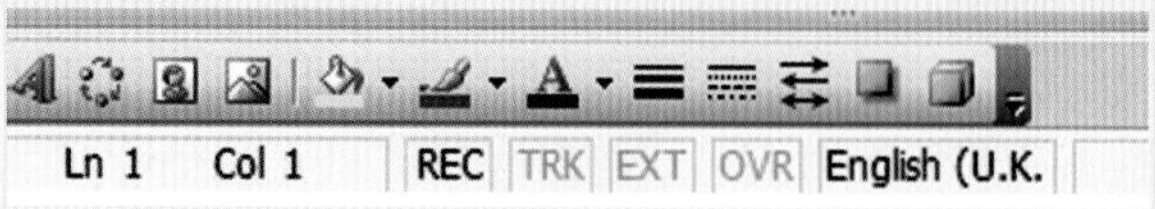

Figure 42

5 Click on the **Align Center** icon. Set the font to **Times New Roman**, size **18**, colour **red**. Type in **PDQ Finance**.
6 Press ENTER. Set the font size to **12**, colour **black**.
7 Type in **Park House Industrial Estate**. Press ENTER.
8 Type in **Sheldon**. Press ENTER.
9 Type in **SA15 2JQ**. Press ENTER.
10 Type in **Phone (01639) 808080**. Press ENTER.
11 Type in **Fax (01639) 808088**. Press ENTER.
12 Type in **finance@pdq.com**. Press ENTER twice.
13 Click on the **Align Left** icon. Click on **Insert > Date and Time**. Choose the version of the date that you want then click on **OK**.
14 Press ENTER twice then stop recording. To do this, you can either click on the **Stop Recording** icon or click on **Tools > Macro >Stop Recording**.

▶ Running the macro

Every time you start a new letter, you can put the address at the top as follows:

1 Click on the **New** icon.
2 a In Word XP or 2003, run the macro by clicking on **Tools > Macro > Macros**. Select the **Address** macro then click on **Run**.
   b In Word 2007, run the macro by clicking on the **Developer** tab. Click on **Macros**. Select the **Address** macro then click on **Run**.

▶ Seeing the coding of your macro

Macros are automatically coded in a programming language called Visual Basic.

▶ In Word XP or 2003, you can see the coding of your macro by clicking on **Tools > Macro > Macros**. Select the **Address** macro then click on **Edit**.
▶ In Word 2007, click on the **Developer** tab then click on **Macros**. Select the **Address** macro then click on **Run**.

The Visual Basic Editor will load and you will see the coding of the macro, as in Figure 43. You can now edit the macro – for example, if you have made a mistake in typing the address.

At the moment, to run the macro you have to click on a number of icons. You can reduce the number of clicks required by customising the toolbars.

```
Normal - NewMacros (Code)

(General)                                    ▼   Address                                    ▼

    Sub Address()
    '
    ' Address Macro
    ' Macro recorded 24/4/2008

        Selection.ParagraphFormat.Alignment = wdAlignParagraphCenter
        Selection.Font.Size = 18
        Selection.Font.Color = wdColorRed
        Selection.TypeText Text:="PDG Finance"
        Selection.TypeParagraph
        Selection.Font.Size = 12
        Selection.Font.Color = wdColorBlack
        Selection.TypeText Text:="Park House Industrial Estate"
        Selection.TypeParagraph
        Selection.TypeText Text:="Sheldon"
        Selection.TypeParagraph
        Selection.TypeText Text:="SA15 2JQ"
        Selection.TypeParagraph
        Selection.TypeText Text:="Phone: (01639) 808080"
        Selection.TypeParagraph
        Selection.TypeText Text:="Fax: (01639) 808088"
        Selection.TypeParagraph
        Selection.TypeText Text:="finance@pdq.com"
        Selection.TypeParagraph
        Selection.TypeParagraph
        Selection.ParagraphFormat.Alignment = wdAlignParagraphLeft
        Selection.InsertDateTime DateTimeFormat:="dd MMMM yyyy", InsertAsFiel
            False, DateLanguage:=wdEnglishUK, CalendarType:=wdCalendarWester
            InsertAsFullWidth:=False
        Selection.TypeParagraph
        Selection.TypeParagraph
    End Sub
```

Figure 43

▶ Customising the quick access toolbar in Word 2007

The quick access toolbar

Figure 44

The quick access toolbar is a customisable toolbar, shown at the top of Figure 44. An icon can be added to the quick access toolbar to run the address macro as follows:

1 Click on the Microsoft Office button then click on **Word Options**.

The Word Options dialogue box appears.

2 Click on **Customize**. The screen now looks like Figure 45 on the following page.

3 Click on **Choose commands** from the drop-down list and choose **Macros**.

4 Select the macro **Normal.NewMacros.Address** and click on **Add>>**.

The macro name appears in the right-hand box as in Figure 46.

You can choose a different icon by clicking on **Modify**. You are given a choice as in Figure 47.

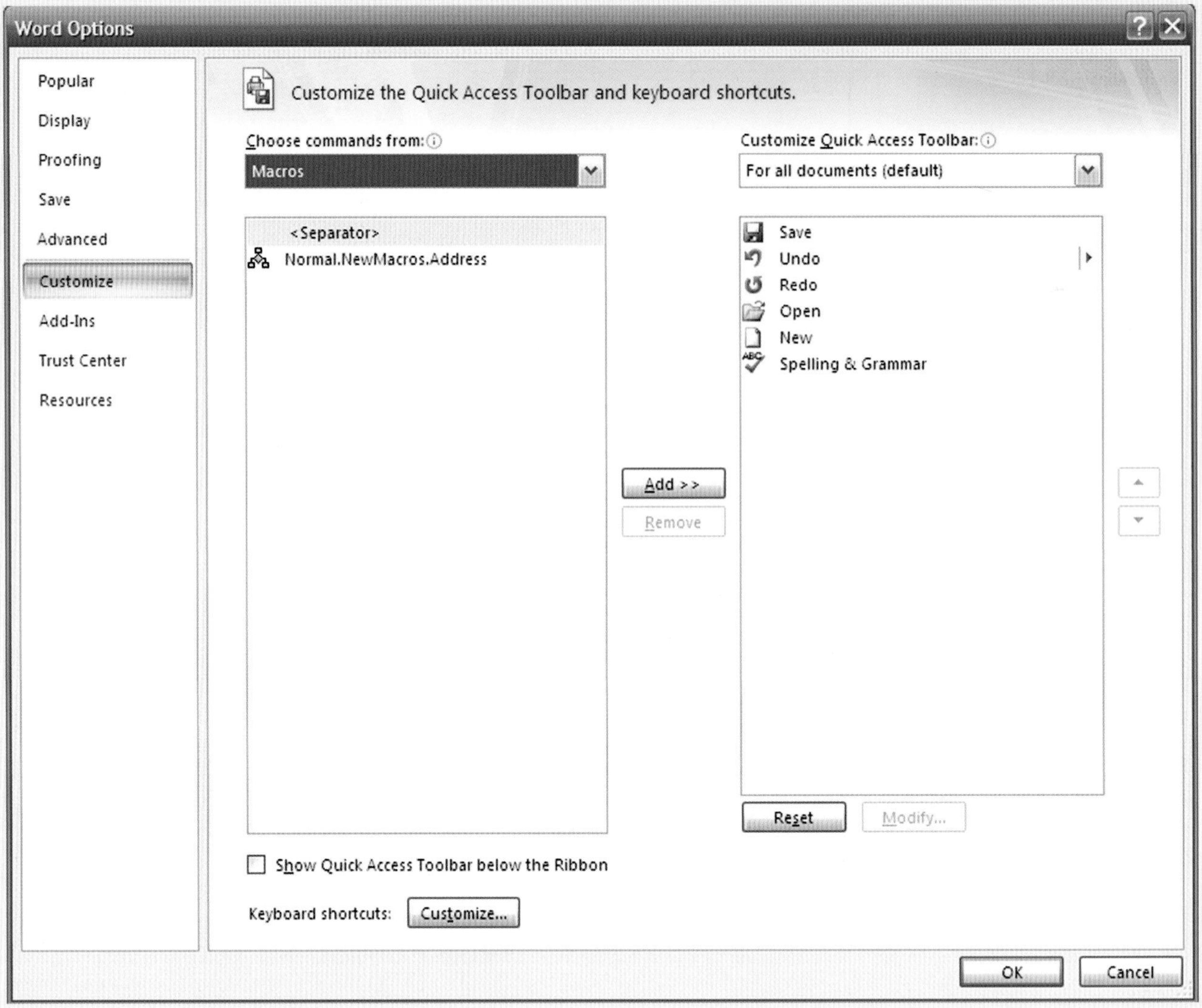

Figure 45

Figure 46

WJEC Information & Communication Technology for AS

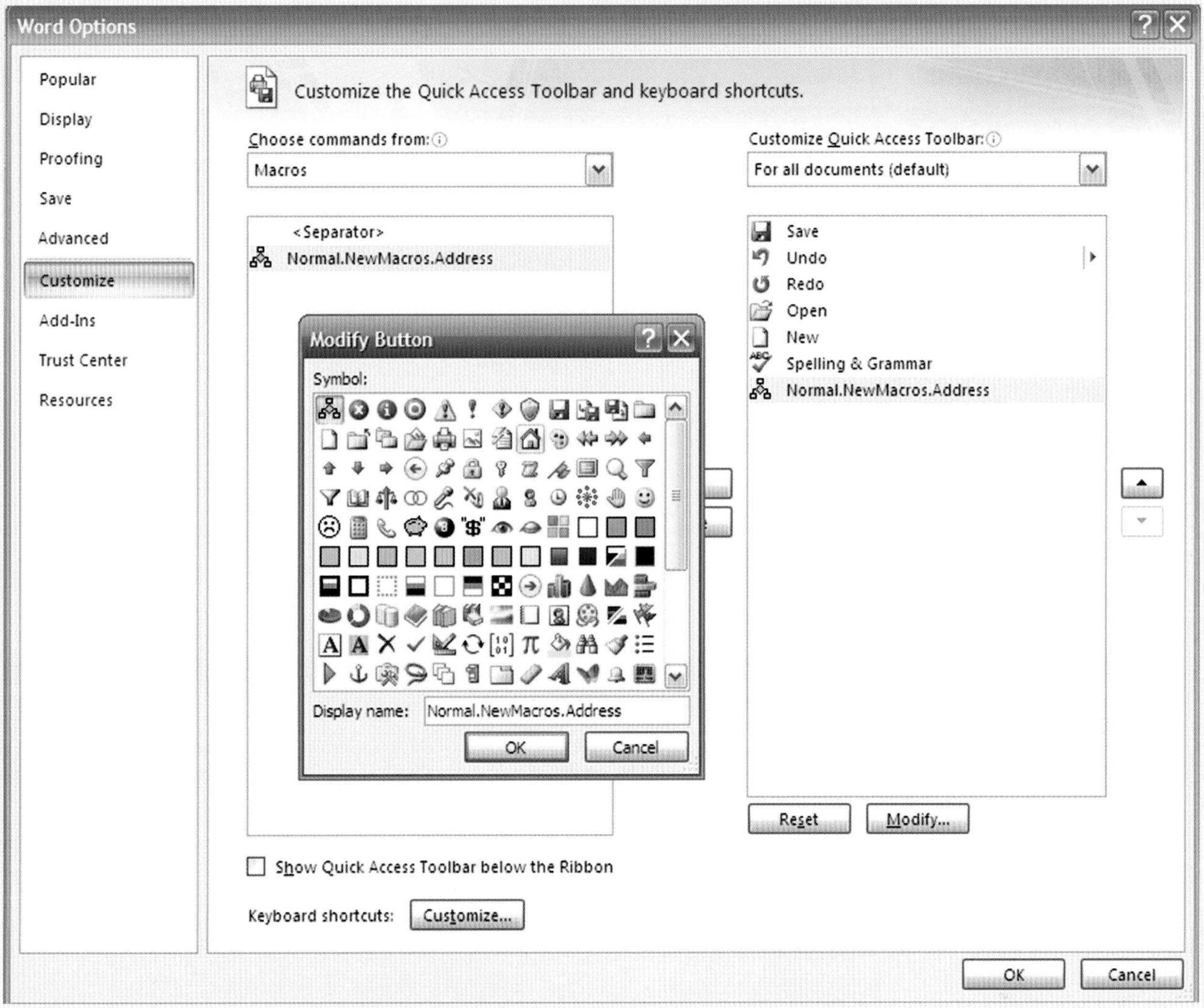

Word Options [?] [X]

Popular
Display
Proofing
Save
Advanced
Customize
Add-Ins
Trust Center
Resources

Customize the Quick Access Toolbar and keyboard shortcuts.

Choose commands from: ⓘ
Macros ▾

Customize Quick Access Toolbar: ⓘ
For all documents (default) ▾

<Separator>
Normal.NewMacros.Address

Save
Undo
Redo
Open
New
Spelling & Grammar
Normal.NewMacros.Address

Modify Button [?] [X]

Symbol:

Display name: Normal.NewMacros.Address

[OK] [Cancel]

[Reset] [Modify...]

☐ Show Quick Access Toolbar below the Ribbon

Keyboard shortcuts: [Customize...]

[OK] [Cancel]

Figure 47

5 Click on **OK**. The new icon selected will now be on the quick access toolbar as in Figure 48.

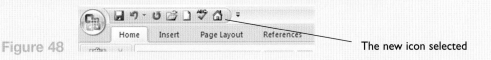

Figure 48

The new icon selected

6 Test that if you click on the icon, the macro runs and the address appears on the screen.

▶ Customising the toolbars in Word XP or 2003

1 Click on **Tools > Customize**. The Customize dialogue box appears as in Figure 49 on the following page.
2 In the **Categories** list, scroll down until you see **Macros**. Click on **Macros** as in Figure 50.
3 In the **Commands** box you will see an icon and **Normal.NewMacros.Address**. Select the icon and drag it to the formatting toolbar. A new button will appear on the toolbar as in Figure 51.

Customize
Toolbars
Commands
Options
To add a command to a toolbar: select a category and drag the command out of this dialog box to a toolbar.
Categories:
Commands:
File
Edit
View
Insert
Format
Tools
Table
Web
Window and Help
Drawing
New...
New
New
New Web Page
New E-mail Message
New Blank Document
Modify Selection
Rearrange Commands...
Save in:
Normal
Keyboard...
Close

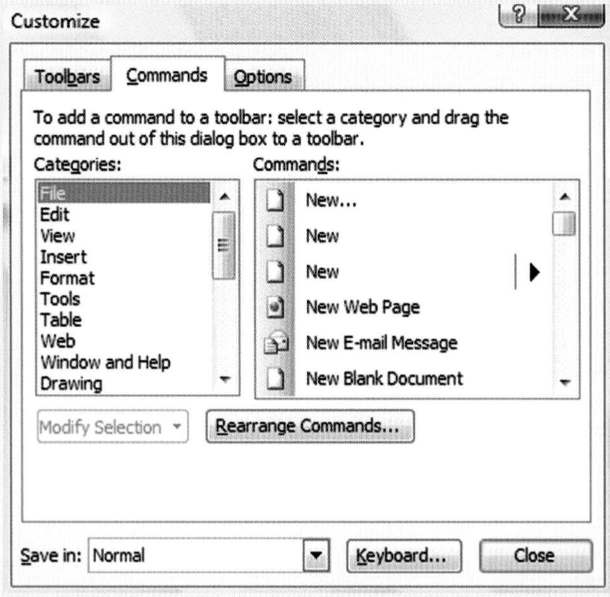

Figure 49

Customize
Toolbars
Commands
Options
To add a command to a toolbar: select a category and drag the command out of this dialog box to a toolbar.
Categories:
Commands:
Mail Merge
Forms
Control Toolbox
All Commands
Macros
Fonts
AutoText
Styles
Built-in Menus
New Menu
Normal.NewMacros.Address
Description:
Save in:
Normal
Keyboard...
Close

Figure 50

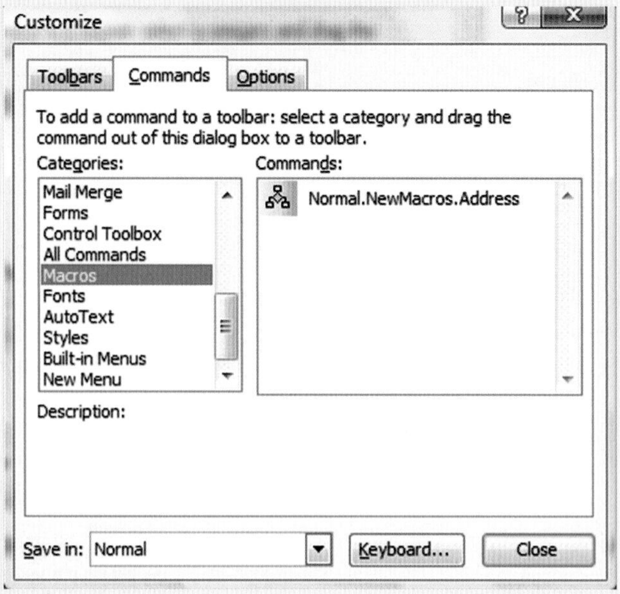

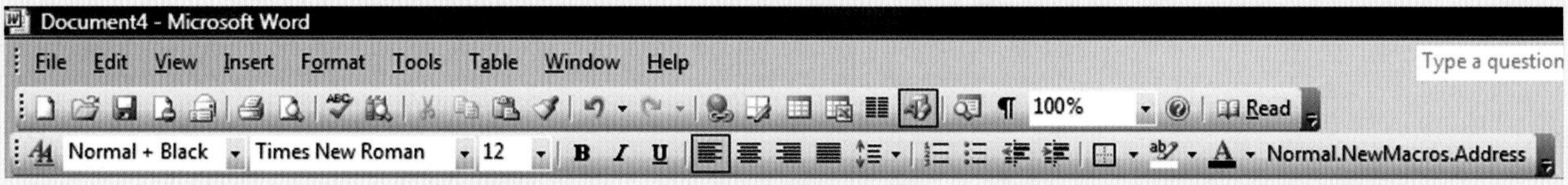

Document4 - Microsoft Word
File Edit View Insert Format Tools Table Window Help
Type a question
100%
Read
Normal + Black
Times New Roman
12
Normal.NewMacros.Address

Figure 51

4 Right click on this button. A drop-down menu will appear as in Figure 52.

5 If you want to have text on your button, just edit the text in the **Name** box.

6 To add an image, choose **Default Style**. The button will be replaced by a small icon.

7 Right click on this icon. Choose **Change Button Image** and choose one of the images that appear, as in Figure 53.

Type a question for help
Reset
Delete
Name: Normal.NewMacros.A
Copy Button Image
Paste Button Image
Reset Button Image
Edit Button Image...
Change Button Image
Default Style
Text Only (Always)
Text Only (in Menus)
Image and Text
Begin a Group
Assign Hyperlink

Figure 52

Type a question for help
100%
Read
Reset
Delete
Name: Normal.NewMacros.A
Copy Button Image
Paste Button Image
Reset Button Image
Edit Button Image...
Change Button Image
Default Style
Text Only (Always)
Text Only (in Menus)
Image and Text
Begin a Group
Assign Hyperlink

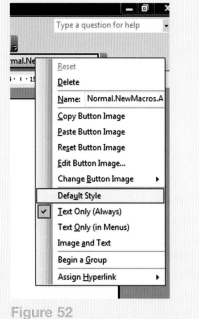

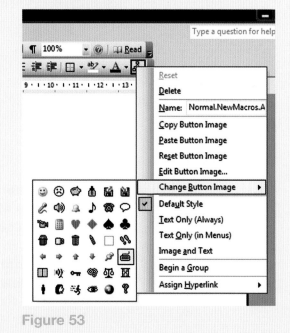

Figure 53

8 You can edit the icon if you wish. Right click on the new icon then click on **Edit Button Image** to load a simple painting program. Click on **OK** when you have finished.
9 Click on **Close**. The icon should now work.
10 Open a new document and click on the icon. Does it load the address?

▶ Unsuitable macros

There is little point in recording macros that perform a function for which there already is an icon on the toolbars, such as:

▶ print   ▶ cut   ▶ copy
▶ print preview   ▶ save   ▶ paste.

Activity 2

1 Record a macro called **MyAddress** to insert your home address at the top of a letter.
2 Create an icon on the formatting toolbar to run this macro.
3 Record a macro called **Yours** that will insert 'Yours sincerely' at the end of a letter then go down five lines and insert your name.
4 Create an icon on the formatting toolbar to run this macro.

Creating new versions of macros involving mail merge

We have set up a mail merge for PDQ Finance for people who have not paid in April. This is only useful for April. For non-payers in May, we will need to set up a different mail merge, similarly for June, July, etc.
You can set up macros to do this automatically. For example, you could record a macro for January as follows:

1 Turn on the mail-merge toolbar, by clicking **View > Toolbars > Mail Merge**.
2 Load the letter file (**PDQ Finance.doc**). You will be asked if you want to take data from your database. Click on **Yes**.
3 Find the word **April** in your letter. Delete it and replace it with **January**. Do this in both places where **April** appears in the text of the letter.
4 Click on the **Mail Merge Recipients** icon.
5 Scroll across until you see the January field. Click on the arrow and

choose **N** from the drop-down list. Make sure that the February field is set to **All** and so are March and April.

6 Save the file as **PDQ Finance January.doc**.
7 Close the file.
8 Start to record a macro. Call the macro **January**.
9 Open the file **PDQ Finance January.doc**.
10 You will be asked if you want to take data from your database. Click on **Yes**.
11 Stop recording.
12 Add an icon to your toolbars (quick access toolbar in Word 2007) to run the January macro.

You could set up similar macros for February, March and April, and add icons to the toolbar for these macros as well, as in Figure 54.

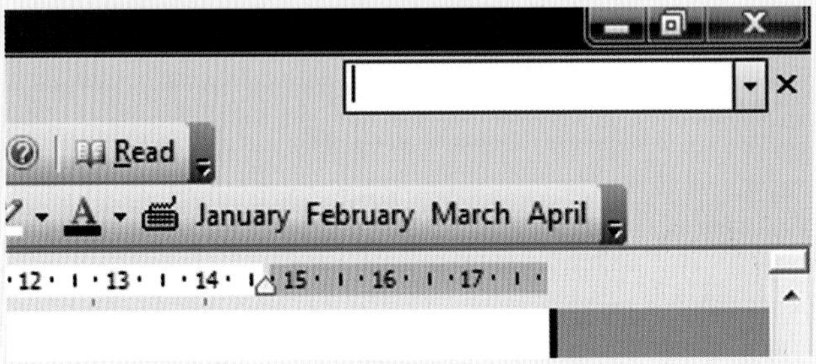

Figure 54

Document templates

Another way of customising Microsoft Word to make it easier to use is to create document **templates**. Rather than starting with a blank document, the user loads a document that is partially filled in. This obviously saves time.

An example of a template is a company letterhead (headed notepaper), where the company address and the date appear automatically. We will show you how to set up and use a letterhead template for PDQ Finance in Word 2007 and Word XP or 2003.

▶ Creating a letterhead template in Word 2007

1 Open a new blank document.
2 Enter the address and other contact details for the company at the top.
3 Enter the date using **Insert > Date & Time**. Choose the date format you want. Make sure that **Update automatically** is ticked then click on **OK**. The screen should look like Figure 55.
4 Click on the Microsoft Office button and choose **Save as**. Choose **Word Template** (see Figure 56).
5 Save the file as **Address** (see Figure 57).

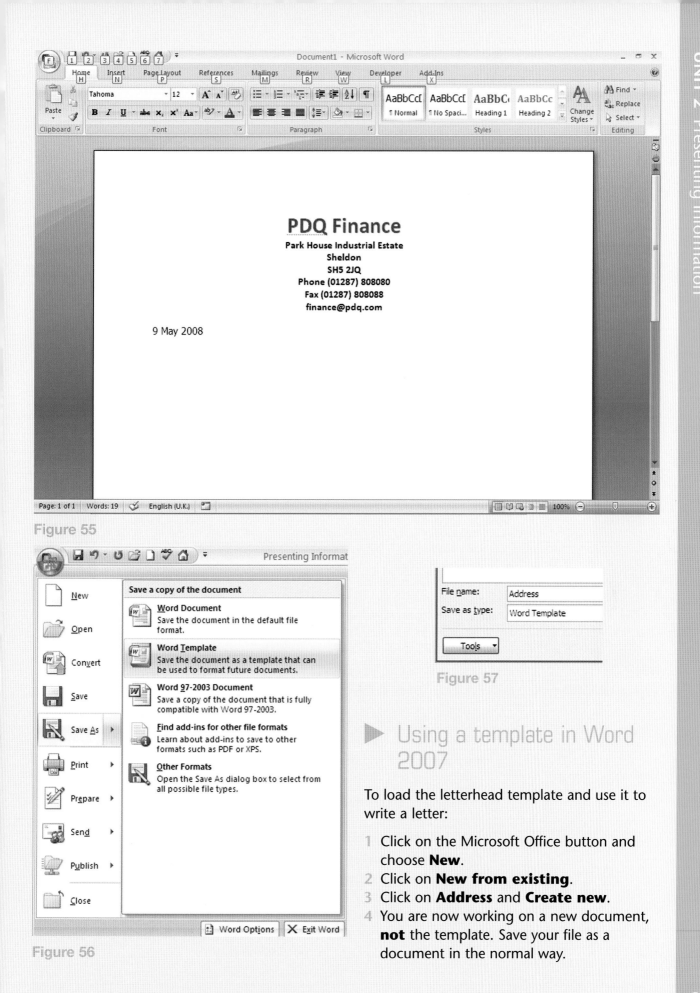

Figure 55

Figure 56

Figure 57

Using a template in Word 2007

To load the letterhead template and use it to write a letter:

1 Click on the Microsoft Office button and choose **New**.
2 Click on **New from existing**.
3 Click on **Address** and **Create new**.
4 You are now working on a new document, **not** the template. Save your file as a document in the normal way.

Creating a letterhead template in Word XP or 2003

1 Open a new blank document.
2 Enter the address and other contact details for the company at the top.
3 Enter the date using **Insert > Date and Time**. Choose the date format you want. Make sure that **Update automatically** is ticked then click on **OK**. The screen should look like Figure 58.

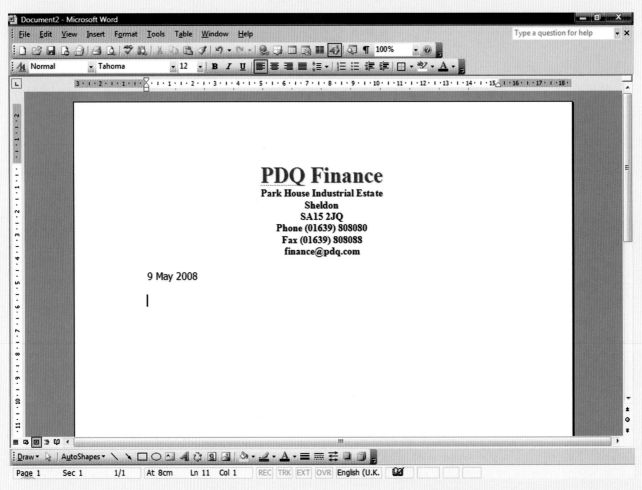

Figure 58

4 Click on **File > Save as**. In the **Save as type** box choose **Document Template** (see Figure 59). Call the file **Address**. Click on **Save**.

Using a template in Word XP or 2003

To load the letterhead template and use it to write a letter:

1 Click on **File > New**.
2 Click on **On my computer** in the pane on the right-hand side of the screen, as in Figure 60.
3 Click on the **Address** icon (see Figure 61) then click **OK**.
4 You are now working on a new document, **not** the template. Save your file as a document in the normal way.

WJEC Information & Communication Technology for AS

Save As

| Save in: | Templates | ⏷ | ⊕ ▾ ⬜ | ⬜ ▾ Tools ▾ |

Name	Date modified	Type	»
Normal			

My Recent Documents

Desktop

My Documents

My Computer

My Network Places

File name: Address   ⏷   **Save**

Save as type: Document Template   ⏷   **Cancel**

Figure 59

New Document ▾ ✕

⊕ ⊕ ⌂

New

- Blank document
- XML document
- Web page
- E-mail message
- From existing document...

Templates

Search online for:

[   ] Go

- Templates on Office Online
- On my computer...
- On my Web sites...

Figure 60

Templates

| General | Legal Pleadings | Letters & Faxes | Mail Merge | Memos | Other Documents | Publications | Reports |

Blank Document   XML Document   Web Page   E-mail Message

Address

Preview

Preview not available.

Create New
◉ Document   ○ Template

[Templates on Office Online]   [OK]   [Cancel]

Figure 61

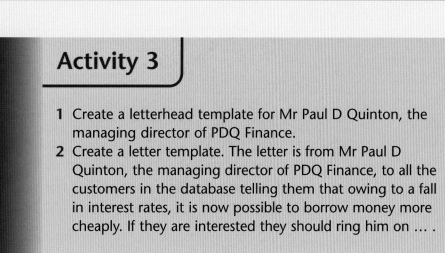

Activity 3

1 Create a letterhead template for Mr Paul D Quinton, the managing director of PDQ Finance.
2 Create a letter template. The letter is from Mr Paul D Quinton, the managing director of PDQ Finance, to all the customers in the database telling them that owing to a fall in interest rates, it is now possible to borrow money more cheaply. If they are interested they should ring him on ... .

Project ideas

1 A cricket club has adult and junior members. Juniors pay a subscription of £25 per season and adults pay £50 per season. Every year in March the secretary of the club writes a letter to all members telling them about practice sessions. Produce:
   a this letter
   b a second letter telling members that their subscription is due. This letter must say how much the member owes.

2 Members of a Christmas club pay into the club every month from January to December. They can pay £20, £50 or £100 per month.
   a Use mail merge to produce membership cards for all members of the club.
   b Write a mail-merged letter to all members telling them that the club is about to restart in January and reminding them how much they paid last year.

3 Set up a system in Microsoft Word that uses five customised buttons on the toolbar to perform the following functions:
   a Pressing the first button opens a new document with a company address and other details at the top of the page.
   b Pressing the second button inserts **Yours sincerely** and the writer's name.
   c Pressing the third button enters today's date.
   d Pressing the fourth button opens a mail-merged letter to all staff saying that because they have worked so hard, they will get either one or two extra days' holiday.
   e Pressing the fifth button closes Microsoft Word.

4 a Use mail merge to produce membership cards for all members of a youth club.
   b Create a mail-merged letter to all members telling them of future events.

What you must hand in

You must hand in the final printout of your document(s). But you must also hand in evidence that you have covered every part of the marking scheme.

You will need to include the following:

1 Data processing activities within the organisation – how the information is processed and communicated at present.

2 The purpose of document(s) you have created.

3 A description of the intended audience.

4 Detailed designs of the document(s), including:
   a designs for any letter templates

b designs for any files from which data will be imported

c designs for any macros. You just need to say what the macro will do – for example, an address macro might put the company name and address and the date at the top of a letter.

5 Printouts/screenshots of completed documents. These printouts should be annotated to point out use of features in the marking scheme. You need to show reuse of your templates, evidence of mail merge and evidence of running the mail merge again for a new use. You must include as evidence:

a printouts/screenshots of the external mail-merge file

b printouts/screenshots of the mail-merge template

c printouts/screenshots of the merged letter

d evidence of recording the macros (make sure that you show both evidence that you have recorded the macros and, in the background of the same screenshot, evidence of the document you have created)

e printouts/screenshots of macro coding for each macro.

6 Evidence of customising the toolbars by adding buttons to run at least three macros (showing evidence of your document in the background).

Marking scheme – Task 2

Components	Criteria	Marks
Design of document	Purpose of document/intended user	2
	Detailed design of document	4
Use of basic features	Import data from an external source	2
	Use of suitable format and layout for data	2
	Ensure automated routines work	2
Use of advanced features	*Each of the following may be awarded 1 mark – up to 3 marks per criterion to a maximum of 5 marks for this section.*	
	Individual macros or modules created using internal programming capabilities of the software package	3
	Individually designed templates (*other than the normal template*)	3
		Max 5

Task

3

Presentation

What you have to do in this task

For this task you have to use an appropriate software application to produce one of the following:

▶ a presentation of at least six slides for an audience
▶ a website of at least six pages for an audience.

You will need to produce evidence of using:

▶ background styles
▶ animation effects
▶ transition effects

▶ hypertext
▶ hotspots
▶ bookmarks.

Explanation of how to use these advanced features can be found on pages 243–245.

To get higher marks you will need to produce evidence of using some of the following features:

▶ sound
▶ original video
▶ original animation such as Flash graphics.

▶ Web pages or presentation slides?

That's up to you. Don't choose something just because it seems easier. Choose the option that will interest you more. That will motivate you and you will enjoy the task. If you enjoy it, you'll work harder.

It is a good idea to have a real project such as:

▶ redesigning an existing presentation or website to make it better
▶ producing a new presentation or website for somebody else.

It is much easier to describe the purpose of the presentation if it is a real presentation for a real business and not something that you have made up.

Designing your web pages/presentation slides

Before you start producing your slides/pages, describe in detail the purpose of the presentation. What will it be used for? Who will see the slides/pages?

Next, produce some rough layout designs. It is best to sketch these using pencil and paper. Draw designs to scale, and for web pages, to the exact size.

You also need to draw a simple structure diagram showing how the slides/pages will be linked.

Your designs should show:

- outline layout of the slide/page
- background format
- use of columns and/or tables
- position of headings/titles, etc., stating the font, colour and size to be used
- position of text frames, stating the font, colour and size to be used

- position of images
- animation and transition effects
- hyperlinks
- hotspots
- bookmarks
- sound
- video
- Flash animations.

Issues to consider

House style

Does the organisation for which you are producing the slides/pages have its own style? Does it have a logo? What font is used? Is there a standard colour for text?

If there isn't a house style, you should create one. All slides/pages must be consistent and use the same style. This means that they should use the same fonts, colours and sizes throughout. (See also *Style sheets* below.)

Fonts

Which font or fonts will be used? This should be determined by the organisation's house style or the house style you have created.

Font size

Which font sizes are best? Study professional web pages and presentation slides to see what font sizes they have used. On web pages text is often as small as 10 point or even 8 point. PowerPoint presentations need much larger text. Slide titles are often 44 point and text 28 point.

Colours

Which colours are best? Does a bright-red background work? Is a pastel-coloured background better? Experiment with different colours. Pale colours are best for backgrounds. But whatever you choose must fit in with the house style.

There can be a little variety here. Reverse colour, which is white text on a dark background, works well for subheadings. But use it sparingly. It is generally OK to use two different fonts on a page/slide.

Style sheets

If you are setting up web pages you can create a style sheet. The style of all your web pages will be based on the style sheet. Change the style sheet and you change all the pages.

If you are setting up PowerPoint slides you can create a master slide. The format of all the other slides will be based on this slide.

Upper or lower case?

Should presentations be entirely in upper case (capital letters)? Lower-case letters are easier to read. They are smaller so they take up less space. Upper-case text is more eye-catching.

Animation

Do you want to animate features? A little animation can be good for attracting the attention of the audience but don't overdo it.

▶ Creating the slide/page design

Once you have made these decisions you are ready to put together some drawings of what your slides/pages might look like. Try images in different positions. Experiment with the position of the title. Produce a few different designs and get some opinions from others.

Look at existing website and PowerPoint presentations to see how they have laid out the text. What size font do they use? Where are the images?

Consider using columns. Text is hard to read if a column goes across a whole slide/page. Have two columns for a PowerPoint presentation and at least three columns for web pages.

Hyperlinks

For web pages you need to consider how the pages will link. Will there be a main home page from which there are links to all the other pages? Will these links be located in a menu? Where will the menu be on the page? Will it be in the same place on all pages? Study some websites to see where they position the menu.

For presentation slides, do the slides have to be seen in order? Is it possible to miss out slides or go back to the start?

Annotating your designs

Your designs should be annotated so that it is clear which features you intend to use, including:

- ▶ styles
- ▶ fonts
- ▶ font sizes
- ▶ images
- ▶ animations
- ▶ videos
- ▶ tables.

◯ Which software?

That's up to you. If you are creating web pages you will need to use a WYSIWYG web editor program. There are several suitable packages on the market, such as Adobe DreamWeaver, Serif WebPlus or Microsoft Expression Web. These programs allow you to set up the web pages easily on screen but you can also edit the HTML script if necessary.

If you are creating presentation slides, Microsoft PowerPoint is likely to be your choice but OpenOffice.org Impress is free and has very similar features. It is possible to import files from and export files to PowerPoint.

Which version?

Again this is up to you. Using the latest version is not necessary as long as you have access to the techniques on page 240.

Backup

Don't moan if you lose your work. Keep a backup on a memory stick. But never work directly from your memory stick. Always copy the latest files onto hard disk.

Advanced features

The marking scheme for this task is shown on page 255.

The marking scheme requires that you use some of the features below. In this section we look at what features are, how to insert them and what to use them for.

▶ Presentation slides in PowerPoint

Hotspots

These are parts of an image with hyperlinks. By clicking in one part of the image you would go to another page. By clicking somewhere else, you could go to a different page.

You can create hotspots in PowerPoint by inserting a text box. Keep the text box blank (so that it is invisible) and insert a hyperlink to another slide. You can also use this feature to play sound or video clips.

Bookmarks

These are where a hyperlink can take you directly to the middle of a page – not just the top of the page.

It is possible to insert a hyperlink to any slide in a presentation. Use **Insert >Hyperlink** then click on **Place in This Document**.

Sound

To insert sounds, click on **Insert > Movies and Sounds > Sounds from File**. Find the file and insert it. It is best to choose to run it **When Clicked**.

Video

To insert video, click on **Insert > Movies and Sounds > Movies from File**. Find the file and insert it. It is best to choose to run it **When Clicked**.

Animation

Click on **Insert > Object > Flash Movie**.

To play a Flash file automatically in your PowerPoint presentation, follow these steps:

1 Display the PowerPoint slide in which you want the animation.
2 Click on **View > Toolbars > Control Toolbox**.
3 In the **Control Toolbox**, click on **More Controls**.
4 In the list, scroll down and click on the **Shockwave Flash** object.
5 Drag a rectangle over the slide to draw the control.

6 Right click on the **Shockwave Flash** object and select **Properties**.
7 Click on the **Alphabetic** tab then click on the **Movie** property.
8 In the value column (the blank cell next to **Movie**), type the full drive path including the file name (for example, **C\:My Documents\MyFile.swf**). This part is absolutely crucial. If you get this wrong nothing will happen.
9 Make sure the **Playing** property is set to **True**.
10 Set the **Loop** property to **False**.
11 Set the **EmbedMovie** property to **True**.
12 Close the **Properties** dialogue box.

To run the Flash animation to test it:
1 Run the slide show from the current slide (SHIFT and F5).
2 Right click on the animation and choose **Play**. To play continuously, click on **Loop** then **Play**.
3 To exit the animation press ESC.

▶ Web pages created in DreamWeaver

Hotspots

These are parts of an image with hyperlinks. By clicking in one part of the image you would go to another page. By clicking somewhere else, you could go to a different page.

In DreamWeaver you need to select the image. The hotspot tool is in the **Properties** area at the bottom of the page. Set the target page in this section too.

Bookmarks

These are where a hyperlink can take you directly to the middle of a page – not just the top of the page.

1 Place the cursor where you want the bookmark – for example, near the bottom of the page.
2 Click on **Insert > Named Anchor**. Call it **Bookmark1**. Click on **OK**.
3 Go to the top of the page. Put the cursor after the title. Click on **Insert > Hyperlink**.
4 The **Link** should say **#Bookmark1**. Set the target to **_self**. Click on **OK**. A # will appear.
5 Press **F12** to test that it works. Clicking on the # sign should take you to the bookmark.

Sound and video

You can set up web pages so that they play sound or video clips – for example, when the page opens.

1 Place the cursor where you want to insert the object (audio or video) in the web page.
2 Click on **Insert > Media > Plugin** and select the required video/audio file. You may need to adjust the height and width of the new object in the **Properties** area at the bottom of the screen.
3 Press **F12** to test that it works.

Flash graphics

You can import animations created in Adobe Flash by clicking **Insert > Media > Flash**. Select the required Flash (*.swf) file. Test that it works as for video/audio.

Designing a website for CMJ Digital

At the beginning of Unit 2, we gave background information on a company called CMJ Digital as an example (see page 185). For Task 1, we used a flyer for CMJ Digital as an example of a document redesigned by a student (see Figure 3, page 193 and Figure 29, page 208).

Producing web pages for CMJ Digital is an example of a suitable project for Task 3.

Example

At present Chris, the owner of CMJ Digital, advertises by posting flyers through people's letterboxes near where he lives. He wants a more modern way of advertising his services and would like a website. He has asked me to help set up a website for him.

The required pages will be:
- a home page about the company and how to contact them
- a page about the digital switchover
- a page about radio
- a page about satellite TV, multi-room and Sky plus
- a page about Freeview and Freesat
- a page showing prices for various services.

They must be eye-catching and include the details that at present are on the flyers.

For this project, you would need to:
- produce designs for all six web pages
- remember to be consistent in terms of colour, fonts, background, layout of the page, etc.
- annotate the designs to show where features such as the following have been used:

a	background styles	f	bookmarks
b	animation effects	g	use of sound
c	transition effects	h	use of original video
d	hypertext	i	use of original animation such as Flash graphics.
e	hotspots		

Figure 1 on the next page shows an annotated design for the home page.

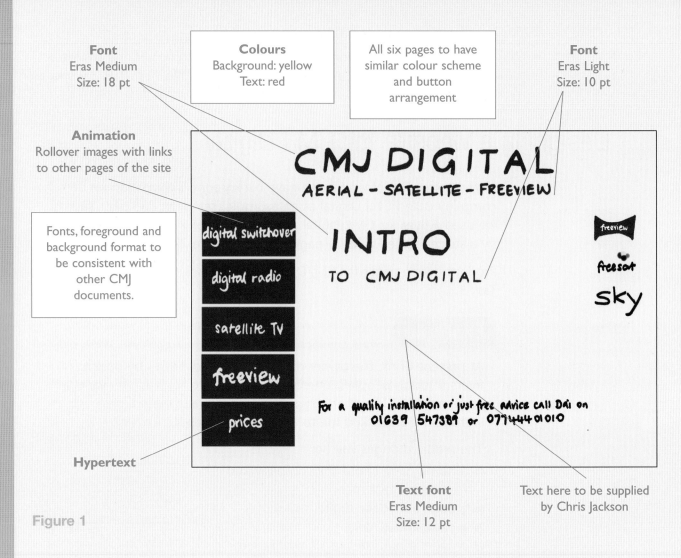

Font
Eras Medium
Size: 18 pt

Colours
Background: yellow
Text: red

All six pages to have
similar colour scheme
and button
arrangement

Font
Eras Light
Size: 10 pt

Animation
Rollover images with links
to other pages of the site

Fonts, foreground and
background format to
be consistent with
other CMJ
documents.

Hypertext

Text font
Eras Medium
Size: 12 pt

Text here to be supplied
by Chris Jackson

Figure 1

What makes a good PowerPoint presentation?

There is no doubt that a computer presentation adds to a manual
presentation. The message of the speaker is reinforced on the screen.
However:

▶ A PowerPoint presentation will not make a dull talk interesting.
▶ The content of the presentation is more important than the methods
used to communicate it. The content has to be right.
▶ A poor computer presentation can lose the audience as quickly as a
boring lecture.

Follow these tips for a good presentation.

▶ Twenty tips for a great PowerPoint presentation

When planning a presentation, remember the following guidelines:

1 **Start with an introduction:** Tell the audience what you're going
to tell them about. Get them interested.

WJEC Information & Communication Technology for AS

2 **Don't overdo it:** The presentation is not an opportunity to show off all the cool features you have discovered or that a friend has showed you. Too much clip-art or too many animations will mean that the audience concentrate on the effects and not the content of the presentation.

3 **Don't overcrowd slides:** The idea of a presentation is not to tell the whole story but to stick to the key points, often called **sound bites**. If you need to make the text small to fit it on a slide, you have too much text. Stick to the 6 by 7 rule. Try to have no more than 6 bullet points and no more than 7 words per bullet point.

4 **Be consistent:** The presentation should have the same look throughout. The same background should be used for all slides, the same font, the same colour of text, the same animation techniques, etc. Components such as logos that may appear on every slide should be in a standard position on each slide.

5 **Choosing colours:** Remember that some colours will work better than others on the screen. Some people find red backgrounds are uncomfortable to look at. Red is associated with anger and danger. Red backgrounds may be best avoided. Yellow text on a dark-blue background works well. Try to use no more than four colours on a slide.

6 **Good contrast:** It goes without saying that you need to use contrasting colours: dark text on a light background or light text or a dark background.

7 **Fonts:** Use large fonts, at least 24 point. If you can't fit all your points on a slide without moving to a smaller font, break up the points onto separate slides. Do fonts like Chiller and Jokerman look professional? Does Comic Sans look professional or babyish? Use the same font throughout the presentation. Generally avoid placing any text on top of a graphic as it may make it less readable.

8 **Backgrounds:** You don't have to use any of the background styles that come with PowerPoint. We've lost count of the number of presentations we've seen that use the *dad's tie* template!

Some of the templates are very good, such as the ocean design (shown in Figure 2). However you may wish to set up your own image to use as the background.

Use image manipulation software such as Adobe PhotoShop or PaintShopPro to adjust the brightness. In Figure 3 the image has been made darker so that the white text is clear. The image has also been blurred to soften the effect.

In Figure 4 the image has been made lighter to make dark text clear.

Your background should depend on the room's lighting. Light text on a dark background looks best in a dark or slightly darkened room. In a light room try dark text on a lighter background.

Using PowerPoint
Conference
March 23

Figure 2

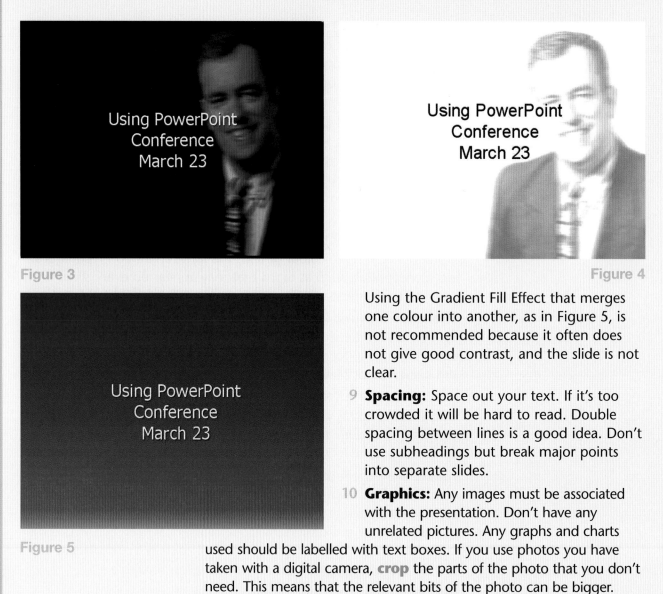

Figure 3

Figure 4

Figure 5

Using the Gradient Fill Effect that merges one colour into another, as in Figure 5, is not recommended because it often does not give good contrast, and the slide is not clear.

9 **Spacing:** Space out your text. If it's too crowded it will be hard to read. Double spacing between lines is a good idea. Don't use subheadings but break major points into separate slides.

10 **Graphics:** Any images must be associated with the presentation. Don't have any unrelated pictures. Any graphs and charts used should be labelled with text boxes. If you use photos you have taken with a digital camera, **crop** the parts of the photo that you don't need. This means that the relevant bits of the photo can be bigger.

11 **Video and audio files:** These can add to a presentation but keep the segments short – it doesn't mean it's interesting just because it's on video. Include a replay button – the audience may want to see or hear the clip more than once.

12 **Transition sounds:** Presentation software offers a library of sounds that can be used to attract attention during transitions to the next slide or animations. Sounds like a gunshot or a camera click are available. They can sound good the first time but the same sound effect heard a dozen times very quickly palls.

13 **Animations:** Presentations can be enhanced by animations. It is good to make text appear exactly when you want but think carefully before using animations. Are they necessary? Do they add to the presentation? Will they distract the audience?

If you use animation stick to the same animation throughout. Try to avoid fancy animations – they just do not look professional. The **Appear** animation is fine.

Never use the **Random** animation effect – it will destroy any consistency of your presentation. Avoid the **Swivel** effect. It takes such a long time to stop that the audience will have lost focus.

14 **Make comparisons:** Don't just say that some new computer system is brilliant. Compare it with what was used beforehand. Does it save time? Is it 25 per cent quicker? Does it save labour? Does it save money? Is it more accurate or more reliable?

15 **Include graphs:** Seeing a graph enables the audience to take in information at a glance. Use graphs instead of tables.

16 **Hyperlinks:** Add hyperlinks to supporting web pages. You can add e-mail links to slides too.

17 **Remember the purpose:** The purpose of a presentation is not to have a presentation. The purpose is to inform the audience.

18 **Good content:** Brilliant use of features will not make up for dull, tedious or inaccurate content. The content must be relevant and interesting and be aimed at the audience.

19 **Remember the audience:** Who will see your presentation? Are they rocket scientists or brain surgeons? Do they have a long concentration span? What do they want/need to know?

20 **Don't forget to sum up at the end:** Every presentation needs a conclusion. You should have a concluding slide with three to five summary points. The audience will gain a much stronger impression. Remember, you can never emphasise or restate your main points too often.

Websites offering advice on presentations

▶ http://www.powerpointers.com/
▶ http://www.presentations.com
▶ http://www.presentersonline.com/basics/visuals/
▶ http://www.rdpslides.com/pptfaq/index.html#TIPS

▶ Ten things you might not know about PowerPoint presentations

1 **Using F5:** Press the **F5** key to start the presentation – much easier than using the mouse. To start the presentation from the current slide press SHIFT and **F5**.

2 **Slide master:** It is a good idea to use the slide master so that all the slides are consistent. Click on **View > Master > Slide Master** and set up the layout for your slides. You can format the background, logos, colour scheme, fonts, font sizes, etc., to create a consistent look.

3 **SHIFT and F3:** While setting up the presentation, use SHIFT and **F3** to cycle between lower case, title case and upper case. Try it. It also works in Microsoft Word.

4 **Slide numbers:** Slide numbers are helpful for easy navigation during authoring as well as during your presentation. Display the slide master and choose **View > Header and Footer** to open the header and footer dialogue box. Tick **Slide Number** and click on **Apply to All**.

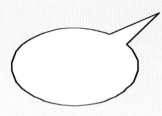

5 **Black out:** You can black out the screen in the middle of a presentation. If you stop to discuss a point and don't want people staring at the screen, black it out by pressing the **B** key. Press **B** again to continue your presentation.

6 **White out:** In a light room, you can white out the screen. If you stop to discuss a point and don't want people staring at the screen, white it out by pressing the **W** key. Press **W** again to continue your presentation.

7 **Callouts:** Experiment with the callouts. These are shapes like speech bubbles and 'thinks' bubbles. Find them by clicking on **AutoShapes > Callouts** on the drawing toolbar. Right click on the callout and choose **Add Text** to enter text.

8 **Alignment:** To align objects perfectly, select two or more objects. From the drawing toolbar, choose **Draw > Align or Distribute**. Select one of the alignment options.

9 **Even distribution:** To distribute three or more objects evenly, select them all. From the drawing toolbar, choose **Draw > Align or Distribute**. Then select **Distribute Horizontally** or **Distribute Vertically**. To distribute objects equally across the entire slide, first choose **Draw > Align** or **Distribute Relative to Slide**.

10 **Automating a movie from a slide:** You can automate running a video clip in a PowerPoint slide, telling it when to start:
  a Right click on the video's icon.
  b Click on **Custom Animation > Timing tab > Automatically**.
  c Set the delay time as required.
  d Test it.

Twenty tips for a great website

1 **Planning:** You'll want to get started straight away but wait a minute. Plan your pages using a pencil and paper. It will save time in the long run by avoiding some mistakes.

2 **Choose a memorable URL:** Use a URL that everyone can remember. A website for CMJ Digital could be www.cmjdigital.co.uk. It could also be www.betteraerials.com, which is easier to remember.

3 **Colour scheme:** Use the same colour scheme on every page. Base it on the company's preferred colours. If there are no company colours already, choose two or three complementary colours and stick with them. If you're still not sure about the colour scheme, find a website that you like. Copy their colour scheme. Most websites use dark text on a light background.

4 **Red on green?** If your company colours are pillar-box red and bright green do not attempt red writing on a green background. Go for better contrast with red and green text on a white or very light grey background.

WJEC Information & Communication Technology for AS

5 **Put the most important information on the home page:** Visitors to your site may only look at one page. So if you have a message to get over, put it here.

6 **Write only one idea per paragraph:** Don't waffle. Stick to the point. People are busy and don't have time to read every word. Keep paragraphs short.

7 **Bullet points:** Rather than using long paragraphs, use bullet points that are easy to read.

8 **Columns:** It is hard to read text that goes right across a web page. So put text into three columns to make the page more user friendly.

9 **Backgrounds:** Keep backgrounds simple. If you do have a background image, check that text can still be read. Avoid bright in-your-face backgrounds. Stick to light backgrounds.

10 **Don't keep moving things:** Keep to a consistent design. Keep images, navigation buttons, menus, logos in the same place on every page.

11 **Write short sentences:** Be concise all the time.

12 **Make the site easy to navigate:** Make the buttons clear. Keep them in the same place on each page. Keep them the same colour throughout.

13 **Across the top or down the side?** If you put navigation buttons across the top, you can fit in about eight. If the buttons go down the left-hand side you can fit in as many buttons as you like.

14 **Keep special effects to a minimum:** You might think that a flashing cursor looks cool but it is professional? Use animation only if it complements your site.

15 **External hyperlinks:** Open links to other websites in a new window. This means that visitors still have a window open with your web page on it.

16 **Don't clutter the screen:** Don't try to cram everything in. Keep some clear white space on each web page. Don't use a tiny font size to get more in. Stick to 10 point for normal text. Use 12 or 14 point for headings.

17 **Scrolling horizontally?** Make sure that your page is not wider than the screen. Visitors won't be able to see the whole page unless they scroll sideways.

18 **Learn from others:** Look at other sites and learn from them. What do they do well? What doesn't work?

19 **Style or substance?** Make sure the content is right. Don't sacrifice the content by spending too long on the layout.

20 **Proofread your work:** Nobody wants to read a web page full of typing and spelling mistakes. Always, always, always proofread your work. Ask someone else to look at it too – they may spot something you have missed.

What you must hand in

You must hand in a final printout of your web pages/presentation slides. But you must also hand in evidence that you have covered every part of the marking scheme (see page 255).

You will need to include the following:

1 The background and user requirements

Example

Chris Jackson is a friend of my father's. He owns a business called CMJ Digital that installs satellite dishes and TV aerials. With the switch to digital, a lot of people need a dish or a new aerial.

Chris is keen to get work from these people. At present he advertises by posting flyers through people's letterboxes near where he lives.

Chris thinks he will get more business if he has a website. He has asked me to design and create the web pages. They must be eye-catching and include the details that at present are on the flyers.

2 The purpose of the slides/pages you have created

Example

The purpose of the website is to inform residents of the services offered by CMJ Digital. The design must be eye-catching. The site should cover all the services offered by CMJ Digital.

3 The intended audience

Example

The audience is any local residents.

4 Detailed designs of the slides/pages

Example

See Figure 1, page 246.

5 Printouts of all your completed slides/pages. These printouts should be annotated to point out use of features in the marking scheme. For example, if you have used hotspots or bookmarks, annotate your printout to say so, as in Figure 6. Include 'before and after' screenshot evidence.

If you have used style sheets or master slides give screenshot evidence of creating them.

Example

Here is my home page [Figure 6]. The colours and fonts used are consistent with flyers distributed by CMJ Digital to local homes.

Animation
Rollover images

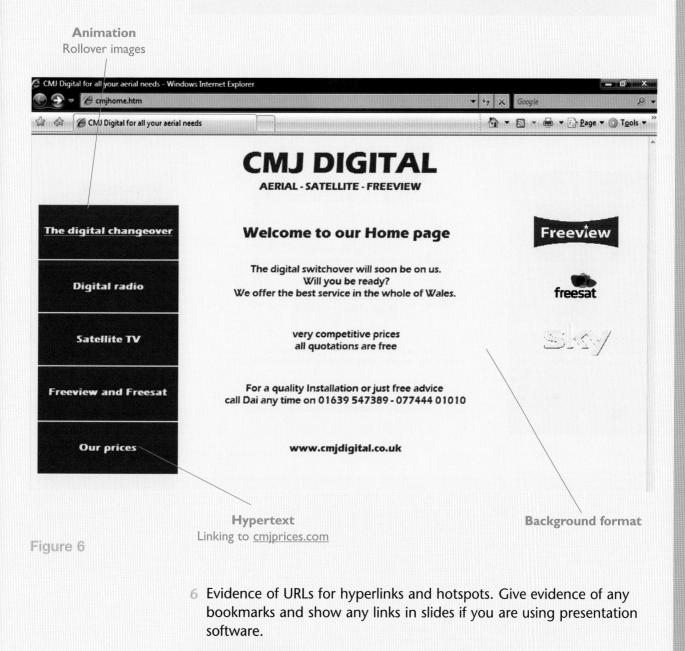

Hypertext
Linking to cmjprices.com

Background format

Figure 6

6 Evidence of URLs for hyperlinks and hotspots. Give evidence of any bookmarks and show any links in slides if you are using presentation software.

Example

In this screenshot [Figure 7 on next page], you can see the alternative image for this button is called prices2.jpg. The URL of the hyperlink is cmjprices.htm. This can be seen more clearly in the enlarged version of the bottom left of the screenshot [Figure 8].

7 The HTML script of web pages if it includes evidence of using features.

Example

The HTML coding for this page looked like this [Figure 9].

8 Annotated screenshot evidence of any sounds, video editing, animations and/or transitions in presentation software.

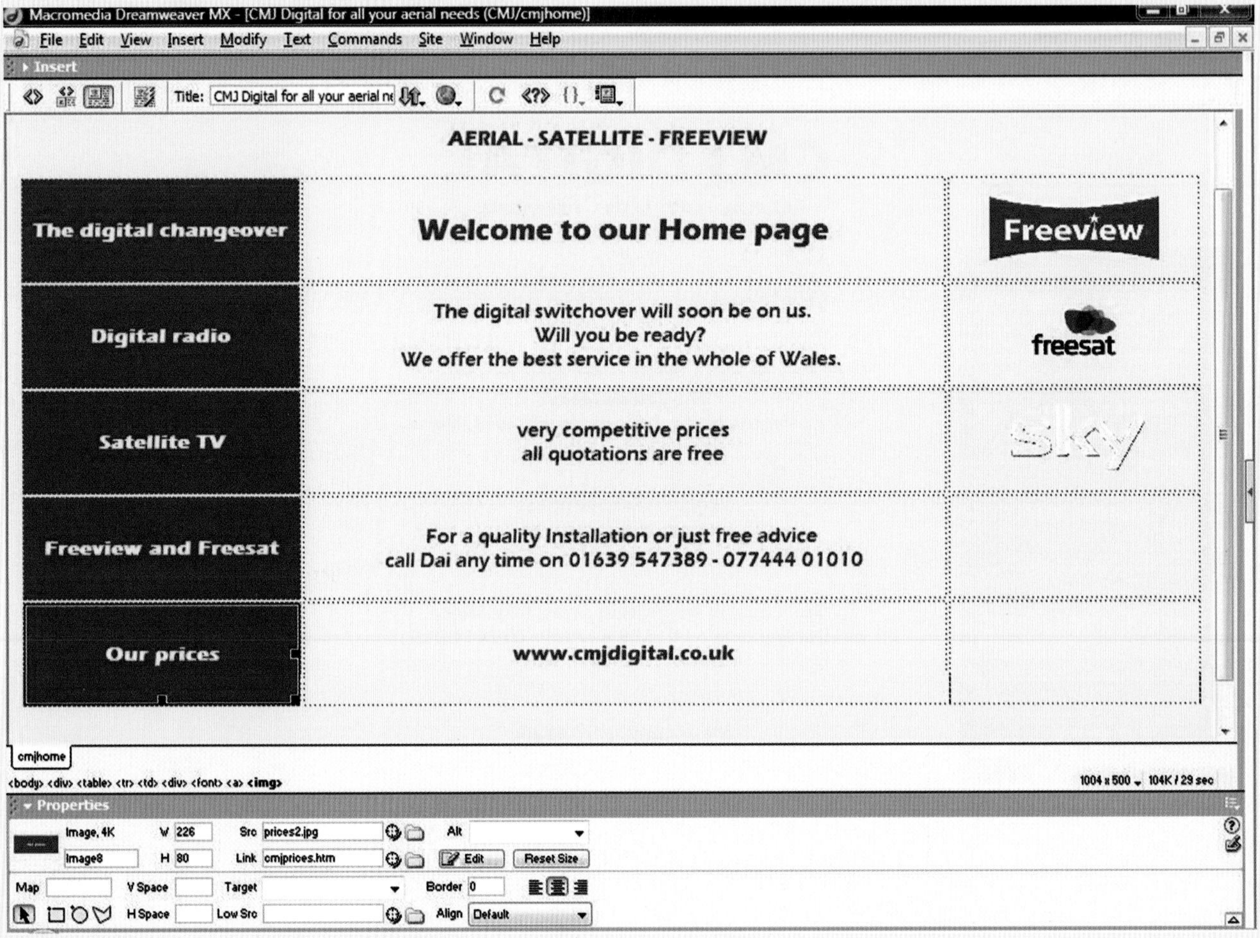

Figure 7

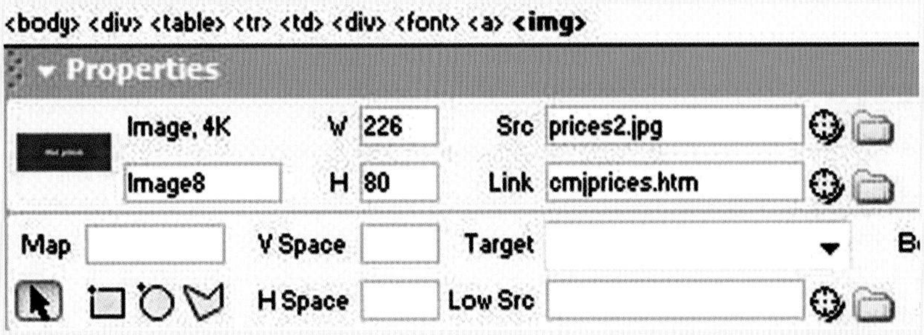

Figure 8

WJEC Information & Communication Technology for AS

```
cmjhome - Notepad

File  Edit  Format  View  Help
<!DOCTYPE HTML PUBLIC "-//W3C//DTD HTML 4.01 Transitional//EN">
<html>
<head>
<title>CMJ Digital for all your aerial needs</title>
<meta http-equiv="Content-Type" content="text/html; charset=iso-8859-1">
<script language="JavaScript" type="text/JavaScript">
<!--
function MM_swapImgRestore() { //v3.0
  var i,x,a=document.MM_sr; for(i=0;a&&i<a.length&&(x=a[i])&&x.oSrc;i++) x.src=
}

function MM_preloadImages() { //v3.0
  var d=document; if(d.images){ if(!d.MM_p) d.MM_p=new Array();
    var i,j=d.MM_p.length,a=MM_preloadImages.arguments; for(i=0; i<a.length; i+
    if (a[i].indexOf("#")!=0){ d.MM_p[j]=new Image; d.MM_p[j++].src=a[i];}}
}

function MM_findObj(n, d) { //v4.01
  var p,i,x;  if(!d) d=document; if((p=n.indexOf("?"))>0&&parent.frames.length)
    d=parent.frames[n.substring(p+1)].document; n=n.substring(0,p);}
  if(!(x=d[n])&&d.all) x=d.all[n]; for (i=0;!x&&i<d.forms.length;i++) x=d.forms
  for(i=0;!x&&d.layers&&i<d.layers.length;i++) x=MM_findObj(n,d.layers[i].docum
  if(!x && d.getElementById) x=d.getElementById(n); return x;
}

function MM_swapImage() { //v3.0
  var i,j=0,x,a=MM_swapImage.arguments; document.MM_sr=new Array; for(i=0;i<(a.
```

Figure 9

Marking scheme – Task 3

Components	Criteria	Marks
Design of presentation slides or web pages	Purpose of presentation/intended user	1
	Detailed design of slides/pages	4
	Structure diagram showing pathways	1
Use of basic features	Background styles	1
	Animation effects	1
	Transition effects	1
	Hypertext	1
	Hotspots	1
	Bookmarks	1
Use of advanced features	Sound	2
	Original video	4
	Original animation/Flash graphics	2

DTP Glossary

alignment refers to the position of text. Left aligned means the lines have a straight left-hand edge but are uneven on the right side. Justified means the spaces between words are adjusted so that both left and right edges are straight.

attributes the properties of an object such as font, size, case, colour.

body text the main text in a document.

bullet a character, often a large dot, that is used to highlight the start of paragraphs. Usually used for lists to attract the reader's attention.

clip-art pictures provided in a library for inclusion in documents.

copyright the right to control the use of images, written text, etc.

crop remove the edges of an image.

cutline the type beneath an image, sometimes called a caption. Tells the reader what is going on in the image.

default an option that is chosen automatically unless an alternative is specified. DTP software often uses a default font of Times New Roman size 12.

draft a rough version of, for example, the layout of a page.

fill property of an object such as the background to text. Fill may be solid, a pattern or blank.

find and replace a useful facility enabling you to find a word and replace it with another word.

folio a printer's term for a page number.

font a set of letters with a consistent typeface, weight and size.

footer information that appears at the bottom of every page, such as a page number.

greeking use of dummy Greek-script text in a mock-up of a document.

gutter the space between columns of text or between facing pages.

halftone refers to images in which shades of colour are reproduced by varying the size of dots that make up each area of the image.

header information that appears at the top of every page, such as the title.

headline a title designed to draw attention to an article and make you want to read it.

import bring an object such as an image or text into a document.

italic slanted type.

justification/justify *See* **alignment**.

kerning the spacing between letters.

landscape paper orientation where the width is greater than the height.

lead the first paragraph in an article – it summarises the article and makes you want to go on reading the article.

leading the space between lines of text. Pronounced *led-ding*.

logo an image used to identify a company.

lower case letters of the alphabet that are not capitals.

margin the area round the edge of a page where printing is not allowed.

master page/view a page which shows objects such as headers, page numbers and borders which will appear on every page of a document.

nameplate the heading on a document such as a newsletter giving its name.

object an item on a page such as a graphic or text.

orphan a line of type on its own at the bottom of a page. *See also* **widow**.

pagination the numbering of individual pages in a multi-page document.

paragraph style a format of indents, line spacing, fonts and sizes applied to a whole paragraph.

pica a unit of measurement used by printers. There are 6 picas to an inch.

point a unit of measurement used by printers. There are 12 points to a pica or 72 points to the inch.

portrait paper orientation where the height is greater than the width.

proofreading checking a document for errors.

rule a printer's term for a line. The thickness of a rule is measured in points. A 1-point rule is very thin; a 10-point rule is very thick.

sans serif term for fonts without serifs, such as Arial.

serif a little extension at the end of some characters in certain fonts, such as Times New Roman.

soft returns holding the SHIFT key while pressing RETURN creates a soft return, but does not start a new paragraph. Often used with bullet lists.

text wrap the technique of flowing text around a graphic object.

upper case term for capital letters.

weight refers to the thickness of type – for example, light, medium, bold or heavy.

widow a line of type on its own at the top of a page. *See also* **orphan**.

zoom enlarge or reduce the magnification on screen.